WOMEN IN CELTIC MYTH

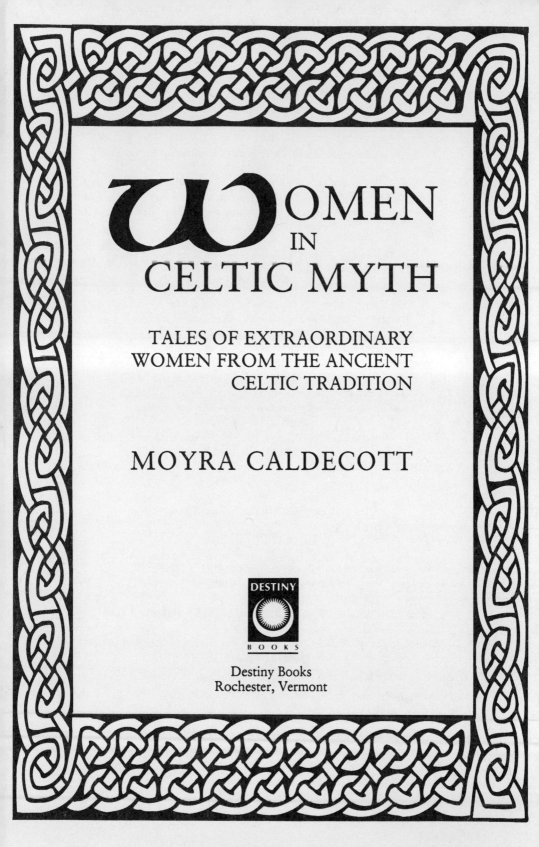

Women in Celtic Myth

TALES OF EXTRAORDINARY
WOMEN FROM THE ANCIENT
CELTIC TRADITION

MOYRA CALDECOTT

DESTINY
BOOKS

Destiny Books
Rochester, Vermont

Destiny Books
One Park Street
Rochester, Vermont 05767

LIBRARY OF CONGRESS CATALOGING-IN-PUBLICATION DATA
Caldecott, Moyra.

women in Celtic myth : tales of extraordinary women from the ancient Celtic
tradition / [retold and explained by] Moyra Caldecott.
p.   cm.
Includes bibliographical references.
Contents: Introduction—Rhiannon—Arianrod and Blodeuwedd—
The tree Etains—Emer and the women who loved Cuchulain—Macha
—The Morrigu—Deirdre—Findabair and Maeve—Grania
—The farmer's youngest daughter—The sea-maiden.
ISBN 0-89281-357-1
1. Women, Celtic—Folklore. 2. Mythology, Celtic. I. Title.
GR137.C29 1992
398.2'0942'0902—dc20   91-42628
                                                                  CIP

Printed and bound in the United States

10 9 8 7 6 5

Cover illustration and design by Amanda Barlow
Text design by Randi Jinkins

Destiny Books is a division of Inner Traditions International

Distributed to the book trade in Canada by Publishers Group West (PGW),
Toronto, Ontario
Distributed to the book trade in the United Kingdom by Deep Books, London
Distributed to the book trade in Australia by Millennium Books, Newtown, N.S.W.
Distributed to the book trade in New Zealand by Tandem Press, Auckland
Distributed to the book trade in Europe by HDG Distrirep,
The Netherlands
Distributed to the book trade in South Africa by Alternative Books, Randburg

Contents

Introduction

Myth is multilayered, like life, and to get the most out of it we have to be aware of many different levels at once. For a long time publishers and booksellers relegated myths and legends to children, perhaps because to be most effective, a myth also has to be a good story; perhaps because they misunderstood the nature of myth and—because it is not amenable to laboratory testing or cross-examination in a court of law—they assumed it was not truth at all. In fact the mythmaker's truth is just as valid but of a different kind. It carries the conviction of a true note in a beautiful melody, and it illuminates the true dynamic of our lives behind the superficial structures.

The truth about living in the universe is elusive, exciting, and mysterious, and it is in the pursuit of mystery that we find all that is worth having, including ourselves. If we catch Truth and put it in a cage—it dies. It only flourishes in flight, in splendid flashes of living light briefly glimpsed through revelational vision, mythic story, and deeply profound poetry.

Many have claimed that they have found Truth, and perhaps some have, but when they try to pass it on to their fellows directly, it falls through their fingers like dust. It was not for nothing that Christ spoke in stories and said: "He who has ears to hear, let him hear."

We are too often given explanations, not understandings, and are condemned, sometimes even killed or imprisoned, because we cannot accept another's explanation. Explanations govern us, clip our wings, and tame us. Stories free us and encourage us to fly. I believe dogma grows from explanation; myth from understanding.

Therefore the commentaries on the stories gathered in this book are not intended as explanations, only as suggestions for ways of looking at the stories, perhaps in order to get a little more out of them.

Like a detective, the myth-reader follows clues eagerly, learning all the while. Unlike a detective, however, we very rarely solve the mystery, for that is not what the mythmaker intends us to do. His or her task is to make us notice the mystery—to make us stop taking things for granted, to look, to question, to wonder.

True myth transmits a recognition of the mystery of being—*not* the whimsical. It deals with the great, fascinating, powerful magic of inner transformation—and anyone who believes its beings are the little flittering fairies of the Victorians is sadly mistaken.

We never stop learning from these stories handed down by our ancestors. They are told over and over again, not because there was, or is, a shortage of stories, but because they had, and they have, something important to say. It is perhaps because our modern myths lack wisdom and we settle for stories without true mythic content— stories that have no profundity, no seed from the great forest to plant in our own plots of ground—that our lives are so often shallow and empty and so many of us have lost our way.

I have chosen to write mainly about the women in Celtic myth, not because I think women are any more important than men but because they are no less important. And I am writing about Celtic myth rather than any other, not because I think Celtic myth is more important than any other but because it is no less important.

It is sometimes difficult to find the pure and ancient Celtic story behind the layers of Christian, Viking, and Germanic influences that have been at work on them in the centuries between their first telling and what they have become today. We may get a strong flavor of the

ancient Celtic society in the stories, but if that were all we were looking for, we would read a straight history book.

We understand these stories, although technologically and in many
other superficial ways our societies are very different, because they
are about human beings who, like us, are on a journey, learning painfully, step by step, to fulfilll their considerable potential—faced then,
as now, with the same essential problems, sorrows, and delights be-
set from within and without by the same dark and violent shadows.

Let us use these myths to step back from the immediacy of our own
cluttered society and see our lives from a different perspective. In Celtic
myth, the very mix of wise spiritual teaching, the power and beauty
of the imagery, and the harsh and gruesome violence makes for a new,
potent, and disturbing vision. To get the full flavor of these myths
you will have to go to the original texts—but let me just point you in
their direction.

The Celtic peoples in whose cauldron of wisdom these myths first
surfaced were thought to be Aryan or Indo-European peoples moving in restless waves from the Middle East and the southwest plains
and mountains of Russia through Scythia, Illyria, Macedonia, and
Thrace toward central and northern Europe, northern Italy, and Gaul.
Isolated pockets were left behind in Asia Minor (Galatia). The flow
continued westward through Iberia (Spain) and Armorica (Brittany)
to the islands of Britain. It is said that one branch of the Celtic
peoples—the Brythonic-speaking branch—settled in Wales, Cornwall,
and Brittany, while the Goidelic branch came to rest in Ireland, the
Isle of Man, and Scotland. They traveled with their stories and their
storytellers, and it is by their stories we can trace them, though they
too have been molded and altered by the changing circumstances of
their migration and the other peoples the Celts have melded with en
route.

It is well known that when the Anglo-Saxons came to Britain in
the fifth century A.D. the Celts melted backward toward the west,
where strongholds held against the invaders. It is also well known
that the Romans never conquered Ireland, and it is therefore easier
for the mythographer to trace the myths in a purer form there than
anywhere else. It may not be so well known that some archaeologists
have found traces of ogham (Celtic ciphers) and other indications that
suggest early Celts made their way across the Atlantic to North

America. This is still a controversial point—but it is intriguing. There are, however, at this time Welsh-speaking areas of Patagonia in South America and Scottish Gaelic-speaking areas of Nova Scotia in Canada. The migrations of the Celts are not over yet.

The Greeks called them the "Keltoi" because they were "the hidden people"—people who had no written records. Their wisemen-priests, the Druids, studied for twenty years to commit all their extraordinary knowledge to memory. Their bards knew by heart stories for every night of the year—and probably more besides.

In 390 B.C. the Celts attacked Rome, and for five years the Romans were subservient to them. The Celts even sacked the great temple of the oracle at Delphi in Greece. They were warlike, fearsome, restless—their women no less than their men. Ammianus Marcellinus described them thus:

> Nearly all the Gauls are of a lofty stature, fair and ruddy complexion: terrible from the sternness of their eyes, very quarrelsome, and of great pride and insolence. A whole troup of foreigners would not be able to withstand a single Gaul if he called his wife to his assistance who is usually very strong and with blue eyes; especially when, swelling her neck, gnashing her teeth, and brandishing her sallow arms of enormous size, she begins to strike blows mingled with kicks, as if they were so many missiles sent from the string of a catapult. (Quoted in Chadwick, *The Celts.*)

The Celts had no religious dogma that we can trace, though accompanying everything they did was a strong sense of the holiness or sacredness of all existence. To them animals and trees had souls, and even inanimate things like swords and stones could speak. Immortality and reincarnation were facts of life, and different levels of reality were taken for granted. Their gods are not easily distinguishable from each other—nor do they respond well to analytical examination. Cernunnos, the great horned god of the Gundestrup cauldron, seems to have been a major deity, gathering to him all our yearning for a healthy and burgeoning nature. In Ireland, the Dagda seems to have been another name for him. Anu, or Danu, was the great mother goddess, giving her name to the Tuatha de Danann, the Children of Danu, who were so known for their magical skills they were possibly not human at all but some kind of spirits or devas or elementals from the Other World. Llyr represented the mysterious and rich depths of the sea. Lugh represented the source of light—the sun; Bel, similarly. Angus Og, associated with Brugh na Boyne (now called New Grange near Slane), was the son of the Dagda and was known to be a being of love and wisdom. He is the divine son who mediates between the realms—rather like Horus in ancient Egyptian mythology.

The sun ruled the year and there were four great Celtic festivals.

Samhain was the beginning of the year, on our November 1: the day of changes, of births and deaths; the day the gate between the worlds is open and spirits can pass freely from one to the other. We celebrate it as All Saints' Day—and even today some fear the walking of ghosts on Halloween.

Imbolg was on our February 1: the feast day of the Celtic goddess of fertility, Brigid.

Beltane was on our May 1: a fire festival in praise of Bel, the sun, the life-giver, for winning over the darkness of winter. It is the time to make fresh beginnings. Hearth fires are extinguished and rekindled anew from the Druid's sacred fire.

Lughnasa was on our August 1: for the sun god, Lugh. Our harvest festival is a celebration of the earth's fruitfulness.

I always think of the Celts as Iron Age peoples because, although their tribal movements began during the Bronze Age, they did not really come to the islands of Great Britain before 700 B.C. It was the Celts who set up the hill forts across the country and conquered the less warlike, indigenous Bronze Age people with their iron swords and spears, cooking their great victory feasts of meaty broth in huge iron cauldrons still to be seen in museums around Great Britain.

The Irish had their *Leabhar Gabhala Eireann* (*The Book of the Conquest of Ireland*), in which they described what was supposed to be the successive waves of invaders. The names, however, bear no relation to any names we know, and the characteristics of the invading forces are often so strange, even macabre, that we cannot believe they are more than vague distorted memories of the flow and flux of ancient tribal movements. The book was written in the twelfth century and was purported to be history. It is of interest to us here because the protagonists described therein are the protagonists of the myths we find so fascinating. A very brief summary of the six invasions from the "dream time" of Ireland follows.

The people of Cesair were said to be the first invaders and were somehow all drowned in a flood except for Fintan, who lived on in various forms—as falcon, eagle, hawk—and saw all that happened.

Partholan and his people followed, driving out the Formorians—half-monstrous creatures already living there—and banishing them to outlying islands.

Partholan's people were mostly destroyed by plague, leaving the stage to the third group of invaders, the people of Nemhedh. After their leader's death the Nemhedhians were conquered by the Formorians—some fled to Greece and others to the northern lands.

Later the Nemhedhians who had fled to Greece returned to reclaim Ireland as the Fir Bolg. They divided Ireland into five provinces: Ulster, Leinster, Munster, Connacht, and Meath.

Later still the Nemhedhians who had fled north returned to reclaim the land. They are known as the Tuatha de Danann—Children of the Goddess Danu—and were famous for the magical lore they had learned while in exile. They were led by their goddess and their god, Danu and the Dagda, and they brought with them four priceless treasures. The first treasure was the Stone of Fal, which cried out when a true king sat upon it. (This is now supposed to be the Coronation Stone in Westminster Abbey, however, some authorities think it never went to Scotland, and thence to England, but stayed in Ireland and now marks what is known as the "Croppie's Grave" near Tara.) The second treasure was the invincible spear of Lugh; the third was the inescapable sword of Nuadha; the fourth was the inexhaustible cauldron of the Dagda.

The Tuatha de Danann defeated the Fir Bolg at the first battle of Magh Tuiredh, driving them into exile among the Formorians. Nuadha lost an arm in the battle and, as he was no longer perfect in form, he could not be their king. He abdicated in favor of Bres, who was half Tuathan and half Formorian. Bres proved to be unsatisfactory as king so was driven out by the curses of the tribal poet, and he fled to his father's people where he set about raising an army. Nuadha, now with a silver arm, became king again and, with the help of Lugh, led his people into the second battle of Magh Tuiredh. Balor of the Evil Eye was defeated and the Tuatha de Danann were the victors.

The sixth invasion was from the Milesians—the sons of Mil—who seem to have come from Spain. They landed on the first of May and were led by their seer and poet Amhairghin. They advanced on Tara and defeated the Tuatha de Danann in spite of the use of a great deal of magic. The Tuatha managed to obtain concessions, however, and the land was divided between them—the Milesians (or Gaels) took the overground part and the Tuatha retreated underground to live on as magical, mystical beings in the "hollow hills" or great burial mounds of ancient times.

According to one particularly interesting legend, one of the Milesian princes had gone from Scythia to Egypt, where he had married "Pharaoh's daughter," and thence to Spain and Ireland. This same pharaoh's daughter, named Scota, is mentioned as having been slain in the invasion battle—her sons became rulers in Ireland and much later her name was given to Scotland when the Irish tribes flowed into that country in great numbers. The old Milesian standard is said to be a snake twisted around a rod, which seems to me a very Egyptian symbol.

Whether the story has any truth in it in the straight historical sense, I don't know, but it is certainly well documented that ancient sea-going peoples, like the Phoenicians, frequently came to Britain and Ireland in search of tin, silver, and gold. We tend to think that these islands, by being remote, were cut off from the great civilizations of the Mediterranean—but they were not entirely.

The dating of this is not at all clear.

We know that St. Patrick arrived to convert Ireland to Christianity in the fifth century, thus the ancient pagan myths belong to a time well before this. Christianity had arrived in Britain earlier with the Romans—but still the myths lived on, fulfilling a very deep-felt need.

From the description of society in these stories, we can tell something of their age. The Tara dynasty destroyed Emain Macha in the fifth century, for instance. And we know that there were no towns or coinage in Ireland before the Vikings arrived in the seventh century. The old royal sites—Tara, Cruachan, Emain Macha—were forts that filled up at festivals or in times of war.

Early Celtic society was hierarchical: A number of small kingdoms agglomerated under several high kings. Below the king there were roughly three divisions. First, the warrior aristocracy, the landowners, and the patrons of the arts. Second, the Druids, bards, judges, physicians, historians, artists, and skilled craftsmen. Third, the ordinary freemen, commoners, small farmers and minor craftsmen. There were also slaves who had been taken in war.

Kinship grouping was extremely important, and most misdemeanors were settled within the group. When a Druid was called in to settle a matter, he was much feared. Fines were standard punishment, and each category of crime had its recognized price. One of the worst things that could happen was to be satirized by a poet, which had the effect of driving the wrongdoer in disgrace from the tribe. It was so psychologically scarring that there were many cases reported of people breaking out in festering sores from such a verbal punishment. Their good name was lost forever—and a good name was one of the most precious things to a Celt, even more precious than life itself.

Fosterage of children was not only common but was used to strengthen links of loyalty and bonding within the tribe. Feuding between families and seeking of vengeance on behalf of one's kin was commonplace. The weapons used were mainly spears (both for thrusting and throwing), slings, swords, and daggers. The chariot was employed with formidable skill.

Kingship was on the whole nonhereditary. Rulers were chosen for their strength and fitness—helped by a little judicious divination!

Women had their place on all levels equal to men—as we shall see from the stories in this book.

None of the written texts recording these myths are from very ancient times. Some of the stories date back three thousand years and for most of that time were passed on bard to bard and never written down. But in the Middle Ages scribes began to try to preserve them. Internal evidence can tell scholars which are original and very old and which are accretions from Roman, Christian, and Viking times. I have drawn on reputable translations for my rendering.

The specifically Welsh stories ("Rhiannon," "Arianrod and Blodeuwedd") were taken from what we today call the *Mabinogion*. the *Mabinogion* is a collection of very ancient Celtic myths and legends handed down by word of mouth for centuries before they were finally collected together and written down in *The White Book of Rhydderch*, c. 1325. Written versions of some of them had existed before but this was the first major collection. I consulted two translations of the *Mabinogion* in particular: one by Jeffrey Gantz and one by Lady Charlotte Guest.

For the Irish stories ("The Three Etains," "Emer and the Women Who Loved Cuchulain," "Macha," "The Morrigu" "Deirdre," "Findabair and Maeve," "Grania"), I again consulted translations by Jeffrey Gantz in *Early Irish Myths and Sagas*. I also consulted works by Lady Gregory, notably *Cuchulain of Muirthemne* and *Gods and Fighting Men*, and T. W. Rolleston's *Myths and Legends of the Celtic Race*.

The original relevant texts from which these translations were made are *Lebor Na Huid Re* (*The Book of the Dun Cow*), a twelfth-century collection of thirty-seven stories, and *The Book of Leinster* (written in 1160), which is much larger and more complete. Earlier manuscripts existed but were mostly destroyed by Scandinavian invaders, leaving only tantalizing fragments.

The stories accreting around Finn, son of Cumhal (for example, the tale of Diarmuid and Grania) seem to have achieved popularity much later and to be as much part of Scottish tradition as Irish. In fact these stories, all stemming from the ancient Celtic myth tradition, are found in different but recognizable versions throughout the Celtic countries of Wales, Scotland, Ireland, Cornwall, and Brittany.

For the Scottish stories of "The Farmer's Youngest Daughter" and "The Sea-Maiden," I've relied on J. F. Campbell's *Popular Tales of the West Highlands*.

I can no longer remember the details of all the books I've read throughout my life that pertain to the ancient Celts and these legends, but I give here a selection of some I have found most useful in the immediate task of writing this book.

Bonwick, James. *Irish Druids and Old Irish Religions*. Reprint of 1894 edition. New York: Dorset Press, 1976.

Campbell, J. F. *Popular Tales of the West Highlands*. Reprint of 1860 edition. Aldershot, U.K.: Wildwood House, 1983.

Campbell, Joseph. *The Masks of God*. 4 vols. New York: Penguin Books, 1982.

Chadwick, Nora. *The Celts*. Gretna, La.: Pelican, 1986.

Cooper, J. C. *Fairy Tales: Allegories of the Inner Life*. Wellingborough, U.K.: The Aquarian Press, 1983.

Dillon, Myles, ed. *Irish Sagas*. Dublin: The Mercier Press, 1985.

Ellis, Peter Berresford. *Celtic Inheritance*. Amsterdam: Muller, 1985.

Franz, Marie L. von. *Shadow and Evil in Fairy Tales*. Dallas, Tex.: Spring Publications, 1974.

Frazer, J. G. *The Golden Bough*. New York: Macmillan, 1974.

Gantz, Jeffrey. *The Mabinogion*. New York: Penguin Books, 1976.
_____. *Early Irish Myths and Sagas*. New York: Penguin Books, 1981.
Gregory, Lady Augusta. *Cuchulain of Muirthemne*. Reprint of 1902 edition. Gerrards Cross, U.K.: Colin Smythe, 1970.
_____. *Gods and Fighting Men*. Reprint of 1904 edition. Gerrards Cross, U.K.: Colin Smythe, 1970.
Guest, Lady Charlotte, *The Mabinogion*. London: J.M. Dent, 1906.
Naddair, Kaledon. *Keltic Folk and Faerie Tales: Their Hidden Meaning Explored*. London: Century, 1987.
Rhys, John. *Celtic Folklore: Welsh and Manx*. Reprint of 1901 edition. Aldershot, U.K.: Wildwood House, 1980.
Rolleston, T. W. *Myths and Legends of the Celtic Race*. London: Harrap & Co., 1917.
Ross, Anne. *The Pagan Celts*. London: Batsford, 1986.
Sharkey, John. *Celtic Mysteries*. London: Thames & Hudson, 1975.
Sjoestedt, Marie-Louise. *Gods and Heroes of the Celts*. Translated by Myles Dillon. London: Methuen, 1949. Turtle Island Foundation, 1982.
Squire, Charles. *Celtic Myth and Legend*. Reprint of 1901 edition. Newcastle Publishing Co., 1975.
Wentz, W. Y. Evans. *The Fairy-Faith in Celtic Countries*. Gerrards Cross, U.K.: Colin Smythe, 1977.

It is usually unwise to try to pin mythic events too closely to physical locations, but when you are traveling in a country it adds a certain twinge of pleasure to recognize a place that has been associated with a story you have read. On this basis I list here a few names and their traditional associations in Ireland.

Almhuin (Finn's dun): near Kildare
Bri Leith (associated with Midir): County Longford
Cruachan (Ailell and Maeve): County Roscommon
Magh Tuiredh (also called Moytura, Mag Tured):
    First battle near Cong (the Tuatha defeat the Fir Bolg)
    Second battle near Sligo (the Tuatha defeat the Formorians)
Mide: County Meath
Temuir: (Teamhair: "Tara of the Kings"): County Meath
Cuailnge (of the Brown Bull): County Louth

Emain Macha (Conchubar's fort): Fort Navan near Armagh
Brugh na Boyne (the home of Angus Og): New Grange, Slane, Meath

I would also like to point out that in all the authorities I have consulted there does not seem to be a standard spelling for the places
and the people in these myths. I claim the right as storyteller to use
the form of the name that feels most comfortable for me. I list a few
examples—the first in each case is the one I have chosen to use.

	Alternate Spelling
Amhairghin	Amergin
Angus Og	Òengus
(Angus the Young)	
Arianrod	Aranrhod
Blodeuwedd	Blodeuedd
Cathbad	Cathub
Deirdre	Derdriu
Diarmuid	Diarmaid
Finn	Fionn
Grania	Gráinne
Gwydion	Gwydyon
Maeve	Medb
Naoise	Noísiu
Usnach	Uisliu

Rhiannon

"You mean to tell me, he lay in the bed with you night after night for a whole year and did not once make love to you?" Rhiannon asked with incredulity.

Arawn's wife laughed. "I know. That a man's sense of honor should be stronger than his desires does seem impossible—but I assure you that is how it was. My lord said when he returned that he had never known a friend so trustworthy or a human so honorable."

"But tell me," Rhiannon persisted. "Did you suspect nothing?" She was fascinated by the story her friend had told her. It seemed a young man called Pwyll had allowed his own hunting hounds to have the kill which had been brought down by the magical hounds of Arawn, the King of Annwvynn. Instead of punishing him for the trespass, Lord Arawn had agreed that he could earn his forgiveness and his friendship by undertaking a difficult task. Pwyll had been eager to comply and, without demur, had exchanged place and form with Arawn for a year and a day. Arawn had told no one, not even his wife, so that when Pwyll came to bed with her at night she had thought he was her husband Arawn.

"At first, when he turned his back to me I let him lie—but when night after night the same thing happened, I began to worry. I did everything in my power to arouse him. Many a time I could feel that he was more than ready; but then he would leap up and walk about, and sometimes even leave the chamber, rather than take me in his arms. There was a time when I became so depressed I wondered what I had done to offend my husband. But in the day he was so affectionate I could not believe he did not love me. Eventually I decided it was his feud with Havgan that was preying on his mind, and as soon as that was settled his manhood would return to him. I let him be—and I proved to be right. At the end of the year the two met at the ford. Arawn (or he who I thought was Arawn) struck the one blow necessary to destroy his enemy. A night later he returned to me with all his old passion and we made love as though we had been parted for a year and a day."

"As indeed you had!" laughed Rhiannon.

"I know that now. But I did not know that then."

"What was he like, this human?"

It was her friend's turn to laugh. "He was exactly like Arawn. I suspected nothing. You can be sure I berated my lord pretty thoroughly for the trick he played on me."

"What did he say to that?"

"He said the test for Pwyll would not have been complete had I known. Nevertheless he was amazed that Pwyll had not succumbed to me. What with ruling the kingdom so admirably, defeating his enemy, *and* respecting his bed, Pwyll really earned Arawn's respect and friendship."

Rhiannon's eyes shone. What kind of human this must be who could do all this!

"Have you no curiosity to go and see what he looks like in his own shape?" she asked.

Arawn's wife laughed. "In human shape? In that clumsy, awkward form? I am only too thankful not to see him as he really is!"

"I would like to know what he really looks like if *I had* spent a year in bed with him."

"Humans are best left well alone. They are inferior beings."

"But Arawn respects him as an equal now."

"Not as an *equal.*"

"A friend at least. And friendship knows no inequality."

"Rhiannon, for me he never existed. Why should I be curious? I love Arawn. There is no one else for me. There never will be."

Rhiannon sighed. She would like to know what the human looked like. She would like to know what it would feel like to lie in bed with him. She even wondered if he would have been able to resist her as easily as he resisted her friend. But she kept quiet now because she could see Arawn's wife was beginning to get annoyed with her. She kept quiet—but from this time on, she nursed a secret longing to see Pwyll. She was determined that somehow she would bring this about.

Rhiannon was the daughter of Heveydd Hên and had lived all her life with her father in the shining realms of Annwvynn. There, until this time, she had had everything she could possibly wish for. Now she began to be restless and dream about a world she had never seen— the world of the humans—a world they talked about as "the dim world, the world of sorrow and strife and shadow."

One day she conceived a plan. She dressed in her finest golden robes and, riding on a snow-white horse, she set off for the borderland between the worlds.

She was in luck—at Beltane, Pwyll and his companions had climbed the mound of Arberth where the two worlds are at their closest. Gazing out across the landscape they saw Rhiannon, a beautiful woman dressed all in gold, riding a white horse. Pwyll, at once curious to know who she was, sent one of his companions after her to find out. The woman wasn't riding very fast and the man expected to catch up with her in no time at all. To his surprise, though he galloped and she did not increase her pace, he found he was no nearer her at the end than he was at the beginning. He returned to Pwyll and reported that he had failed. Pwyll laughed and teased him for his poor horsemanship.

The next day Pwyll and his companions returned to the mound and again saw the woman riding. Pwyll dispatched a different man to find out who she was and began to be annoyed when the second rider returned with the same excuse that he had ridden as hard as he could yet still could not catch up with the lady.

Pwyll began to suspect that there was some enchantment at work, and on the third day when the same rider appeared he set off after her himself on his fastest horse. Everything happened as before. It appeared as though she were not riding very fast and yet, no matter how hard he drove his own steed, he could not catch up with her. At last, exhausted and frustrated, he called out to her: "Lady, for the sake of the man you love, stop for me!"

"So I will gladly," she said, stopping at once. "And you would have been kinder to your horse if you had spoken those words earlier."

Then Rhiannon saw the man she loved before her, beads of sweat on his forehead from the hard riding, eyes as green-blue as the ocean, hair as brown as hazelnuts. And Pwyll saw before him the most beautiful woman he had ever seen, so beautiful indeed that he doubted she was mortal.

"Lady, what is your errand, for I have seen no one like you before in any of my lands. Are you a messenger for Arawn?"

"No," she said. "I am on an errand of my own."

"What errand may that be?"

"To find the man I love best."

"And have you found him?"

"Yes," she said quietly.

Then there was a long silence between them, Pwyll not daring to hope she meant what he thought she meant.

"If I am that man," he said at last, "then Pwyll, Lord of Dyved, is the happiest man alive."

"You are that man—and Rhiannon, daughter of Heveydd Hên, is the happiest woman in the two worlds."

Then Rhiannon told Pwyll that if he did not take her as wife she would be married to a man she did not love, and Pwyll promised that he would not let that happen. They spoke a long while and arranged that Pwyll would come to her father's kingdom in a year and a day and claim her as his bride.

When he returned to his companions the prince was silent and thoughtful but told no one what had transpired.

Rhiannon returned to her realm and set about the long and delicate process of persuading her father that she was going to marry Pwyll instead of Gwawl. It was not easy, but at last all was arranged and the marriage feast was set. Pwyll arrived with his companions and was greeted joyfully. He sat in the place of honor between Heveydd and Rhiannon. The musicians plucked their harps; the minstrels sang; the bards intoned their long and heroic verses.

Suddenly a tall, auburn-haired youth entered the hall and stood before Pwyll. Pwyll at once invited him to sit down and join the feast, but the youth refused, saying that he had come to make a request rather than to sup with him. Pwyll by this time was so flushed with wine and the pleasures of the day he was prepared to grant anyone anything.

"Ask," he said grandly. "Whatever it is, if it is within my power, I will grant it."

The youth smiled, and Rhiannon threw up her hands in horror. She had been pulling at Pwyll's sleeve to try to attract his attention since the young man had entered the hall, but Pwyll had been too drunk to take any notice.

Now she rounded on him angrily. "Why did you say that?" she cried. "I have never heard anything so foolish!"

"He has given his word in front of all these nobles," the youth said quickly. "He has to abide by it."

"What is your request?" Pwyll asked, somewhat taken aback by Rhiannon's anger.

"You are to marry the woman I love," the youth said. "It is to ask for her, and for this marriage feast, that I have come."

Pwyll looked at Rhiannon, shocked.

"You had better say no more," she said sharply. "You have done enough mischief. This is the man I wanted to avoid. This is Gwawl, son of Clud. You have given your word—now you have to give me to him."

"Never!" muttered Pwyll. But he was troubled, for he knew he would be dishonored if he broke his word.

"There is only one way out of it," Rhiannon whispered. "I have a plan, and if you will do what I say, I will never belong to Gwawl but only to you."

She told Gwawl haughtily that he couldn't have this feast as his wedding feast because she had already given it to the companions of the Lord of Dyved. She reminded him that it was not in Pwyll's power to give as it was she and her father who had provided it. She told him that a similar one would be prepared for him when he returned to wed her in a year and a day.

Gwawl rode off with his companions and Pwyll with his. In his hand Pwyll had a small leather bag that Rhiannon had told him to guard carefully and to bring back at the appointed time. She had instructed him in how it was to be used and made him promise to follow her instructions exactly.

❖

On the day that had been arranged Pwyll and his ninety-nine men arrived early and hid in the orchard above Heveydd's court, as Rhiannon had instructed them.

Gwawl arrived with his men in all their finery, ready for the wedding feast. The young bridegroom took his place at the head of the table between Heveydd and Rhiannon in great good humor. The old man greeted him warmly. He was not sorry that his daughter had been tricked into marrying the man he had chosen for her. He was not sorry that Pwyll had shown himself to be so foolish the year before. He had warned Rhiannon about humans and she had seen for herself. There was only one thing that marred his enjoyment of the feast and that was the way Rhiannon was treating Gwawl. She greeted him with apparent enthusiasm and was smiling and talking as though there were nothing in the world that she wanted more than to be wed to him this night, but . . . there was something in the brittleness of her smile, the slightly mocking ambivalence of her remarks, that worried her father. He had the feeling that everything was not as it seemed and that she was plotting something.

When the feasting and the carousing was at its height, a ragged beggar came to the door and, because no one was barred from the celebration, he was allowed in. He stood before Gwawl, as once Gwawl had stood before Pwyll, and craved a boon. Gwawl at once generously promised to grant it, if it was reasonable.

"Indeed it is reasonable, my lord," said the beggar, "for all I ask is that you fill this little bag here with food."

Gwawl smiled at the slightness of the request and instantly commanded that the man's bag be filled.

Heveydd looked across at Rhiannon when this was being done and was uneasy to notice that her eyes were shining and she was having difficulty suppressing laughter.

The servants soon found that no matter how much food they stuffed into the bag, it seemed never to be full. At first Gwawl laughed at the difficulties they were having and then became annoyed.

"Man, will your bag never be full?" he demanded.

"It will only be full, my lord," the ragged man replied, "when a nobleman, rich in land and possessions, steps into the bag and presses the food down with both his feet, saying as he does so: 'There is enough inside.'"

"My lord," said Rhiannon quickly to Gwawl, "do it or there will be no food left for our guests."

"Gladly," said Gwawl, and he leapt up lightly to step into the bag. No sooner had he done that than the ragged man pulled the drawstring tightly over his head and imprisoned him in the bag. Then Pwyll triumphantly threw off his tattered garments and stood before the assembled throng with a horn to his lips.

Before Gwawl's men, somewhat the worse for drink, had fully grasped what had happened, the great doors swung open and Pwyll's men, fully armed and sober, sprung into the hall.

"Now will I bargain the freedom of Gwawl against the lady Rhiannon!" Pwyll cried.

But his men, in high spirits at the turn of events, began to sport with the bag and kick it about the hall.

"Daughter, what have you done!" Heveydd whispered to Rhiannon, shocked. But she was standing, reaching out her arms to Pwyll and oblivious of all else.

Helplessly, Gwawl's men watched as their lord was kicked and battered ignominiously in the bag. At last Gwawl cried out that such a death was no death for a nobleman.

"He is right," Heveydd said angrily to Rhiannon. "Such is no proper death for him. Last year you saw that humans are foolish—and now you see that they are wantonly cruel. Do you still want to live among them?"

She did not reply, but Heveydd could see by her expression that she had not intended the trick to take the turn it had.

Pwyll called a halt to the savage game and moved to release Gwawl from the bag.

"One moment," said Rhiannon quickly. "Before that is done we must have assurances that he will make no more claims and seek no revenge. And," she added, "that he will give the presents our guests are entitled to on your behalf."

Gwawl agreed to everything and was released, bleeding and with many bones broken. Heveydd and Rhiannon watched him go, carried by his men, and wondered if, in spite of the assurances, they would not one day have to pay dearly for the uncalled for savagery of Pwyll's men.

That night Rhiannon's thoughts were not on human foolishness or cruelty, but on the pleasures of making love, at last, with the man of her choice.

At the end of the long-protracted festivities it was time for Pwyll to return to his own land. Heveydd suggested Pwyll should go on alone and that Rhiannon should follow later.

"My father," Rhiannon said fondly. "When are you going to give up this attempt to part us? You can see how it is with us. . . . Accept it."

Heveydd sighed deeply.

"You were ever headstrong," he said. "So be it. But the time will come when you will know what I have been trying to save you from." He turned to Pwyll. "Take care of her, human. She is more precious than all the gold and silver in your world."

"I will take care of her, my lord," Pwyll answered soberly. "For she is more precious to me than the world itself."

Rhiannon went with Pwyll to Dyved, and there at Arberth a feast had been laid out to greet the new bride. Rhiannon was surprised that the singing was almost as sweet as in her own realm. Pwyll introduced her proudly to his people. She generously gave gifts to all who came, and not one went away but had a word or two to say about her beauty and her graciousness. But later, when they were at their own hearths, they wondered that their prince had chosen an alien princess from Annwvynn rather than a wife from one of the neighboring kingdoms. "No good will come of it," they said. "Their ways are not our ways."

For two years things seemed to go very well. Neither Pwyll nor Rhiannon, locked as they were in their private idyll, noticed that some of the more pompous members of the court were annoyed that Rhiannon sometimes seemed to be laughing at them. Neither Pwyll nor Rhiannon noticed that sometimes Rhiannon's impatience with the slow and cumbersome way things were done in this world, compared to the way they were done in hers, annoyed some of the courtiers and their wives.

In the third year a deputation came to Pwyll and pointed out that Rhiannon had not yet shown any signs of bearing a child, and they strongly advised that their prince put her aside and take a wife more likely, as they put it, to bear him children. Pwyll refused . . . but he said, in answer to their persistence, that if no child were forthcoming in another year, he might possibly consider what they had suggested.

Before the following year had run its course Rhiannon had given birth to a son.

That night after the exertions of labor, the sleeping mother and child were put in the care of six women. One by one the women who were supposed to be on watch fell asleep, and when they woke in the morning they found to their horror that the infant had disappeared. Rhiannon herself was still peacefully asleep and unaware of this. The women anxiously consulted as to what was to be done, for they knew they would be blamed. One came up with a grisly plan to escape punishment and easily persuaded the others to it. They seized the newly born pups of a deerhound, slaughtered them, and smeared the blood all over Rhiannon and themselves, leaving the remnants of the pups around so that they looked like the dismembered pieces of the baby.

When Rhiannon woke refreshed and looking for her baby, they told her that they had fought to save its life, but that she, being from the Other World, had proved too strong for them. All six women swore that they had witnessed her ripping her child to pieces.

Distraught as she was at the loss of her child, Rhiannon tried to plead with them to tell the truth, promising that whatever had happened they would not be punished. But the house was roused and the terrible news spread like wildfire; the six women protested so loudly and swore the truth of what they said with such formidable oaths that the people found it easier to believe their six voices than the single protestations of a woman who was from an alien world and had never really fit into theirs.

Angry people gathered outside Pwyll's castle and shouted for Rhiannon's death. She heard them chanting as she lay in bed, weeping for her lost child. So adamant were the women and so skillfully had they told their story that Rhiannon herself began to wonder if there was not some truth in it. Who knew what terrible things she might have done in her sleep? She often felt torn between the two worlds and perhaps . . . perhaps some fell being had taken over her mind when she was hovering between neither and made her harm her child.

Pwyll listened to the story of the women with a white face. He couldn't believe his beautiful Rhiannon had done what they said . . .

but all the evidence seemed to be against her. Besides—and here he was influenced by his companions—she was not of their world, and who knew what Other World people were capable of? She had been extremely angry when she found out his companions had suggested she should be put aside if she did not produce a child. Perhaps she had produced the child and then killed it to spite them.

Everyone demanded her death. But Pwyll pulled himself together enough at least to refuse to do this. He would not put Rhiannon to death, but he agreed that she should be punished.

Rhiannon lost her place at his side and was doomed to live in disgrace at the gate for seven years, there to confess her crime to every traveler who came by and, in penance, ask them to allow her to carry them on her back into the presence of her lord.

At this time it was hard to know who suffered more, Pwyll or Rhiannon.

At first loutish people spat at her and sneered, but gradually the sorrowful dignity of the queen softened every heart.

Many a time Rhiannon thought of her ancient home in the shining land of Annwvynn and longed for the life she had led there. She remembered her father's parting words but knew that even he would not derive satisfaction from the way his prophecy had come true. She thought of going home, but her love for Pwyll was not dead—and her fear that she had done what she was accused of still haunted her.

Now there was a nobleman called Teirnon Twrvliant who lived some way from Pwyll's castle and had a mare of which he was inordinately proud. Every May Eve she foaled, but every time the foal had disappeared by morning. This particular year Teirnon determined to solve the mystery and lay in wait, hidden in the stable all night. Suddenly a horrible claw appeared at the window, seized the colt, and started to drag it away. Furiously, Teirnon hacked at the claw with his sword and managed to cut it right off; the claw, and the foal, fell within the stable. Outside he heard a terrible scream and rushed out to see what manner of beast might have such a claw. In the darkness he could see nothing, but he could hear it crashing away in the undergrowth. He hurried back to the stable to see how the foal was faring and at the door almost stumbled over a bundle. When he looked more closely, he saw it was a small boy covered in blood and mucus and wrapped in a silk mantle. Teirnon at once took the child to his wife, and they agreed to rear it as their own. They called him Gwri Golden Hair and were astonished at how quickly he grew. At one year he was as sturdy as a three-year-old. They gave him the colt they had rescued on the same night as they found him.

One day Teirnon heard the sad tale of Rhiannon and how she was in disgrace and what had occurred to put her there. He listened attentively and began to think about Gwri. He and his wife looked at the boy closely, and it seemed to them that there was no doubt he resembled Prince Pwyll. They agreed that it would be wrong for them to keep the lad any longer, much as they loved him. They sat him upon his horse, and Teirnon and three companions rode with him to the court of Pwyll. There they found Rhiannon at the gate sadly telling her tale and offering to carry them into the castle. They spoke gently to her and led her into the presence of Pwyll. There they explained how they had found the boy.

Rhiannon stared at the child and felt all the sorrows she had suffered lifting off her. There was no doubt in her heart that this was the son of Pwyll and herself. Nor was there doubt in the heart of anyone else.

Then there were tears of rejoicing . . . and pleas for forgiveness . . . and the child was proudly installed as prince between his father and his mother. He was given the name Pryderi, and he swore to honor his foster mother and father as much as his own mother and father to the end of his days.

Rhiannon's golden youth was gone. She was thinner than she had been, and her eyes no longer shone with humor and mischief—but she was back where she wanted to be and her son was at her side. Pwyll couldn't do enough for them to make up for what they had been through.

When Pwyll came to die, an old man, Rhiannon was still a woman in her prime. She sat beside his grave and mourned, thinking back over the years. She had loved him in spite of everything he had done—the foolishness of his promise to Gwawl, his tardiness in checking his followers when they were humiliating and tormenting a helpless victim, and, above all, his blindness in not seeing her innocence in the matter of their son. He had been a hero to his people, a friend to the King of Annwvynn, a mighty warrior, a noble prince, a handsome and a loving man, but . . . he had been human, and her father had warned her about humans.

Rhiannon picked up a handful of loose earth from his grave mound and sifted it thoughtfully through her fingers. This earth—this strange, solid earth that humans clung to and fought over as though it were the only reality they had. Pwyll had been wiser than that: he had reached after other things, albeit in the wrong way. In his youth Pwyll had tried to steal the stag from the magical kill of Arawn. He had tried to seize something that belonged to the supernatural realms without being granted the right—and for this he had been put to a long and difficult trial, from which, Rhiannon thought with satisfaction, he had emerged with flying colors. She smiled, remembering her conversation with Arawn's wife and her own youthful curiosity that had started the whole long chain of events.

It is true she had shown herself first to him and deliberately enticed him into her realm. But he had told her later that he and his companions were on the mound of Arberth that day knowing that strange wonders were sometimes seen from there and wanting themselves to witness such a wonder. It was only because he was already seeking the supernatural realms that she was able to appear to him at all.

His rashness at the first wedding feast had shown that he was not yet ready for her, and so he had had to wait until he was. His second attempt was more successful. That his men behaved as they did was the only flaw. As their leader Pwyll was responsible for not having taught them the true nature of honor. For this he should have had to wait another year. Her father had tried to insist on this—but she could not wait and had taken him, flaws and all, because she loved him.

And here she was without him, marooned in neither one world nor the other. She couldn't leave her son Pryderi—anchored as he was by his human blood to this world.

Over the years Rhiannon and her son ruled Pwyll's cantrevs well. She kept a shrewd control at home while he campaigned and added to his lands. But when he took a wife—Kigva, daughter of Gwynn the Splendid, son of Gloyw Wide Hair, son of Casnar—Pryderi began to think that it would be best if his mother had a life of her own to lead so that his own wife could take her rightful place at his side in court matters.

Pryderi thought about Manawyddan, one of the sons of Llyr and brother to Bran the Blessed who had been killed in Ireland fighting

24

for their sister Branwen. Manawyddan was a man Pryderi greatly respected and one who had his origins in the supernatural realms, as had Rhiannon. As Bran's brother he should have inherited his place as High King of the Island of the Mighty on the death of Bran's son— but this place had been usurped by Casswallawn, son of Beli. Pryderi and others had offered him help to regain his lost lands, but Manawyddan was not interested. He had had enough of war and killing and wanted to settle down in peace.

Pryderi suggested he should come to meet his mother. He spoke of her beauty, of her wisdom, of her intelligent conversation. He suggested that if Manawyddan liked her they should marry and rule over seven cantrevs of Pryderi's land. If later he wanted territory of his own, Pryderi would help him get it.

Manawyddan agreed at least to meet the lady, and Pryderi took him home where Kigva and Rhiannon had prepared a magnificent feast of welcome. At the high table Manawyddan was placed next to Rhiannon.

Rhiannon had no inkling of what was in her son's mind as she talked to the stranger with the wise and gentle face. She liked him at once and found it easy to converse with him. They covered matters ranging from the passing of the seasons in this world to the timeless ideals of the shining realms of Annwvynn. In every matter they found the comfort of common ground.

Late in the evening Pryderi leaned across to Manawyddan and asked if he had decided to accept the offer or not.

"What offer?" Rhiannon asked at once.

Pryderi told her what he had suggested and Rhiannon was angry.

"Was I not to be consulted in this?" she asked sharply.

"My lady," Manawyddan said at once, "we did not tell you before only because we wanted to save you embarrassment. If you had known what we had in mind, you might have been wary of me and we would never have conversed as freely as we have done."

Rhiannon looked at him searchingly. She saw a handsome, mature man; one who understood her very well; one who carried the wisdom of her own shining realms with him; one whom she already liked more than any man she had seen since Pwyll's death. It was true there was none of the racing of the heart she had experienced with Pwyll ... but racing of the heart is not always the criterion of real and abiding love.

"Well," she said sternly to Manawyddan. "What have you decided?"

He smiled at her haughtiness. "Lady, if you will have me, I would be honored to be your husband."

Rhiannon was silent for a moment or two longer—just enough to cause Manawyddan and Pryderi some anxiety—and then she too smiled. Pryderi breathed a sigh of relief. Like his father before him, he tended to rush into things without proper consideration—and for a moment he thought he had spoiled a beautiful plan.

"My lord," Rhiannon said in a voice bordering on the mocking, "my son Pryderi had a good idea for once. I would not want to ruin it for him!"

Manawyddan laughed.

"Lady, we will do well together."

"Ay," she said. "I think we will."

And so it was that Rhiannon entered on a new marriage and a new life.

There followed some very good years. Rhiannon, Manawyddan, Kigva, and Pryderi were the greatest of friends, and the four spent a great deal of time together in pleasant and satisfying pursuits.

One evening the four companions were at Arberth enjoying a feast when they felt the urge to climb the mysterious mound from which Pwyll had first spied Rhiannon. There was something of nostalgia in Rhiannon's decision to visit the place and something of curiosity in Pryderi's.

It was summer and the sun had not yet set. The land lay under its golden light and they stood on the top and admired the neat pattern of the cultivated fields, the little plumes of smoke from the homesteads, the herds of cattle quietly grazing. From this height they could see their own castle with the tiny figures of men and women, dogs and geese, passing in and out.

Suddenly they heard thunder and looked up at the sky, puzzled that such a sound should come from a clear sky. When they looked down again they saw that a thick mist was creeping over the land, and they were soon engulfed in it themselves. Kigva held Pryderi's hand tightly and whispered that she wanted to go back to the castle. There was a strange eeriness about this mound that she had always hated.

"That we will, my love," her husband promised her, "as soon as the mist lifts a little and we can see our way."

But the mist did not lift, and Rhiannon advised them all to keep close together and hold fast to each other, for she sensed that this was no ordinary evening mist rolling in from the sea. She found herself strangely excited—half wanting to slide back into the magical world of her youth, half dreading to part with the happiness she had now found in the land of Dyved.

When the mist finally disappeared she was a little disappointed, but also a little relieved, to see that they were not in Annwvynn. The land of Dyved still lay at their feet, but—and here they gasped, Manawyddan putting his arm around Rhiannon's waist and Kigva clinging even tighter to Pryderi's arm—the landscape was totally changed. There were no cultivated fields, just wild forests and hills as they had been in ancient times. There were no herds, no homesteads, no plumes of smoke. The castle was no more than a ring-mound with a few charred remnants of wooden huts. No man, woman, or child—no dog, goose, or horse —moved on the face of the earth. They were totally alone.

They were so shocked they said nothing to each other, but each hurried silently down the mound toward the place where their castle had been—still hoping that when they were off the magical mound, all would be as it had been. But it was not. The desolation was complete in every direction. The castle was as they had seen it from above. There were no signs of their occupation of it. All their clothes, jewels, and fine furniture were gone; all their friends and companions lost.

Night was coming on and they were afraid.

That first night they huddled in the shell of the ancient buildings. They set a fire against the cold and slept close together, hoping that in the morning all would be back to normal.

But in the morning they were no better off.

Day after day passed, and they remained in this strange, deserted land. To eat, they had to hunt and scratch about for roots and berries like primitive people. Each morning they woke hoping to find a change. Each morning they were disappointed.

At last they accepted the fact that their own country was somehow lost to them, and they decided to leave the area and travel east, hoping that some other parts of the world had been left untouched by the enchantment.

They found a place at last where there were people and farms and villages such as they had once known. They were at a place called Hereford in England. Where they were not known and where they had no trappings of power and privilege. They had to start as strangers in a strange land and find work as best they could. They chose as their profession the making of saddles and, under Manawyddan's expert guidance, soon earned such a reputation for the beauty and comfort of the saddles they made that all the other saddlemakers in the district became jealous and plotted to murder them.

When this came to their notice, Manawyddan at once suggested that they leave the area and try their luck somewhere else. Pryderi wanted to stay and fight—but he was dissuaded.

In the next town they tried their hands at shieldmaking, and again their work was so skillful that the other shieldmakers grew jealous and threatened to run them out of town. Pryderi was furious and again wanted to draw his sword—but once again Manawyddan prevailed upon him that the best policy was to leave peaceably and start again. Grumbling audibly, Pryderi followed the others to another town.

Once again they settled down, and this time they became shoemakers. When this too earned them the enmity of the local shoemakers, even Manawyddan agreed to give up trying, and sadly they made their way back to their beloved Dyved. There they hunted and gathered berries as before.

One day their hunting dogs entered a copse and then rushed back to the men trembling with terror. Astonished, Manawyddan and Pryderi looked to see what the trouble was—and were almost run down by a huge, shining white boar that broke cover and went storming off down the valley. The dogs pursued it, and the men pursued the dogs. Before long they were brought up short before the high walls of a large building, and they stood amazed—for no such building had been seen in Dyved since the enchantment began. Manawyddan put his hand on Pryderi's arm to stop him from rushing in headlong after the boar and his hounds.

"Be careful," he said. "This building was not here before. This could also be enchantment."

"I cannot lose my hounds," said Pryderi impatiently. "I must go and see what is happening." And he shook off Manawyddan's hold and followed the hounds and the boar into the building.

Once inside, there was no sign of the animals nor of any living thing.

Pryderi walked bemused through deserted hall after deserted hall, down corridor after corridor. At last he came to a great courtyard with an elaborate white marble fountain at the center. Hanging from a gold chain above it, as though to be used for drinking, was an exquisite golden bowl. Delighted, Pryderi reached up and seized the cup. At once he stuck fast to it and couldn't move a muscle in his body.

Meanwhile, Manawyddan waited outside for Pryderi to reappear. He could hear no sound from within the castle nor see any movement. Filled with sorrow and foreboding he returned to Rhiannon and Kigva and told them what had happened.

Rhiannon was at once furious that he had left her son there and made no attempt to rescue him.

"There is strong magic there, Rhiannon," he said. "It would not profit you two women if you were left entirely alone."

"I am going to fetch him out," she said scornfully.

Manawyddan tried to dissuade her, but she would not listen. She could think of nothing but that her son was in danger and she must do everything in her power to rescue him. She rushed away from her husband and entered the strange new building. Like Pryderi, she wandered through halls and corridors for some time before she came to the courtyard where she found the white marble fountain with Pryderi leaning against it, reaching up to a golden cup—he had apparently turned to stone.

Knowing at once that it was because Pryderi had tried to grasp the golden cup from the shining realms without invitation or proper preparation, Rhiannon impatiently rushed forward and tried to take it from his hand, intending to return it to its rightful place. But as soon as she touched her son and the cup, she too stuck fast and couldn't move a limb. At that moment there was a clap of thunder and a thick mist rolled in over the building. When it lifted, neither the building nor Rhiannon and Pryderi were to be seen.

Manawyddan and Kigva stared in dismay at the place where the building had been.

Rhiannon and Pryderi found themselves at the center of a jeering crowd and were jostled and pushed until they were brought before the high throne of the ruler of this land. They were greeted coldly by the prince and his lady, and orders were given for heavy burdens and chains to be put upon them.

"Why do you treat us so?" Rhiannon asked haughtily. "What harm have we ever done you, sir?"

"No harm to me," the prince replied, "but to one who is very dear to me."

"Who could that be, my lord?" Rhiannon asked. "We have no recollection—"

"That is enough!" the prince snapped. "Take them away and let them be used as beasts of burden . . . for beasts have no recollection or understanding of what they have done either."

And so another long period of suffering started for Rhiannon. As they went about their chores, she tried to think who it could be that they had wronged—but she could remember no one. She saw the prince occasionally, and every time he noticed her weariness and pallor he smiled with satisfaction.

Rhiannon observed that every night at a certain time everyone in the court and around it disappeared—only the pregnant wife of the prince remained behind.

Because the princess was lonely at these times, she would wander out to the yard where Rhiannon and her son were chained for the night, and sometimes she would talk with them. It did not help Rhiannon to question her, for it soon became clear that she had as little idea as to why they were being punished as they themselves had. Pryderi tried to persuade her to speak to the prince about their release, but Rhiannon could see that she was too timid to do that.

Having given up trying to find out why they were there, Rhiannon asked the young woman where everyone went at night, and why, when they returned, they were so full of noise and mirth. The young woman at first refused to tell them, but one night she seemed particularly lonely and in need of company, and she softened enough toward Rhiannon to tell her that all the others had temporarily transformed themselves into field mice so that they could go into the human world to eat up all the wheat belonging to Rhiannon's husband.

"Do you not want to go with them?" Rhiannon asked calmly. "They seem to have such great sport."

"My husband will not allow me to go," the woman replied sadly.

"What? Will not allow you? I would not let my husband rule my life like that. If there were something I really wanted to do, no husband in the world would keep me from doing it."

There was no more time for conversation that night, because the others had returned.

The next night Rhiannon remarked to Pryderi that it looked as though the princess had got her wish after all and gone with the others.

She had indeed; and when the others returned, Rhiannon and Pryderi noticed at once that there was a great deal of agitation and none of the usual celebrating and carousing. They overheard someone say that the princess had been captured and had had to be left behind.

Rhiannon smiled. "I thought that would happen," she said softly to Pryderi. "She is very pregnant and cannot move as fast as the others. That is why her husband did not want her to go."

Pryderi looked at his mother with admiration—even in extremes of adversity she was quick to think up a plan.

Back in Dyved, Manawyddan had at last captured one of the mice that had been devastating his crops every night. It was a fat little one . . . too fat to move as fast as the others.

"As an example to its companions," he said to Kigva, "I am going to hang this mouse." And he set about gathering the wood to build a gibbet.

"Surely it is not dignified for a man in your position to go to the trouble of hanging such a small and insignificant creature," Kigva said in surprise. But Manawyddan insisted that he would do it.

He returned to the mound of Arberth and began to set up the gibbet. He was just working on the construction when a youth appeared and asked what he was doing. Manawyddan explained, and the young man said he would not have thought it would bring much honor to a man of Manawyddan's standing to take revenge on such a tiny creature in that way.

"Nevertheless," Manawyddan said, "I will do it—for this mouse and its companions have all but made me starve."

Before the gibbet was complete, a man accosted Manawyddan and offered gold for the mouse—to save Manawyddan, he said, from the disgrace he would bring upon himself by doing such a mean and paltry thing.

Manawyddan gave the same reply as he had given before.

Now an old man appeared, and after the same conversation and the same reply, Manawyddan actually fastened the thong about the mouse's neck.

The man then offered Manawyddan anything he cared to name for the release of the mouse.

Manawyddan smiled grimly and paused with the noose still around the mouse's neck.

"Would you give me the release of Rhiannon and Pryderi in exchange for this one small mouse?"

"I would," the man replied at once.

"Would you also remove the enchantment from the land of Dyved?"

"You shall have anything you ask—only free the mouse!" the man cried desperately as he saw the noose still around the tiny neck.

"Not until you tell me who the mouse is and who you are."

And then it all came out. The mouse, of course, was the man's pregnant wife, and he himself was Llywd, son of Kil Coed, who had avenged the wrong Rhiannon and Pwyll had done his best friend Gwawl, son of Clud, when he had been tricked into a leather bag and then ignominiously kicked by Pwyll's men. Gwawl himself could not take revenge because of the assurances that he had been forced to give at the time.

"Ah," said Manawyddan. "Before I release your wife, I want assurances that all is now settled between Gwawl and Rhiannon and that no more harm shall come to us because of that old quarrel."

"I swear," cried Llywd, and he reached out his hands for the mouse.

"Not so quick," Manawyddan said sharply. "Where is my wife?"

Then he saw Rhiannon and Pryderi coming toward him, and in the rejoicing he released the mouse and they saw no more of Llywd or his wife.

The rich and fertile land of Dyved returned to its old form. No one but the four of them had noticed that anything had ever been any different or that any time had passed since they went together to climb the mound of Arberth.

────── Commentary ──────

While out hunting, Pwyll, a prince of the ordinary world, has run down the prey of Arawn, King of Annwvynn of the Other World, who was also out hunting. Instead of punishing him for his presumption, Arawn sets Pwyll a task. He asks him to exchange places with him for a year and a day, to take on his appearance and to live as though he were indeed Arawn in Arawn's own palace. It must be a year because, as we so often find in Celtic myths, the entry into a realm or world different from one's own can only occur at specific magical times, usually coinciding with the great sacred festivals of the year—a time when the gate between the worlds is open.

The concept of the hunt in the physical sense is often used in myth as a symbol for the search in a spiritual sense. In the forest—the dark and shadowy (but fertile, rich, and fruitful) region between the worlds—Pwyll is out searching for something; he is not sure what, but it will be something better and different from what he already has. We know it will not be material riches because, as prince, he already has those. He is in the right frame of mind for an encounter with the higher realms, but because he is new to this kind of searching, he blunders and takes on some knowledge that he is not yet ready to handle.

Arawn has two choices: He can punish Pwyll and send him back to where he was before—in which case he might be discouraged and not try again—or he can give him the training necessary for him to handle the new knowledge. Arawn can see Pwyll's potential and decides on the latter course. Note that it is Pwyll who makes the first move (as he does later by climbing the mystic mound of Arberth). He is already seeking. He is not just randomly picked by Arawn.

Pwyll has to prove that he can rule the higher levels in himself as well as he can rule the ordinary, worldly ones. He is a good and just prince in the ordinary world; can he now become even greater by passing severe tests on the inner planes? Not only has he to take on the nature of Arawn, but he has to go to bed with Arawn's wife and not touch her. This is not spelled out, but Pwyll has the sensitivity to understand how he must conduct himself. As women are usually associated with the intuitive faculty, Pwyll has to learn to live with intuition—to respect it but not seduce it or be seduced by it. This is a warning to some of us who are tempted to go off on wild tangents from reality, claiming that we are following our intuition.

The fact that Arawn claims he needs human strength to overcome an enemy is interesting and is not uncommon in Celtic myth. We see it again in the story of Cuchulain and Fand (page 95) in the Irish tales. It might be interpreted that Arawn pretends he needs human help in order to put the human through a demanding and crucial test—a spiritual battle—or that the incorporeal, but nevertheless not-so-far-from-human, beings inhabiting the next realm up from us need physical vehicles to work through.

We are used to the idea of spirit entities taking over physical bodies to do their work in this world, from popular horror movies to spiritualists and faith healers. Perhaps more unfamiliar is the idea that a physical human being can go the other way. Some people who have come back from momentary death have reported seeing extraordinary visions of the Other World—albeit heavily colored by memories of this one. It does not surprise me that people who report having had glimpses into the Other World describe it much as our own—as did the ancient Celts, ancient Greeks, and ancient Egyptians. . . . After all, the more unfamiliar a thing is the more we strive to understand it through familiar images and symbols. A primitive tribesman who sees an airplane for the first time sees it as a particularly noisy bird.

The Other World in Celtic myth is not the remote Heaven where God the Father, God the Son, and God the Holy Ghost exist in inexplicable splendor beyond our imagining. It is the next realm up in a hierarchy reaching from one even darker and heavier than our own, through several realms of ever-increasing rarification, until the ultimate Source of All is reached, about which even the Celtic myths are silent.

The Other World in which Pwyll finds himself—the Other World of the Tuatha de Danann in Ireland—is not unlike our own, and yet it is not the same. The two worlds interact, and experiences of great importance to the evolution of the human soul occur from their interaction.

Both Rhiannon and Pwyll—explorers of each other's worlds—are changed by their contact with each other.

For our protection, the two worlds are not open to each other all the time. There are certain places where it is almost as though there is a gate to the Other World. Many have found this gate in a circle of standing stones; on the top of a mountain at dawn; in a forest or on an ancient burial mound, as Pwyll did; or in a church, temple, synagogue, or mosque that has had a long history of sincere worship. There are also only certain times when the gates are open, and the ancient Celts believed these times occurred most frequently at Beltane or Samhain or some other of the major solar festivals—at mid-June or mid-December, for instance. It is no accident that we celebrate the birth of Christ in mid-December or that the rising of the sun at the winter solstice shines in a thin needle of orange light into the long dark tunnel of New Grange in County Meath, Ireland—the ancient burial mound known as the Brugh na Boyne in Celtic legend.

Note that Pwyll and his companions seek a marvel on the mound of Arberth at Beltane and that Pwyll has to wait a year for the next Beltane before he can visit Rhiannon's world and have the wedding feast. When the feast goes wrong, he has to wait another year until the gate is open again before he can return.

Note also that one cannot send a substitute once one decides to reach toward the Other World. At Beltane, Pwyll's horsemen cannot reach Rhiannon—and, indeed, Pwyll cannot himself until he speaks the magic words; that is, speaks to her from his own heart and not in idle curiosity.

A marriage of the two realms is not easy, and conditions have to be fulfillled before it can take place. Pwyll must wait to mature longer and to be sure it is what he really wants. Then he has to overcome a rival. He is outwitted and fails, and then he must go away and wait again—presumably growing wiser as he waits.

It is very important in the process of spiritual evolution that each step taken is a conscious one. We must know what we are doing and why we are doing it.

It is worth noting here how time and again in mythic stories the precise wording of what is said is of crucial importance, and any carelessness can get one into trouble. We all know of the genie who offers three wishes and the difficulties some people get into because they do not word their wishes thoughtfully enough. In this story, Pwyll is careless in not noticing how he lays himself open to giving up Rhiannon by offering to give Gwawl anything he asks for that is "in his power to give." Rhiannon saves herself by studying the wording of the contract as skillfully as any modern lawyer. She rules that she cannot be married this year to Gwawl because he asked for her *and* the marriage feast, which is not in Pwyll's power to give. But she does not notice at their next encounter that she lays herself open to the vengeance of Gwawl by not extracting assurances that *no one ever* would avenge his humiliation. By the end of the story the characters are being much more careful in their use of words.

Rhiannon helps Pwyll outwit his rival at the replay—but it is clear he is floundering in this Other World, and it is only Rhiannon's love of him and her determination to be with him that makes it possible. It is a combination of grace, in the Christian sense, and his own worthiness that allows Pwyll to reach for the rewards of the spiritual realms.

Then there is the unpleasant incident of the bag. The trickery that goes on between the worlds is also a feature of Celtic legend. In the realms just one step ahead of our own, we are still subject to much that is of a distinctly worldly nature. The vivid familiarity of it—combined with that little extra something that makes it unfamiliar—is what leads us to respond so immediately to Celtic myth and subjects us, whether we realize it or not, to the alchemy of its inner message.

Once Rhiannon has given up her own world and, for love of Pwyll, has entered ours, she takes her time to have a child, as though she knows what difficulties it will entail.

Notice that both the foal and the boy are taken on May Eve—the time when all nature is reborn and the gate between the worlds is again open.

The boy is eaten and yet regurgitated whole and alive—like Jonah and the whale in the Bible and like the fisherman's son and his wife in "The Sea-Maiden" (page 207). He is not being eaten in the normal physical sense but is being subjected to a form of isolation for initiatory purposes—a sojourn in the regions of the unfamiliar, the unknown. The monster represents the formative second womb. Pryderi is a son of two worlds and as such has to have two births. The second birth seems so monstrous to us only because it is not the same as ours.

The ordinary people at the court cannot understand the process of Other World testing and rebirth. They are frightened, horrified, and shocked and demand that the mother be punished. Rhiannon herself—because she has now taken on human characteristics—suffers deeply for her child and has feelings of doubt and guilt.

Rhiannon's punishment for what they think she has done is to last seven years—the magical number for Celts, as for so many peoples. The punishment takes two forms: conscious and verbal remorse, and physical hardship. It is interesting that her physical punishment—offering to carry travelers on her back—harks back to her ancient links with the Celtic horse goddess. In a sense Rhiannon is being punished for her very Other Worldliness. They are mocking her for her alien nature—just as an intelligent, sensitive child at school is bullied and mocked by the stupid and insensitive rabble who sense his or her superiority and fear it.

I don't think the ancient Celts thought the horse *was* a goddess—any more than we think a dove is the Holy Spirit or the ancient Egyptians thought Horus was a falcon. At a time when the Celtic tribes relied heavily on the horse, it would be natural for them to use this as symbol. And as it was still close to the time when the greatest of all mysterious and unknown beings was thought of as female—the mother—the abstract horse symbol was made more accessible by giving it a woman's name: Epona, Rhiannon, Macha . . . .

Pwyll wishes he did not have to put Rhiannon through her punishment. But he is bewildered and confused. He is, after all, only human. Consequently, he sees very little of the overall pattern of life and is very easily misled by vociferous but ignorant compatriots. Part of him wants to conform to the demands of his fellow men, but another part of him, his higher self, wants to break free of them. At least he keeps enough of his integrity by not allowing her to be put to death.

Note how quickly the foundling boy grows in the care of Teirnon and his wife—a sure sign that he is not an ordinary child. Arianrod's son Llew Llaw Gyffes does this too (see the folowing story).

Fostering is the norm in Celtic families of this time. Pryderi is fostered out—but without the knowledge of his parents. Teirnon, a noble and an honorable man, brings up the child after his second birth in a way perhaps his own parents, with their emotional problems, would not have been able to. Pryderi thrives.

The foal that was taken by the monster, to be given a second birth like the boy, becomes Pryderi's steed. They have shared an experience—they understand each other. If Rhiannon is thought of as being connected with the ancient horse goddess—as she often is—it is appropriate that her child and a foal should both be submitted to the same initiation and brought up together. In Celtic myth animals are often helpers and guides on inner world journeys and adventures, lending their particular instincts and strengths.

One of the things about Celtic myths and legends that makes them so readable and enjoyable is that whatever high and esoteric teaching they might contain, the basic structure is a good and very human story. We can recognize ourselves at every turn—though some of us will be more surprised than others at what we find.

After Pwyll's death, Rhiannon lives on as mother/mother-in-law in her son's household. She is a strong and intelligent woman and is by no means the type of mother-in-law that appears so frequently and so boringly in modern jokes. Nevertheless, we all understand Pryderi when he wants to find a husband for her.

Rhiannon's curiosity about Pwyll's world led her to serve a difficult apprenticeship in it, just as Pwyll's curiosity did in Rhiannon's world. Rhiannon's reward for coming through it with honor and reaching a wise maturity is that she is now paired with a being of her own world who, like her, is as much at home in this world as he is in his own. Manawyddan is one of the sons of Llyr, the great sea-god. He is one of those beings who has come to help us, teach us, and guide us but, because, like Christ, he has taken on human form, he has to suffer human limitations and troubles.

Rhiannon and Manawyddan meet, respect each other, love, marry. Note that Pryderi mentions his mother's wisdom and good conversation as much as her beauty when he is trying to encourage Manawyddan to meet her. One of the things I find refreshing in the Celtic myths is that women are honored as much for their minds as for their bodies. The dumb blonde would not stand much of a chance in ancient Celtic society! Nor would the woman who denigrates the femaleness of her body. The whole woman and the womanness of the whole woman are taken into account—as is the manliness of the man—in mind *and* body. Mind and body are not often set up as rivals against each other but as necessary and complementary sides of a whole.

One evening in summer—probably at the summer solstice, when it is believed the gates between the worlds are not as tightly closed as they are at other times—the four companions choose to climb the mound of Arberth. In other words, they deliberately choose to seek a mystical/spiritual/Other Worldly adventure. They should not have been surprised therefore when a Druid mist rolls in and the ordinary world disappears. Nearly all esoteric teachings will tell you that you should not call at the gate out of idle curiosity but only after careful preparations and with a good and serious motive. In this case it seems almost as though the four, feeling lazy and bored on a long summer's day, decided to attract an Other World adventure to themselves, not having thought it out properly before. Or perhaps I'm doing them an injustice and they felt the readiness manifesting as an urge to continue further on the path to higher realms. Perhaps Rhiannon and Manawyddan were homesick—or perhaps they wanted to impress the youngsters with a marvel. Whatever their motives they were not careful and specific enough, and they found themselves caught up in an adventure that did not turn out to be as pleasant as they had hoped.

But—as another esoteric teaching will tell you—nothing happens by mistake or by chance. They might not have known what they were asking for and they might not have liked what they got, but what they got was what they needed. Other World beings may well be in a higher state than we humans, but they also are on a journey upward through the realms toward the Ultimate One—and they need to be tested and trained on the way just as we do.

Kigva, the only purely human one of the four, is the most frightened. The others face up to the situation as best they can.

It is significant that the landscape around them looks exactly like the one they are familiar with and yet is completely different. How often have we been going about our business—hurried, harassed, unthinking—when suddenly something seems to snap inside and we see the same familiar things in a wholly different way? We start to see the meaning of it all. We see ourselves in a different perspective. We remember in one sense we are on a planet hurtling through space and in another that we are incorporeal in essence—and eternal. The huge and pompous buildings of our modern cities and all they stand for suddenly look like *nothing!* They can be blown away, but we cannot!

The four spiritual adventurers have reached a new plane—and on it they have none of the advantages and privileges they had on the previous one. They are no longer known to be of a respected royal family. They are not known in any capacity at all. To survive and make their way, they have to start from the beginning with only their innate intelligence and skills. Any refugee who has fled from one country where he or she was respected and successful and finds him- or herself at the bottom of the ladder in a new country, despised and ignored, knows the feeling. Only very exceptional people can climb up again—and those who do, receive as their reward the jealousy and enmity of the locals who are *not* so exceptional.

Wherever the four go and settle and try to make good, they are up against jealousy and prejudice. Pryderi is ready to punch a few faces, but Manawyddan insists they rise above it and try again. Three times (the Celtic magic three!) they make good, and three times they have to move on. At last, discouraged, they go back to where they started. But no one can ever go back to where they started. They are different and the land is different. It appears the same as when they left it, but there is a mysterious building that was not there before. Manawyddan can feel the difference; but Pryderi, impulsive and thoughtless like his father, will not listen to the warning and follows his hounds, who are pursuing a great white boar. Not only is the boar one of the most magically significant animals of Celtic myth—usually associated with the darker side of the great mother goddess—but this one is *white!* That should certainly have alerted Pryderi to the fact that it was not of this world.

Pryderi enters yet another plane of reality by going into the mysterious house. It is at once a trick organized by Gwawl in revenge for an old wrong and, at the same time, an independent magical/mystical/initiatory trial through which Pryderi must pass.

Pryderi is faced by a fountain or well, above which is suspended a golden cup on a golden chain. The well occurs again and again in Celtic legend and is associated with the earth goddess—the source of fertility, inspiration, and life. The well almost always has a guardian—usually female—to prevent the unworthy and the unready from drinking the potent and illuminating waters. Here there is no visible guardian. The cup reminds us of the Holy Grail—that mysterious chalice sought so feverishly by the knights of King Arthur's Round Table and by all men and women in the secret recesses of their hearts; the chalice whose liquid contents will give them the true meaning of life. The fact that the cup and chain are of gold suggests, of course, that it is something special, precious, and associated with light. This is not just any old cup.

Although there is no visible guardian, the unworthy and unready *are* prevented from drinking. In his impatience Pryderi seizes it without thinking—and sticks fast. Another familiar teaching is that something that is good for the initiate may well be bad for the noninitiate.

Rhiannon, forgetting all her own wisdom and going against wise Manawyddan's advice, rushes after her son, her mother's love blinding her to the deeper significance of what may be at stake here. She too sticks fast, and in this dangerous state, halfway between two realms, they are vulnerable to Gwawl's plan to have them seized and subjected to humiliations roughly equivalent to those which Gwawl himself suffered at Rhiannon's hands.

The punishment of Rhiannon and Pryderi—and therefore, obliquely, of Manawyddan and Kigva, who are associated with them—serves a double purpose. It teaches that one never escapes the results of one's actions, that old debts have to be paid off before one can move on. This theme of punishment for several generations is common in Celtic mythology and may have something to do with their belief in reincarnation, which was so strong that debts incurred in one life were sometimes required to be repaid in another. In the story of the three Etains (page 73) the theme is used again. Conare, the son of the third Etain, is punished because his grandfather dug up and desecrated the sacred hollow hills of the Tuatha. Macha (page 127) curses to the ninth generation. One wonders if the biblical warning that the sins of the fathers will be visited on the sons might possibly have had something to do with that same belief in reincarnation that was said to have been edited out of the Bible at the great synods of the early fathers.

The second purpose the punishment serves is that it brings about yet another initiation trial for the four. The two Other World beings, Manawyddan and Rhiannon, with cunning and wisdom in equal proportions, succeed in breaking the spell and freeing them all. That Manawyddan is approached three times for mercy—by a youth, a man, and an old man—suggests that all through one's life one is faced with decisions to make: personal good name among one's fellows set against justice in an abstract sense (the mouse, after all, was caught stealing and therefore due for punishment). Manawyddan is even offered great financial rewards to divert the natural course of karma, but he ignores (or pretends to ignore) all offers until the right man, the man whose other half is the mouse, is prepared to sacrifice every-thing (including himself) to undo what he has done.

Older and wiser, the four return to Dyved—or rather Dyved returns to them. No one else has noticed any time passing. In other words, all these trials and adventures have happened on the inner planes—outside time and space—as they always do.

Based on the following branches of the *Mabinogion:*
  "Pwyll, Lord of Dyved"
  "Manawyddan, son of Llyr"

Sources used:
  Gantz, Jeffrey. *The Mabinogion.* New York: Penguin Books, 1976.
  Guest, Lady Charlotte. *The Mabinogion.* London: J.M. Dent, 1906.

Arianrod and Blodeuwedd

"**Y**ou come to me still bearing the wolf smell upon you!" said Arianrod haughtily. "You, who have disgraced our family and brought the wrath of Math ab Mathonwy upon us."

"Sister, Gilvaethwy and I have paid for our deed in three long years of suffering. We have been changed into deer and swine and wolves. We have learned to survive without any of the comforts to which as men we had grown accustomed. I ask you now, for the sake of our mother, to seal Math's forgiveness by accepting the honor he offers our family through you. Take Goewin's place as his footholder, his comforter, and his confidant."

"What makes you so sure I am a virgin?"

"You live in this castle with your women. The white sea beats at your doors. No man comes nigh you from Samhain to Samhain."

"Ay, no man comes nigh me. Do you ask me to give this up and live in the king's presence among the noise and turmoil of the court, where men smell of horses and horses of men?"

"Come, princess—there is no higher honor than to serve the greatest sage and seer there has ever been. Math is a master of magic no man has ever or can ever surpass. He is as great of wisdom as of strength. Of how many men can that be said?"

"If he is so great of wisdom, how could he be so easily tricked by you into war with Pryderi?"

"He is wise and he can hear a whisper from a hundred miles away if he chooses to listen—but he trusts where perhaps he should not trust; he forgives where perhaps he should not forgive."

"A rapist and a trickster," she said pointedly.

Gwydion, her brother, smiled ruefully.

"Our brother Gilvaethwy is not a rapist. He loved Goewin truly and only her. Love of her had made him ill," he replied.

"He took her by force," she said scornfully, "when you had tricked Math, her protector, away from her side!"

"Sister, we are not proud of what we have done. If we could undo it, we would."

"Pryderi, son of Pwyll and Rhiannon is dead! You murdered him with your tricks. Nothing you can do can bring him back."

"He chose to fight for his pigs."

"He chose to fight to be avenged on the one who had swindled him out of his special gift from Arawn of Annwvynn. Those smooth and delicious pigs were a gift from the shining realms—they were not the bristling swine of the forest. Shame on you, brother, for using the lofty magic Math had taught you to rob a man—and a man as honorable as Pryderi! His father was a mortal, but his mother was of the Tuatha de Danann, like us. She will not rest until you have paid for your part in this."

"I have paid! Math has seen to that."

"And what did you learn," she demanded scornfully, "in your year as a deer?"

"I learned what it was to be hunted and to have little defense but fleetness of foot. I learned what it was to have nothing provided but have to find every morsel of food and water myself—and while doing that to be always in danger. I learned the powerful urge of the rut—and knew that my brother Gilvaethwy, in taking Goewin, had behaved as the animals behave, not as a man. I took him as he took Goewin and he suffered as she suffered. A fawn was born to us, the deer and the doe, and Gilvaethwy, our brother, suffered in the bearing."

"And where is this fawn now—this offspring of such a strange union?"

"Math touched him with his wand of yew and he became a human child. He lives now among Math's women. His name is Hydwn. He will not suffer for our misdeeds. He will have the fleetness of the deer, the sensitive ears, the gentle mien. But he will not rut as they rut nor be hunted as they are hunted."

"And what did you learn in your year as a wild forest boar?" Arianrod persisted.

"I learned to forget fine silks and soft couches. I learned the smell of rotting vegetation and animal feces. I learned to push and fight. I learned to hide. Gilvaethwy, as sow, felt the thrust of my desire and the pangs of bearing a huge litter. Only one survived. He is now with Math, a boy called Hychdwn, strong and fierce. He has a geiss against hunting boar—but he will not suffer for our misdeeds."

"Your third year was spent as a wolf. Did you learn aught from that?"

"We learned to work with the pack. We learned that we should not go off on our own but always listen to our leader. Our deeds rebound on our fellows. If we do not work together, all suffer."

"And the child of the year?"

"He is with Math, a boy called Bleiddwn. He will be a leader. He will not suffer for our misdeeds."

"Ah, brother, I see Math is indeed a wise sage. No punishment could have been as effective as the lessons he has taught you and Gilvaethwy. I can see that you have changed."

"Will you come with me and serve him—the pure virgin who holds his feet in her lap when he is weary; the wise virgin who listens to his troubles; the beautiful virgin who pleases his eyes when he has gazed too long on the savageries of the world; the maiden whom no man has touched save himself, who cannot tell his secrets because no man lies in her bed to listen; the unblemished barrier through which no unwanted energies pass from one realm to another?"

"I will come, brother—and I will be honored to serve such a man."

Arianrod left her crystal chair and her circular shining castle beside the silver sea, and traveled with her brother Gwydion to Caer Dathyl in Arwon, where the High King of Gwynedd—Math, son of Mathonwy, the greatest magician in the Island of the Mighty—dwelt.

Math was so attuned to the invisible realms that he could only bear to dwell among humankind if his feet never touched the ground. In war, when he was forced to walk upon the earth, he wore special shoes to lessen the damaging effect of the powerful chthonic energies of the earth. When he was seated at home, his feet were prevented from touching the ground by resting in the lap of a specially chosen virgin. It was said that if he chose he could hear the thoughts of any in his kingdom, and there was no magic too sensitive or subtle for him to perform. But this was only because he took the precautions he did. If he let his powers seep away into the ground of this material world— or if he allowed the energies of this world to overwhelm those he carried within himself from the other—it might be a very different story. In seducing and raping Goewin, his nephew Gilvaethwy had done more than dishonor a maiden and her family—he had put Math's own powers at risk and hence the safety of his whole kingdom.

Gwydion had noticed that his brother Gilvaethwy was pining for love of Goewin. He had thought up a scheme to get Math out of the way so that Gilvaethwy could approach her. He had traveled south to Powys, where another great king ruled: Pryderi, son of Pwyll and Rhiannon. Disguised as a traveling bard, Gwydion told such wonderful and heroic tales at the court of Pryderi that the king offered him any reward he cared to name. Gwydion named the beasts Pryderi had recently received as a gift from the king of the magical realms of Annwvynn. Pryderi regretted that this was the one thing he could not oblige Gwydion with because he had promised Arawn that he would not sell or give them away until he had bred the same number again from them. Gwydion suggested that an exchange of gifts might get around the problem, and he offered Pryderi twelve magnificent and richly caparisoned chargers and twelve black greyhounds, each white-breasted and each with pure gold collars and leads. He added for good measure twelve amazing golden shields. Pryderi was tempted and agreed to exchange his few pigs for Gwydion's costly gift.

Delighted, Gwydion left at once, driving the pigs quickly northward.

Within twenty-four hours Gwydion's gift of horses and dogs and shields had disintegrated, returning to the original bits and pieces of rubbish out of which he had conjured them.

Pryderi led his hosts north, seeking to reclaim his pigs and punish Gwydion.

Word of their approach reached Math. Without knowing what

Gwydion had done, he raised his army to defend his country against what he thought was an unprovoked attack.

A terrible battle took place and many good men on both sides were killed. Pryderi, in order to save more slaughter, suggested he meet Gwydion in a single combat as his quarrel was not with Math but with Gwydion alone.

It was agreed. And using sorcery, Gwydion killed the noble king of Powys.

While Math was away at battle Gilvaethwy forced Goewin to bed with him in Math's own bed.

Math had paid compensation in cattle and gold to Goewin's family as soon as he heard from the girl what had happened, and he had honored her by marrying her himself. But this had left him without a suitable foot-holder. Gwydion, in trying to recompense him for what he and his brother had done, offered the king their sister, Arianrod, a young woman of extraordinary beauty and very high rank. Arianrod, Gwydion, and Gilvaethwy were the offspring of the Great Goddess Don, Math's own sister.

Math agreed to see Arianrod and waited for her with some impatience in his great oaken chair. His trust in the children of Don had been somewhat shaken, and there was an edge of wariness to his impatience. Gwydion had been his favorite pupil and he had let Math down. The boy had shown such promise, learning in leaps and bounds anything that Math chose to teach him. As a young man his mind was brilliant and subtle. Gilvaethwy was simple beside him. He knew there was great affection between the brothers, and Gwydion on more than one occasion had helped Gilvaethwy overcome some difficulty— but this latest escapade was too damaging to too many people to condone.

Arianrod stood in the great hall before the chair of Math ab Mathonwy. Beside the king sat his new wife, seemingly a calm and untroubled young woman. There was no sign on her face of the dishonor she had suffered. Her eyes met those of Arianrod and she looked deeply into them. Her profession had not been an easy one. It had required patience, dedication, loyalty, and, above all, self-sacrifice. But the rewards had been great. She had noticed Gwydion and Gilvaethwy looking at her in the great hall. She had felt the pull of her own blood too—but she had fought it. The honor of her family

47

rested on her virginity. As family of the chosen one of Math they enjoyed great respect in the tribe. All knew she had the ear of the king and what she asked for she would surely receive. She was ashamed that she had not been able to stop her heart leaping when the hooded young man drew her into Math's chamber—and she was not proud that she had felt a sharp twinge of disappointment when she saw it was not Gwydion himself. Would she have fought for her virginity so fiercely and been so quick to run to Math with the tale had it been Gwydion rather than Gilvaethwy?

Perhaps it was as well it was the lesser man—for she knew that there was no way of deceiving Math. Indeed, she was amazed that Gwydion had managed to do what he had done without Math suspecting anything. Was the pupil outstripping the master?

Would Arianrod be a suitable substitute for herself? She looked at Arianrod. She was tall and slender. Her red-gold hair fell like golden rain from a diadem of pearls around her head . . . purple silk flowed over silver arms . . . eyes as green as the sea boldly gazed out from an exquisite face.

Arianrod was proud. Goewin could see that by the way she held her head, by the way she stood before the king. Gwydion stood beside her—dark eyed and dark browed, handsome and fiery—holding his sister's arm and leading her forward. She sighed. She loved Math and was proud to be his wife now, but . . . .

Gwydion presented Arianrod to the king, and Math with his old, wise eyes gazed at her thoughtfully. There was something about her that belied she was a maiden—a wordly wise twist to her lips, an arrogance to the tilt of her head. She would not be the mild, gentle, loving creature Goewin had been. She would not be restful.

"Why did you bring me this woman, Gwydion?" he asked. "I think she is not a virgin."

"No man has touched my maidenhood," she said coldly. "Why do you doubt it?"

"I swear she is a virgin, my lord," Gwydion insisted. "No maiden more beautiful or of higher rank would serve you better."

"Step forward, lady," Math said to Arianrod, and Arianrod flowed toward him with a rustle of fine silks, her hair gleaming in the firelight, redder than the flames themselves.

In his hand Math held the yew rod that was his wand. Carefully he moved it from hand to hand and then bent it almost double between two fingers—all the while never taking his eyes off her.

"There is a test," he said quietly, "that I expect all who serve me in this role to take."

Goewin looked surprised. She had not been tested. Her word and her father's word had been sufficient.

A shadow crossed Arianrod's face.

"A test, my lord?"

He nodded.

"Do you not trust the word of your own kin?" she said haughtily.

He smiled and cast a sidelong glance at Gwydion and Gilvaethwy, her brothers. She knew it was their fault he was hesitating now.

"I will take no test," she said icily. "The word of Arianrod, the daughter of Don, should be enough."

"She will take it, lord," said Gwydion hastily. "My sister knows it is not *her* word you mistrust but my own."

Arianrod gave him an angry glance and would have protested once more had not Math, before she realized what he was planning to do, leaned forward and swiftly touched her between her legs with his wand. She felt a rush of water as though the floodgates of a dam had opened, and from her womb, before the astonished eyes of the assembled throng, fell a golden-headed, golden-skinned infant boy. Shocked, Gwydion stared at him. Almost instantly something else fell from her. This time Gwydion reached forward and, before anyone else could see what it was, he gathered it up, wrapped it in his scarf and hurried it from the room.

Furiously, Arianrod glared at Math and the staring faces around her.

"It would seem you lied," he said quietly.

"I did not lie," she said between clenched teeth and turned angrily on her heel. No one stopped her as she swept down the full length of the hall and out into the night.

Crying, the golden-haired boy was taken up in Goewin's arms—but he would not rest there, pushing and struggling to be free. Even as they watched he grew and grew until he was of a size to walk and run . . . and then he ran out of the hall too and over the hills to the sea, crying for the wild ocean and the great moon that pulled the waters hither and thither.

Math made a sign over his head to name him "Dylan," and the boy swam away in the sea like a fish.

"Arianrod's son," Math murmured. "His father must have come from the sea."

"No man has touched my maidenhood," she had said, and no man had.

Arianrod was burning with shame and resentment. She had been humiliated in front of all those people. Why had she let Gwydion talk her into going to court! She was better off here in this wild place—this familiar, beautiful place. Here no one called her to account, no one questioned or tested her. She could still see the faces, the staring eyes, the gaping mouths. Damn Gwydion and his ideas! Why had she listened to him! She had been curious—half wanting to change her way of life. She had been ambitious, too. It would have pleased her to be the High King's special confidant. She would have been close to a man whose magical skills outstripped any she knew. She would have been able to observe, to learn. Was it that she wanted to please Gwydion? There had always been something between them . . . a stirring, an awareness, an interest that was more than it should be.

Arianrod had chosen to live so isolated from the world because her restless spirit could find nothing there that satisfied her. The petty quarrels and gossip of the court bored her. Beside her handsome, brilliant brother, no man pleased her. Shadows . . . puppets all! Her heart needed a greater stimulation than any there could give. Perhaps Gwydion's description of Math had led her to hope that here at last would be a man worthy of her—immortal as herself, with a mind to match her own.

Arianrod walked on the strand below her castle. She flung her sandals off and felt the cool sand beneath her feet. She loosened her silken robes and they slipped unnoticed from her. She flung her diadem of pearls into the sea from whence they had come. Naked, she entered the water.

The white sea frothed over her flesh, the blue water caressed her limbs. Sighing, she floated in the embrace of the great, the powerful, the mysterious. . . She felt his touch in every part of her. She knew him and he knew her. This mighty being was her lover. This was the father of her child.

It was a long time before they drew apart, and she, satiated with lovemaking, crawled up on the beach and lay in the last rays of the evening sunlight.

Her skin was golden and on her lips lingered the taste of salt.

One day Arianrod was walking around the perimeter ramparts of her castle when she saw two riders approaching. She was about to withdraw when something made her pause. One of the two was Gwydion, and beside him rode a young boy. She hesitated. She watched them as they rode—now in sight, now out of sight—up the winding, almost overgrown path that led to her remote and isolated retreat. Of all the men in the world she least and most wanted to see, it was her brother Gwydion! She had not seen or heard anything from Caer Dathyl since her humiliation and had given instructions to her women that no one was to be allowed to approach her castle. If any word reached any ears, they were to say nothing about it to her. Caer Dathyl and all who lived there had ceased to exist as far as she was concerned. But something stopped her this day from sending out the women warriors who guarded her gate.

"Let them approach," she whispered. Whether it was a spell of Gwydion's or her own loneliness that gave the order, she was not sure—but it was not long before Gwydion and the young lad were standing before her, dusty and travel-stained.

"Greetings, sister," Gwydion said, his dark eyes looking into her own so intently that she felt his gaze as disturbing as a touch.

She turned her shoulder to him and moved away.

"What brings you here, brother?" she asked bitterly. "Have you not done me enough harm? Are the companions of the king still laughing at Arianrod the virgin?"

"No one is laughing, sister. But some have wondered why you sought to deceive the king."

She turned to face him, her face livid with anger.

"State your business, brother, and be gone. You have not traveled this far solely to taunt me."

"No, I have not."

Gently Gwydion pushed the young boy forward.

Arianrod looked at him. She saw a child with the eyes of the golden eagle. She saw a child clothed in light. Somewhere in her heart stirred the memory of a dream. She was standing on the ramparts of her castle and high, high above her a golden eagle circled, lowering with each spiral until the beating of its great wings lifted her clothes around her. She felt the heat of his breath. She felt the power of his body. His claws and beak touched her but did not harm her, though they could have torn a wolf apart.

"This is your second son," Gwydion said, his brown, strong hand on the boy's shoulder protectively, his eyes never leaving her face. "I love him as my own."

Her green eyes blazed with golden fire.

"I have no sons," she snapped. "No man comes to this castle. No man touched my maidenhood."

"Nevertheless, he is your son and he has come for his name."

The boy shifted uneasily from one foot to the other. As long as he could remember he had looked on Gwydion as his only parent. Gwydion had loved him, reared him, trained him, protected him. He was the object Gwydion had rushed from the hall wrapped in his scarf. He had been kept in a chest at the foot of Gwydion's bed until he was ready for the world. Then he had cried out as a babe cries out for its mother's milk, and Gwydion had found him a nurse to feed him. But it was Gwydion who did everything else for him that a mother and a father would do.

Now the boy had been brought before this formidable lady and told that she was his mother. She was a stranger with a stranger's fierceness; her eyes looked on him with loathing, her jewels spat fire, her white limbs trembled with an emotion he could not define. She strode about the room angrily.

"So you have come to taunt me after all," she snarled. "Take this creature from my sight!" she snapped. "He is no child of mine, yet he will have no name lest I give him one."

Gwydion looked on her darkly.

"Why do you fight the truth so bitterly, my sister? This is your son. You know it."

"I know it not!" she screamed. Yet, in her rage, she fancied she felt the beating wings of the golden eagle upon her limbs, her breasts, her maidenhood.

"Deny him as much as you will," Gwydion said sternly, "yet he will be named by you. Come, child," he said more gently to the boy who was trembling at his side. "Your mother is not yet ready to give you your name—but she acknowledges you by saying that no one will name you save herself!"

Arianrod picked up a crystal goblet that stood upon the table and flung it with all her might at her brother's head. With a mocking laugh he stooped out of its way, and it smashed to a thousand glittering fragments against the wall behind him. Before she could pick up anything else, he and the boy were out of the chamber, running down the long corridor to the inland gate, and away on their waiting horses.

It seemed to Arianrod that for a long time she heard Gwydion's laughter in her ears.

One day, breathing in the fresh sea breezes from her battlements, Arianrod spied a strange and elegant boat drawn up at the small quayside, its sail of many colors unlike any she had seen before. No one used her small harbor but those who were bringing supplies to Caer Arianrod. She called her women and questioned them, but none knew anything about the boat.

"Is it not some lover come to fetch one of you away?" she demanded.

"No," they said. "None of us have seen such a boat before or know any of the crew who sail in her."

"Go down," Arianrod then said to one of her women. "Find out what she is doing at my quay."

Arianrod watched the young girl run down the steep and rocky path, watched her as she questioned a man standing on the deck, watched her as she clambered back up the hill.

"Well?" she asked impatiently.

"They are foreign shoemakers, my lady. I have never seen such leather—crimson and gold, finer than doeskin and yet as strong as ox hide."

Arianrod looked thoughtful. "Go back," she said. "Take the measurements of my feet to him and ask him to make me a pair of shoes—the best he can."

She retired into the castle and went about her business.

It was not long before her maid presented her with a pair of shoes more beautiful than she had ever seen before.

She sat on her crystal chair and lifted her slender foot.

The shoe did not fit. It was too large.

"Go back quickly before the boat sails," she said. "Tell him he is to make a smaller pair."

But the second pair was too small.

When Arianrod's maid was sent to complain to the shoemaker, he replied that he could not make the shoe fit unless he saw the lady's feet.

"The man is incompetent," said Arianrod impatiently. "Tell him to go away."

But she looked at the two pairs of shoes again and saw they were the best-made shoes she had ever seen—the leather the finest and the design the most beautiful.

She called for her light cloak, flung it over her shoulders, and set off down the path to the quayside.

"I am surprised you cannot make shoes to measure," she said scornfully to the shoemaker.

He bowed politely. "I could not, lady, but now I shall be able."

Beside him sat his apprentice boy stitching away at the leather.

At a signal they both climbed out of the boat onto the quayside.

Suddenly, a tiny bird, a wren, landed some way away from them on the deck, and, with extraordinary skill, the apprentice shot at it with his catapult. He hit it in the leg between the sinew and the bone.

Arianrod was impressed and smiled.

"Surely the golden-haired one has a skillful hand," she said.

Suddenly, the strange shoemaker seemed to melt away, and in his place was her brother, Gwydion, laughing triumphantly.

"You have been tricked, sister. You have named your son. From hence forward he will be known as Llew Llaw Gyffes, the golden one of the skillful hand."

She swung around to look at the boy. It was the same child Gwydion had brought to her castle to be named.

"A curse be on you for your deceit," she snapped angrily. "You will not profit from this trick. He has a name but he will never have arms but those I give him. And I will *never* give him arms!"

The boat had become a floating mess of sedge and kelp. The shoes she had so admired stank of rotting red seaweed. All had been illusion conjured by Gwydion.

Arianrod turned on her heel and strode back to her castle, her red hair floating out behind her like so many tongues of flame. Again her brother's laughter rang in her ears.

Gwydion and Llew Llaw Gyffes returned to Gwydion's castle, Dinas Dinllev, where the boy grew up under the guidance and tutoring of his uncle.

But when he was on the verge of manhood, Llew Llaw Gyffes pined for his own weapons, and no weapons felt right in his hand. Gwydion, seeing that he was ready for armor and none could be found for him, took him once more to visit his mother.

This time they appeared as two youths at the gates of Caer Arianrod. Arianrod was told that two bards from Glamorgan requested audience.

"What manner of men are they?" she asked suspiciously, for men were not encouraged to visit Caer Arianrod.

"Not men, my lady," was the reply, "but youths. The one staid and serious—the younger more lighthearted."

"Show the youths into the great hall, and gather all in the castle. Tonight we will have feasting and heroic tales, singing and dancing."

Arianrod's women were delighted, and the two young bards were quickly ushered into her presence. The more serious of the youths sat at her right hand and they spoke of the various tales stored in his memory.

"You are young to be a bard, sir," she said.

"Ay, my lady," he said. "But my friend and I have been with the Druids of Glamorgan since birth and we imbibed the ancient tales with breast milk. We could tell you a story for every day of the year and two on the feast days—and never repeat one that you had heard before."

"Tell me one now, bard, one that I have not heard before—and you shall have a feast such as you have never had before and a night to remember."

The youth bowed and stood up before her.

He began a tale, but Arianrod claimed that she had heard it before and he had to change to another. She had heard that also, and again he had to start another. So it went on until at last he told her a tale of a golden eagle who loved a woman and gave her a child that she rejected. She did not stop him, and he saw that she had tears in her eyes—but so strong was his enchantment that she still did not suspect that he was Gwydion and his companion was Llew Llaw Gyffes.

In the early hours of the morning a chamber was prepared for the two youths, and all went to their rest.

No sooner were they all asleep than they were awakened by the fearful sound of battle. Arainrod, rushing to the window of her chamber, was horrified to see that her castle was under attack. A fearsome host was gathered in the darkness. Fire arrows were raining down on her roof of wooden beams and reeds, spears piercing the breasts of her guards.

Half-clothed, distraught, Arianrod rushed through the castle, calling all her women to don their armor.

Gwydion and Llew heard her hammering on their door.

"What is it, my lady? What is that terrible sound?"

"We are under attack," she cried.

"By whom, my lady?"

"I know not and I care not. Come out and help me defend my castle."

"We cannot, my lady—we are bards, not warriors. We have no arms."

Impatiently she flung some spears and shields and swords into the room.

Gwydion started picking them up and began to arm himself.

"Please help my friend," he said. "He has not borne arms before and does not know how to strap them on."

With trembling hands as smoke filled the corridors and the sounds of shouting and screaming grew nearer and nearer, Arianrod fastened the youth's armor, placing a sword at his side and a thrusting spear in his hand. As soon as he was fully armed, the sounds of battle ceased. The smoke disappeared.

Shocked, Arianrod stood before Gwydion and Llew Llaw Gyffes, knowing that she had been tricked into giving armor to her son. She could see him testing the sword in one hand and then the other, feeling its weight, smiling that it suited him so well. She ran to the window and looked out. The hills lay sleeping in the moonlight. There was no movement, no sound but the hooting of an owl in the distance.

She rounded on Gwydion.

"This is the last time you trick me," she snapped, "and you will regret that you ever started this dangerous game. I put a curse upon this boy now from which you will never free him. He will never have a wife of the race that inhabits this earth!" And she ordered them both from her sight and forbade them ever to return.

This time Gwydion did not laugh. Llew, looking at his face, knew that the game was over and they were the losers.

As the boy grew to manhood he longed for a wife, and Gwydion, watching his suffering and knowing that this time he had not the skill to outwit Arianrod, turned to Math at Caer Dathyl. He told Math all that had happened and complained bitterly of Arianrod's attitude toward her son.

"You may have the cunning of a great magician," Math said, "but you have not the wisdom to go with it. Could you not see that by your tricks and your triumphs you were driving her further and further away from the boy? Arianrod is a proud and independent woman. She hates being outwitted and she hates being manipulated. Now your meddling has brought a very serious curse upon Llew's head. Who knows? She might have come to accept the boy as her own if she had been left to discover him for herself."

"But how? She lives isolated in that castle and hardly ever sets foot outside it."

"Nevertheless, if she had heard tales about him she might have wondered. . . . If you had tried to keep him from her, she might have wanted to take him away."

"It is unnatural that a woman should not acknowledge her own child."

"Arianrod must have her reasons."

"What reasons?"

"She will have to tell you those herself when she herself knows what they are."

"Meanwhile?"

"Meanwhile we must find a wife for Llew Llaw Gyffes."

"But. . . ."

"But she cannot be of the human race."

"How then . . . ?"

But Math ab Mathonwy had a plan, and he and his student Gwydion, two great magicians, joined their powers together to create a wife for the young man.

In her eyrie Arianrod peered up at the sky with tears in her eyes. Where was the golden spirit of the eagle now? Why was he not there to watch over the boy and prevent her from destroying him with her fierce and wayward heart?

"Strange the feelings I have, strange the thoughts. There is no breeze to move my branches and yet my branches move."

Math and Gwydion had fashioned a wife for Llew out of flowers—

using in particular the oak, the broom, and the meadowsweet. They named her Blodeuwedd.

The flower maiden opened her eyes, and the sky on a summer's day was not bluer. She smiled, and the sunlight on a fresh, clear pond did not sparkle more.

She turned her face wonderingly, looking at the three men who stood over her. The old, the younger, and the young. The two older spoke to the youngest, and he blushed and stepped back from her. They spoke more sternly to him and pushed him forward. Blodeuwedd could not understand what they said. They did not speak with the wind's voice nor the voice of the bees.

The young man drew nearer and stooped over her where she lay. His face was shy and tender, his eyes full of wonder. She saw herself reflected in his eyes and she was no longer a flower but a woman. She marveled at the transformation.

She thought about moving her branches, and they responded. She lifted them, and the young man reached down his own to her. Intertwined like vine and trunk of tree, she felt his strength, his desire, his love flow through her. He lifted her and the two older men smiled. Her tendrils floated down, soft as silken hair, over his shoulders. He brushed her petals with his lips, and she felt a warmth coursing through her body she had never felt before.

He carried her away from the other two and laid her in a soft and sheltered place. He lay down with her, and with his body he touched her so exquisitely that it seemed she floated in a sea of feelings each one more delightful than the last. When he withdrew from her she was sad and wished he had not stopped. She reached out for him— but he was tired and sighed and would not touch her again.

She lay quietly thinking . . . and she knew she was no longer thinking flower thoughts but the thoughts of a woman.

Llew Llaw Gyffes had a wife.

Gwydion told Math ab Mathonwy that now that the young man had a wife it was only right that he should have property, too. Math gave Llew Llaw Gyffes a cantrev to rule and he set up his castle near Ardudwy. There he won the hearts of all his people and was greatly honored and respected.

Blodeuwedd sat at his side like a mist of blossom in the spring, and everyone wondered where Gwydion's nephew had found such a beautiful and dutiful wife. She never talked back. She never complained. She served the wine to his guests and smiled and sang. No shadow ever crossed her brow, no harsh word crossed her lips. When Llew took her hand she followed him to bed. She never tired of his touch, and she never demanded more than he could give.

One day the young chief had to leave his cantrev to attend the High King at Caer Dathyl. Blodeuwedd stood at the gate of the castle and watched him go, waving her white hand until he was out of sight, and then walked slowly back into the castle. She sat at her window and waited for him to return—knowing no other life but the life of pleasing him.

She was sitting thus one day when she heard horns blown in the forest.

"What is that sound?" she asked her women.

"It is Gronw Pebyr, the lord of Penllyn, hunting in the forest," she was told.

She leaned forward to see what she could see, and she saw men on horseback pursuing a stag. One was ahead of the others and soon left them all behind, disappearing out of her sight.

At sunset, one of her women told her that the hunters had finished the hunt, but it was so late that it would not be possible to return to Penllyn before nightfall. Blodeuwedd said at once that she was sure her lord would be glad if she made them welcome in the castle and gave them chambers for the night.

Gronw Pebyr thanked Blodeuwedd warmly for her hospitality and sat down opposite her at the long table for the evening meal. In the firelight his skin glowed golden brown. When he lifted his arm, the velvet of his tunic sleeve fell back and she saw the ripple of his muscles. His jaw was strong, his nose straight—but it was when his eyes looked into hers that she thought her whole body would melt away.

They ate their fill and downed more honey mead than was usually served at her husband's table. Blodeuwedd and Gronw saw no one else but each other, and when it was time to retire, the lady of the house herself took the lamp that would lead him to his chamber.

She opened the door and led the way in, setting the lamp on the table beside the bed but making no move to leave.

Gronw stood looking at her. Her hair was of so pale a hue it was almost silver her skin appeared almost silver too. The silk that flowed over the soft curves of her body was the color of young spring leaves. . . . Blodeuwedd seemed like a young sapling rich with its first blossom.

Gronw stepped forward and took her roughly in his arms. All evening she had told him with her eyes that this was what she wanted, and now he did not hesitate and she did not resist. All night they lay and made love, rested and made love again.

In the morning they drew apart, and Blodeuwedd returned to her own chamber.

At noon she rose and went down to the kitchens to tell the servants to prepare another feast for their guests.

"Are they not leaving for Penllyn, my lady?" she was asked.

"No," she said. "My husband would want me to show his neighbor hospitality. They will stay one more night."

The servants looked at each other but said nothing. They prepared the feast.

That night the feasting ended earlier than before, and the mistress of the house took up the lamp and led her guest to his chamber. The door was barely closed before she had let slip her silken robes and his hands were on her breasts.

"Ay," she whispered, "would that there was nothing else in life but the lovemaking that you give me."

"Tomorrow I must go," he replied. "Your husband will be back from Caer Dathyl."

"Not tomorrow," she cried. "One more night. One more, I beg of you."

He stayed another night, and at the end of this she was even more insistent than before.

"I cannot live without you," she said. "You cannot go."

"I must go," he said. "While your husband is alive we cannot be together."

"There is some spell on him," she said thoughtfully. "I am not sure what it is. But his uncle once let slip that he could not be killed by ordinary means."

"Then you must find out by what means he can be killed," Gronw said. "For the only way we can be together every night is if he is dead and gone."

When Llew returned from Caer Dathyl, he took his wife to bed but found her in a strange mood. She seemed to shrink from his touch and turn her face from him.

"What is it?" he asked. "What is the matter?"

A tear seeped out from beneath an eyelid as blue-white as a snow-drop petal.

He looked at her tenderly and with concern, but because he could see she did not want it, he did not touch her.

"My lord," she said sadly. "I was so lonely when you were away that it made me afraid as to what would happen to me if you were killed and I was left alone."

He smiled in relief. Was ever love like hers?

"You must not fear this, my love," he said gently, "for I cannot be easily killed. Math and Gwydion have seen to that."

"What do you mean, my lord?" she asked, her large eyes looking into his with such innocence, such anxiety, that he was almost in tears himself.

"I can only be slain by a wound received in a very unusual and par-ticular way."

"What way is that, my lord?"

"There is no need to concern yourself about it," he said and reached out his arms for her. But once again she withdrew.

"I am concerned, my lord, and I cannot sleep for worrying about being left without you."

He sat up and rested his chin on his knees.

"I will tell you—but you must tell no one."

"No one, of course, my lord."

"The spear with which I am struck must have taken a whole year to fashion, and the work done on it must only be done when holy rituals are being performed."

"That would be a rare spear indeed. Is that the whole of it?"

"No. There are more safeguards. I cannot be slain within a house nor without. I cannot be slain mounted—nor on foot."

"It sounds as though you can never be slain, my lord—for how could such conditions ever by met?"

He laughed. "You see," he said. "I told you there was no need to worry. Only if someone were to put a cauldron by the river and thatch it over with a roof and then bring a buck and put it beside the caul-dron; if I were to stand with one foot on the cauldron rim and one on the back of the buck and someone were to pierce me with the spear that had been fashioned in the way I have described—then, and only then, could I be slain."

Blodeuwedd informed Gronw at once of this complicated ritual and Gronw set about working on the spear.

A year from that time he met Blodeuwedd at their trysting place in the forest and told her that the spear was ready.

That night, while caressing her husband, Blodeuwedd still pretended to be concerned that he should die and leave her alone.

"If you leave me," she said, "perhaps I will cease to be."

"You are a woman," Llew said firmly. "You will live whether I live or not."

"But what would life be without you?" she sighed.

"I will not die and leave you."

"I want to see for myself that it is impossible to kill you."

He smiled fondly. Perhaps it is in her nature to worry about such things more than other women, he thought, remembering how she was made.

He decided to set her mind at ease and allowed himself to be persuaded to set up a cauldron on the bank of a river. She attended to every detail with an anxious face—the thatching over the cauldron so that he would be neither inside nor out; the catching of a young buck goat to be held beside the cauldron for him to stand with one foot on the rim of the cauldron and one on the animal's back so that he was neither mounted nor on foot.

Satisfied that everything was prepared correctly, she clapped her hands.

"Now I see how impossible it would be for you ever to be in such a position," she said contentedly.

At that moment, Gronw, hiding in the bushes, flung the spear he had worked so long and hard to fashion. Straight and true, it flew to its mark and pierced Llew's side. The haft fell away, but the point stayed in.

With a terrible scream Llew fell to the ground.

Blodeuwedd shut her eyes, trembling at what she had done.

When she opened them, there was no sign of her husband. In his place was a wounded eagle staggering about, striving to raise itself into the air.

Shocked, Blodeuwedd stared at it.

Then, with another piteous cry, it finally summoned up the strength and flapped away.

Those who were nearby saw the creature disappear over the hills and wondered at the almost human shrieking of the bird.

Gronw took Llew's place and joined Llew's lands to his own. He and Blodeuwedd were rarely seen, spending much of the day and night in lovemaking. When he emerged red-eyed from his chamber, his temper was short, and anyone who came to him for counsel or succor was sharply dealt with.

"My lord, stay," Blodeuwedd pleaded. "You spend less and less time with me these days and nights."

"I have spent too much time," he said brusquely. "My hunting dogs grow fat, my servants insolent. I have things to do apart from pleasuring you."

"My lord, I thought you too enjoyed our time together."

"Yes, yes," he said impatiently. "But I have a life to lead apart from you, and I have been neglecting it. Work on your tapestry. Talk to your women."

"When will you come back?" she cried, dragging on his arm.

Roughly he pushed her aside.

"I will come when I come," he said sharply. "Do what other women do. Let me go."

Blodeuwedd sat at the window as she had done for Llew and watched for his return.

Meanwhile, it came to the attention of Math and Gwydion that Gronw Pebyr had taken over Llew's wife and lands. The story of the eagle was told to them—though no man had seen it since that fatal day.

Math and Gwydion knew that Llew had lost all that he had lost through his own foolishness, and it was he alone who must win it back.

"I feel in my bones," Gwydion said, "that the boy is still alive and needs help. I will not rest until I have found him."

He set off, thinking bitterly about Arianrod, whom he blamed for what had happened to his nephew. He wondered if he should go to her and ask her help. He could not believe that somewhere in her heart there was not a place for her son.

But he did not go to her.

He traveled the land, inquiring about an eagle with the voice of a man in agony . . . but no one had heard of such a thing.

One day Gwydion was resting on a farm and heard how the farmer's sow ran away every morning as soon as the sty was opened, and no one could follow her or knew where she went. She returned every evening well fed and satisfied.

"We have tried to follow her to see where she finds her food, but every day she gives us the slip. No one yet has found out where she goes."

"Tomorrow I will follow her," Gwydion said. He knew that here was a mystery that might help him find Llew. Because Gwydion had stolen the magical pigs from Pryderi, Llew's destiny had taken the turn it had. It was not surprising to Gwydion that the magical beings of the Other World would draw the circle from the first step to the last.

When the sow ran from the sty at dawn, Gwydion followed her. This time she could not keep her route hidden but led him straight to a tall oak tree that grew beside a river. There she stopped and began to feed. Gwydion quickly crept forward to see what she was eating and saw that it was putrid flesh that seemed to be dropping from the branches of the tree.

He looked up and there he saw an eagle, barely alive—the flesh the sow was eating was falling from its wounds.

"Ah, Llew Llaw Gyffes," he whispered. "You are found."

He began to sing softly to entice the suffering bird down to his hand. He sang of the oak, the sacred tree that sheltered him and grew strong and fine beside the river. He sang of the nine score tempests that had shaken its branches through the years without ever succeeding in destroying it. Stately and majestic it stood—sheltering Llew, his friend and nephew.

It seemed that the bird was listening, and with each of the three verses of the song, it hopped down to a lower branch—until at last Gwydion could take it in his hands.

There he comforted it and took it back to Math at Caer Dathyl. With his wand Math returned the poor creature to its human form and called physicians from far and wide to minister to him.

It was a year before Llew was strong enough to take his place in the world again, and then he spoke about reclaiming what had been stolen from him. Math and Gwydion offered help, but it was Llew himself who made the decisions about what had to be done, and it was Llew himself who led his men toward Ardudwy.

Blodeuwedd, sitting at her window watching for Gronw, saw the hosts led by Llew approaching.

"Is he not dead, my husband?" she cried, wringing her hands. "Is he not dead?"

"My lady," cried one of her women, rushing into the chamber. "The Lord Llew Llaw Gyffes is returning with warriors more than we can count."

She saw the crowding, frightened faces of her women. She felt the beating of her heart. What she had done, she had done for the love of a man, and now, where was he—this man who had given her so much pleasure?

"We must flee!" the women cried, and Blodeuwedd took her white cloak from their hands and ran with them down the echoing corridors of the castle and out by the western gate. They ran over the fields toward the mountains.

Seeing them, Gwydion broke off from the others and turned his horse in pursuit.

"Ah, beautiful lady, white and predatory as an owl . . . where is your flower softness now? Where the petal-silk of your skin?"

The women, clustering and crying, still ran, but looked fearfully over their shoulders as Gwydion rode them down, his great cloak swirling behind him like a shadow. They missed their footing and fell into the lake. Like so many petals, they floated for a few moments and then were gone.

Only Blodeuwedd still ran, crying for the life she had chosen to throw away.

She saw Gwydion lift his wand.

"No," she cried. "No . . . no . . . Oo . . . oo . . ."

Her voice was the owl's voice and her owl-wings lifted her above the fields, the forest, and the mountains.

"I will not take your life, for some of your blame rests on me for creating you. But you will live in the night where you belong."

"Oo . . . oo," she cried, weeping for what might have been and could never be. "Oo . . . oo . . ."

She felt the wind in her wings and wheeled and soared: Blodeuwedd—the owl—her eyes dazzled by the sun, blinded by the light.

Llew met Gronw and refused to accept compensation for what he had done. He agreed, however, that they should meet under exactly the same circumstances as they had met before. This time Gronw would stand with one foot on the cauldron and one on the back of the goat, and Llew would be the one to throw the spear.

Gronw tried to make one of his men take his place, but all refused. He was a lord who had not won their loyalty and their respect.

"Seeing that I was persuaded by your wife to do what I have done," Gronw pleaded with Llew, "will you allow me to hold this slab of stone between me and the spear?"

Llew agreed, and prepared to throw.

Gronw held the slab of stone between himself and Llew, but the spear passed right through it and slew him. It is said that the stone still lies on the bank of the river Cynvael, in Ardudwy, with the hole in it pierced by Llew's spear.

Blodeuwedd, watching from the trees, saw that Llew ruled his cantrev well and honorably. Sometimes in the night he heard her cry forlornly, and his heart ached for the woman of flowers he had known.

Arianrod, in her remote castle by the silver sea, was well content that her son had passed through all the tests she had set for him and had become a strong and wise man.

Commentary

One of the features of Celtic myth is the rhythmic patterning of number symbolism. The number three was of particular importance to them, as it still is for us—birth, life, death; past, present, future; thesis, antithesis, synthesis. It is said that it was this particular obsession of the Celts that made their acceptance of Christianity, with its three-in-one God, so quick.

The constant repetition of the theme of three is not arbitrary. It has an important and dynamic role to play in the story. The triad, the trinity, the trilogy . . . all give the impression of a progression that leads to a whole—a meaningful pattern rather than randomness and chaos.

In this story we have three women: Goewin, Arianrod, Blodeuwedd.

Goewin, Arianrod, and Blodeuwedd are three very different individuals, and their contrasts can be taken as major themes of the myth—or they can be taken as different aspects of the one complex being: woman.

Goewin is the humble but strong, self-effacing woman content with her place in life and doing her duty with pleasure and pride. Arianrod is the free-ranging spirit, the wild element, the self-assertive and restless being, voyager between the worlds. Blodeuwedd is the nature sprite and earth woman, the amoral fertility deva.

Three men in the story pit their wits against Goewin, Arianrod, and Blodeuwedd, and in each case the men come off worst. Gilvaethwy (aided by Gwydion) rapes Goewin. She does not crawl away into a corner, a disgraced woman, never heard of again. Instead, she speaks out against them and they are punished. She is given compensation and becomes the High King's wife.

Gwydion tries to trick Arianrod and at first appears to succeed, but in the last bid he is outwitted. He cannot get around her final curse, and by trying to he almost destroys the nephew he loves.

Blodeuwedd is created to be the perfect docile wife (like the Stepford wives) for Llew. But she is also a cold-blooded murderer. Even when she flies off as an owl, defeated, she has won in a sense because she has not been executed as her lover was and lives on, hunting in the night.

There are three occasions in which pigs are importantly involved in the story. The war is fought over Pryderi's pigs; one of the punishments meted out to Gwydion and Gilvaethwy is to serve a year in the form of swine; and it is a sow who helps Gwydion find Llew.

Gwydion and Gilvaethwy have to pass through three animal transformations in punishment for their crime—as deer, as swine, and as wolves. In each case there is a son; therefore, there are three sons of these strange unions.

There are three deceits practiced. Gwydion conjures rich gifts to cheat Pryderi out of his pigs. Arianrod claims she is a virgin. Blodeuwedd deceives Llew.

Gwydion tries three times to outwit Arianrod—as shoemaker, as bard, and by making a woman of flowers.

Llew has to take three important initiatory steps. In the first he seeks and finds a name. In the second he seeks and finds his arms. In the third he seeks and finds a wife. These three steps, however, are merely the preliminaries. Only when he has been through three further tests is he considered to be a strong, mature, and wise ruler. He is wounded by the betrayal of his wife. He takes refuge in the form of an eagle (his right as the son of the eagle god), but he is not ready to escape suffering and take his place as a ruler until he listens to the wise teaching of Gwydion, given in the form of three verses of song. Note that Gwydion mentions the oak, the sacred tree in which Llew is learning wisdom, three times.

Llew has allowed himself to be pushed hither and thither by other people and, until he was wounded, he had not taken his destiny into his own hands. After his recovery he is ready to make his own decisions.

To return for a moment to the significance of Llew receiving his name, there is no doubt that a name is of vital importance to any human being. In some ancient Aryan languages, as John Rhys points out in his book *Celtic Folklore,* the words for breath, soul, and name appear to have the same root. In ancient Egypt, a person's name was believed to be one of the nine vital elements of his being, without which he would fall back into the void and cease to exist. In some cultures the father breathes the name of the child into its ear as it is born, while some cultures choose a name based on the first word the mother says after delivery.

In many cultures the onset of puberty calls for a new name, and at various stages of initiation names are given. Arianrod's son has no doubt been called something by his family and friends during his infancy, but his important name—the name that will mark him for his journey through eternity and that is given at the beginning of the initiation process—*has* to be given by his mother. I wondered if his father could have given him this vital name if his father had been known.

Some authorities think that Gwydion was the father of Llew by incest. I think not—and I think that, at any rate, the Celts at this stage of their culture were still so close to the mother goddess cult that it was the mother who had to name the child.

Arianrod, Gwydion, and Gilvaethwy are themselves called "the children of Don." Don was the goddess—not the god—known as Danu in Ireland. Arianrod has many features of a great goddess. Her name is often associated with the words "silver circle" or "silver wheel," and the Welsh name for the constellation of the Corona Borealis is "Caer Arianrod"—the castle of Arianrod. Silver wheel and silver circle may refer to the great Wheel of Fate, of Life, of Wholeness celebrated in the ancient stone circles of pre-Celtic peoples. It may be silver because it is associated with the moon and the stars. Arianrod is no ordinary woman and her son is no ordinary son. The naming of him has to have deep and magical significance. It might also be worth mentioning here that the Druids were often called on in this capacity of naming at significant times in the individual's life—and they usually based the name on incidents associated with the person, as Gwydion and Arianrod do here.

When I first read this story I was surprised by the idea of a virgin "foot-holder," but then I learned that this was a fairly well-established office in Celtic courts. It seems to me to have its roots in a very ancient and widespread belief in the sacred, magical powers of the divine king, which could be drained away by contact with the earth.

That the foot-holder of Math has to be a virgin is presumably because a virgin is thought to be a pure and unsullied buffer between the transcendental and the earthly states.

I find it interesting in this connection that Llew, who was a divine being in training for sacred kingship, said he could only be slain while his feet were *off* the ground. Was this another of Gwydion's tricks? Was it that he, in fact, could *not* be slain if his feet were off the ground? All the conditions for the death of Llew were meticulously arranged by Blodeuwedd and Gronw—and yet he was *not* slain but transformed into his divine form from which he later emerged as a noble and honorable king.

Faint echoes of the same philosophy are found in many other Celtic stories. In one story a mortal prince, Laeghaire, entered the Sidh and lived among the immortals. When he wanted to return briefly to say goodbye to his earthly family, he was told to stay mounted and on no account to put his foot upon the earth or he would never be able to return to the shining realms.

✧

Nothing in Celtic myth is meaningless. Meanings may have become obscured over the centuries of passage through one bardic rendering after another, but they can usually be teased out again by intrepid symbol hunters.

The yew out of which Druid wands are usually made is important. The *New Celtic Review* (No. 34, November 1983/January 1984) describes the yew as "the Celtic symbol for rebirth, since the yew tree, like the human soul/spirit cannot be given an accurate age. The yew grows its branches down to the earth, where they form new trunks, the old centre of the tree rots and fresh seeds grow again from within the soft centre. So yews are commonly of great age. The Bretons believe that each corpse in the graveyard has a root of the yew tree growing in its mouth. The soul/spirit of the Celt is transmigrated into the next life in a remarkable way parallel to the life cycle of the yew tree itself."

Like all good symbols, the yew's very ambiguity lends it its magical potency. Much of the tree is deadly poisonous, and yet it is the symbol of eternal life.

It is no accident that the wounded Llew is found in an oak tree and that Gwydion sings its praises in three englyns. The oak is sacred to many people—particularly the Celts. To the Druids the most sacred of all the trees was the oak, and when mistletoe was found on oak it was thrice blessed. While he is in the oak tree, Llew is in the process of absorbing Druidic wisdom.

"The summer solstice is the flower time of the oak," writes Kaledon Naddair in *Keltic Folk and Faerie Tales*. "It is a magical time of transformation and invisibility. . . ." Note that Blodeuwedd is made of oak flowers, broom, and meadow-sweet. Broom, according to Naddair, is a "Faerie Bush and has hidden magical powers when used with knowledge. Its first power-station is when its erotic and heady smelling blossoms waft over sunny braes in spring."

Meadowsweet shows its feather-white and salmon-pink flowers from June to September in marshes, in fens, and beside rivers. Life-giving water is its habitat. It is also known to have been a sacred herb of the Druids, noted for its fragrance and its healing properties.

All three plants are sacred, blooming at different times of the year in different habitats; all are charged with magic properties. It is likely that Blodeuwedd was not created with one wave of the wand out of flowers chosen at random but with careful use of Druidic knowledge and studious observation of magical ritual.

One might also look for significance in the three animal forms Gwydion and Gilvaethwy are forced to take as punishment for their crimes. The deer, the wild pig, and the wolf are the three chief animals of the wild forest of the time. All are richly featured in Celtic legend. The deer (stag) is associated most with Samhain (November 1), when the rut is at its height and the powerful energy of the beast is at its peak. Many magical quests begin with the sighting of a deer in a forest, and the pursuit of it takes on a deeper significance than the hunt for food. In the story of Rhiannon, it was while hunting a deer that Pwyll, Pryderi's father, inadvertently slipped into the Other World. It was while hunting a deer that Gronw, in this present tale, came into the life of Blodeuwedd.

The wild pig is associated with spring and summer, the forest, fertility. Many forms of the Celtic earth goddess are associated with the milk-giving sow who bears many offspring.

The wolf is associated with winter, wild howling winds, snow. February, according to Naddair, is called "the wolf-month, storm-month, the month of bleak death." The wolf is associated with power and strength and persistence. One fears and respects a man with a wolf totem.

I find it interesting that Gwydion and Gilvaethwy began as helpless, hunted animals, passed through a period as animals that are both hunted and hunter, and finished their apprenticeship as animals that are strong and fearless hunters. Was it necessary for them to learn humility before they were allowed to learn pride?

Llew takes on the form of an eagle. The name Llew is the Welsh form of the name Lugh, which is associated with the god of light, the shining and bright one, the sun. The eagle is sometimes called "the eye of the sun" because it soars so high, sometimes hovering, it seemed, in the very heart of the sun. At the height of their power, Druids were said to be capable of taking eagle form. In this way they could spirit-travel across the world and observe all that needed to be observed. Llew apparently took eagle form when he was not quite ready for it and, until Gwydion found him and rescued him, lived only halfway transformed—hence his suffering and his unhealing wound.

Goats were sacred to a great many ancient gods and often, as Naddair points out, because of their "renowned fertility and sexual capacities" they were associated with various fertility goddesses. Blodeuwedd is certainly a fertility figure in more than one aspect. It is not surprising, therefore, that she chooses the goat. The cauldron of plenty is also a fertility symbol. So what have we here? Llew—whom Blodeuwedd wishes to destroy—is placed on two fertility symbols and shot with a ritually prepared spear. The king is sacrificed so that the strong fertility urge of the earth mother may be satisfied. His flesh later feeds a sow—another Celtic symbol for the earth goddess. He does not die, however, because he has no human part. He is the son of Arianrod, a divine being, and the eagle/sun, also a divine being. (Note that in the story of Rhiannon Pryderi dies because he is part human through his father, Pwyll.)

The owl is associated with the dark side of the world . . . with death . . . with the earth goddess in the third of her aspects—the hag. Blodeuwedd has passed through the other two aspects—the maiden and the woman—and now she becomes the hag. The night predator, the owl, is not thought of very favorably by the Celts.

I have by no means exhausted the symbolic possibilities of this story. Every time you read it, in whatever version comes to your hand, you will find more to tease the mind, more to seek out and find.

Based on the following branch of the *Mabinogion*:
  "Math, Son of Mathonwy"

Sources used:
  Gantz, Jeffrey. *The Mabinogion*. New York: Penguin Books, 1976.
  Guest, Lady Charlotte. *The Mabinogion*. London: J.M. Dent, 1906.

The Three Etains

The First Etain

E tain, daughter of Etar, a warrior from the province of Conchubar, was bathing in the river when she and her companions saw a rider approaching. Never in her life had she seen a man so beautiful.

He was wearing a green cloak over a tunic embroidered elaborately in red, fastened at both shoulders with a single gold brooch of exquisite workmanship. His shield was silver, studded with gold and with a rim of gold. It was slung across his shoulder on a silver strap with a gold buckle. His spear was five-pronged and striped with gold along its whole length. His long hair was as gold as the band that held it from his face; his eyes gray.

He reined in his spirited horse and sat for a while, gazing down on them.

Some of the young girls retreated under the water, embarrassed by his presence; others flaunted themselves and called out to him. Etain stood half in and half out of the water, motionless, aware that she was the one on whom his attention was fixed. She felt very strange, as though she had seen him before—yet she knew she had not. He too was looking at her as though he knew her. Her companions at last fell silent, realizing that he saw no one but Etain. They drew back from her and watched what would happen.

Etain's heart beat very fast and she felt that this was a moment that would never leave her and a moment beyond which nothing in her life would ever be the same. But was there sorrow in his eyes?

He began to speak in a rich, deep voice, his words strange and haunting.

"Etain is here today as a fair woman among children; but it is she who healed the king's eye from the well of Loch Dá Licc; it is she who was swallowed from the cup of the wife of Etar. Because of her, a king will break his geiss and chase the birds of Tethbae, because of her, a king will drown his two horses in the waters of Loch Dá Airbrech, because of her, there will be fighting against Echu of Mide, and the mounds of the Sidh will be desecrated. There will be no end to her story, no end to the celebration of her name."

With this he raised his spear arm in salute and turned away. Suddenly he was gone and the girls were alone in the river with the sunlight glinting on the water.

They looked at Etain and she was shivering.

"What does it mean?" she whispered. "Is it a prophecy? Shall I be the cause of a war?" She was frightened—but already she longed to see the young man again.

A few years later, Echu of Mide, High King of Eriu, proposed to hold the feis of Temuir, when all the scattered kings and noblemen of Eriu would gather at Temuir. It would be a time of music and feasting, of storytelling and of exchanging costly gifts. But it was also a time of stocktaking. The High King would renew the acquaintance of his enemies and his friends, and his tax collectors would assess what taxes should be imposed. It would also be the occasion for the performance of an ancient ritual in which the High King would be obliged to make love to the representative of the goddess, the mother of the earth.

Because Echu had no wife, the other kings and the noblemen refused to bring their wives to the feis, complaining that the High King might well choose one of them for his partner in the ancient ceremony. Echu was urged by his companions to take a wife. He agreed but stipulated that he wanted to see a fresh face—not one already known to him and his nobles. He sent messengers out across the land to bring back reports of possible candidates. The young woman who all seemed to agree was the most suitable was Etain, daughter of Etar of Indber Chichmane in the province of Conchubar.

Rather reluctantly, Echu left the comfort of his home and set off to see the young woman for himself. He first came upon her as she was preparing to wash her hair where the fresh, clear water sprang out of the hillside in a bower of ferns and mosses. She was clad in a tunic of green silk stiff with embroidery in red and gold and fastened over her breasts with clasps of silver and gold. Over this tunic was a fine mantle ornamented with silver fringes, and over this again, flung back over her shoulders, was a heavier mantle of glowing purple. When Echu came upon her she was unbinding the plaits of her long golden hair, loosening the little golden balls at the end of each one of them, a silver comb in her hand. Her arms were lifted and the cloth had fallen back, revealing her skin as white as the foam of a wave and as smooth as silk. Her eyes were as blue as hyacinth and evenly set, her eyebrows the blue-black of a beetle's shell. Her neck was long and slender; her thighs, her knees, her ankles firm and smooth. She seemed more akin to the shining beings of the Sidh mounds than to the human race. Beside her was a basin of silver with a design of four birds chased upon it, its rim studded with little bright gems of carbuncle.

Echu watched her for some moments before she realized he was there. When she did, she turned her head and looked at him calmly, curious but unafraid. She saw a man, neither young nor old; neither ugly nor handsome. A strong-looking man with a kind face and the clothes of a king. She saw the admiration in his eyes.

"Etain, daughter of Etar," he said quietly, and his voice pleased her. That was the beginning of the wooing.

Etain was not unhappy to be married to the High King. There were times when she thought with longing of the beautiful young stranger she had seen by the river—and sometimes she tried to remember the words he had spoken to her. Her heart had stirred for him as it did not stir for her husband; but she told herself that the young rider had been a prince of the Sidh and that his world was not her world, his time was not her time. Nevertheless, whenever he came to her mind, waking or sleeping, she was disturbed by a terrible sadness and a sense of loss.

✧

Now Echu had two brothers of whom he was very fond. One of them, Ailill Angubae, fell hopelessly in love with Etain when he first saw her at the feis of Temuir. Out of respect for his brother the king and Etain herself, he said nothing to anyone but tried to conquer the longing which was rapidly becoming an obsession. He fell ill and Fachtna, Echu's Druid doctor, was brought to him.

"You have an illness no doctor can cure," he said. "It is either love or jealousy." But to the king Fachtna said no more than that he could not cure what ailed his brother.

Echu at this time had to leave the court to make a progress around his lands. He was worried about his brother and charged Etain to look after him most carefully. This she promised to do.

"If he should die," Echu charged Etain before he left, "make sure that his funeral is worthy of him. See to the digging of the grave, the mourners, and the slaying of his cattle yourself." Etain promised to do everything she could for her husband's brother, and Echu left, knowing that he could not neglect the duties of his position, no matter how anxious he was.

Etain visited Ailill every day, bathing him and feeding him. At times he seemed to be almost on the mend, but at other times there seemed no hope for him. Etain began to notice that it was her presence that made him better and her absence that made him worse.

"So, Ailill Angubae," she said one day. "I begin to understand the cause of your trouble." And they spoke for the first time directly and honestly, and Ailill admitted to her that it was his hopeless desire for her that was causing his decline.

"If only you had told me before," she said. "I am sure your brother would not want me to be the cause of your death." And out of pity for him she arranged to meet him that night on the hillside away from the house.

Eagerly Ailill awaited the moment, bathing and preparing himself carefully for the tryst. Etain walked about her chamber until the appointed hour, thinking about her husband and about Ailill and wondering if she was doing the right thing. She had no desire for Ailill, only compassion. Would Echu praise her or blame her for what she was about to do? She had a deep affection and respect for Echu, but neither he nor anyone else had ever stirred her blood as had the young prince of the Sidh.

That night, when the time came to leave, Ailill fell into a deep sleep and did not wake until the third hour of the next day.

Meanwhile, on the hillside a young man of the appearance of Ailill met Etain. He apologized for the weakness his illness had brought about, and they did not touch.

When Etain saw Ailill the following day he was lamenting that he had not been able to meet her the night before because he had slept through the trysting hour. She was puzzled but thought that perhaps it was to avoid embarrassment that he pretended he had not been at the meeting place at all. She agreed to be on the hillside at the same place again that night.

This time Ailill sat up in front of a fire waiting for the appointed time, with water ready nearby to splash his face as soon as he began to feel sleepy. But in spite of his determination, he was fast asleep yet again when the meeting time came.

Again Etain was met by a young man with the appearance of Ailill.

The third time this happened Etain chided the stranger in the guise of Ailill. "It is not you I come to meet but an honorable man who is in danger of death and whose health I seek to restore."

"It would be more fitting you came to meet me," the stranger replied, "for I was once your husband and I love you still." Etain looked at him in amazement as the likeness to Ailill faded and the beautiful young prince of the Sidh she had once seen stood before her. "When you were Etain Echrade I paid a great bride-price for you," he said. "I drained marshland and rerouted rivers for your father, and in the end I paid him your weight in silver and gold."

Etain clasped and unclasped her hands, trying to make sense of the wisps of memory that floated through her mind at his words. It seemed to her she remembered his arms around her and the pleasure of their love for each other—but she was disturbed by the strange haunting visions that seemed to make no sense. At one time she felt herself to be a huge scarlet butterfly kept among beautiful flowers in a cage of crystal. At another time she felt the pain of exhaustion as she battled against a wild storm wind that blew her butterfly wings to tatters but would not let her die. She felt great longing for him, and yet he seemed no more than a figment of her dreams.

"What is your name, sir?" she asked at last, deeply troubled by the feelings his presence were stirring up in her.

"Midir of Bri Leith," he said quietly, watching to see if his name meant anything to her. It sounded in her ears like a melody she had heard long ago—a sweet melody that filled her with pleasure.

"If we were together," she asked quietly, "why were we parted?"

"My first wife, Fúanmach, was a sorceress trained by her foster father, the Druid Bresal Etarlám," he replied. "She was jealous of you and cast a spell with a red rowan wand that first turned you into a pool of water and then, when that evaporated in the sun, into a worm that later turned into a scarlet butterfly."

Etain sighed. She remembered folding her velvet wings against the breast of Midir. She remembered his tender care of her and how, no matter where he traveled, she had been with him, sharing his thoughts, his life. At night, with the power of his love, he could briefly transform her back to her human form.

"You might have been safe with me even then, had not the spite of Fúanmach conjured a tempest to blow you from my side," said Midir.

Tears came to Etain's eyes as she remembered her struggles to return to Midir, the long years of battling against wind and storm. But there had been a time of calm; she remembered a crystal cage with flowers . . . but it seemed to her the man who was with her then was not Midir of Bri Leith.

"You never came back to me," Midir said, "though my foster son, Angus, son of the god Dagda, found you and would have returned you to me, had Fúanmach not once again swept you out of our reach with a tempest."

"When was this? When did all of this happen?" asked Etain. "I am the daughter of Etar, and it seems these things you tell me are more dreams and visions than memories."

Midir stretched out a hand and tenderly touched a curl of her hair.

"You could say these things happened in the ancient days, my love, long centuries before Etar's wife swallowed you in a draft of ale and gave you birth. Or you could say they happened in a realm where there is no time. But they happened to you and me nevertheless, and now that I have found you again I cannot let you go. You do not belong to this land and to these people. Your home is with me in the golden land, the realm of the Sidh, invisible to these people but never far away. Come with me."

"I cannot," she said sadly.

"Come," he said, reaching out his hands. "Our land is full of music, our people without blemish—hair primrose-yellow, bodies white as snow, the color of the foxglove on every cheek. Age never withers us. There no one speaks of "thine" and "mine" . . . and children are not born in sin or pain. The land of Eriu is green and pleasant, but it is a desert to our land. Sweet water flows through it, and the mead and wine are headier than any served in Echu's house. Come with me, my love, and take your rightful place. From there you will see all that is to be seen in the land of the mortals, yet their shadow will not fall on you."

Etain looked deeply troubled. "My husband in this life is a good and noble man. I love him and I will not cause him pain."

"If he were to agree to your leaving him, would you come with me?" Midir asked.

Etain looked at him. She longed to go with him. Although all that he had told her was as strange as an ancient tale, she felt their love had long roots and was very strong.

"If my husband says I may go with you, I will go," she said quietly.

Midir bowed and was suddenly gone.

When she returned to Ailill the next day she found him dressed and ready to ride. His illness had left him completely. She told him something of what had occurred and they agreed his debilitating passion for her must have been caused by Midir's spells and nothing more. They were both glad they had been prevented from betraying Echu.

One spring day, Echu, Etain's husband and the High King of Eriu, was gazing out over the rich and fertile plain that surrounded the royal hill of Temuir, admiring the blossom that floated like mist over the rich green grass, when he sensed that someone had joined him. He looked around to find a young warrior, a stranger of extraordinary beauty, beside him. His tunic was purple; his hair long and golden; his eyes lustrous and gray. In his one hand he held a five-pointed spear, in the other a shield with a white central boss surrounded by gems of gold. The king knew this young man had not been in the palace fortress the night before, and it was too early for the gates to have been opened for travelers.

"Greetings, stranger," the king said. "What is it you want of me?"

"Not much, my lord, but to know you better and to play a game of chess with you."

"How can you know me better, sir, when you don't know me at all?"

"I know you, my lord."

"What is your name?"

"Midir of Bri Leith."

"It is a name not known to me."

"It will be henceforward. Will you play, my lord?"

The young warrior was calm and well spoken, and the king felt no fear of him.

"I will gladly play," he said, "but the set is with the queen and she has not yet woken."

"I have my own set," Midir said, and produced one at once: the board of silver and the men of gold. A precious stone shone in each corner of the board, and the bag for the men was woven of interlocking fine bronze rings.

Midir set up the pieces and asked if they should begin.

"Certainly," the king said, "but we must play for a stake."

"What stake do you wish to play for?" inquired Midir.

"It is all the same to me," said the king.

"If you win," said Midir, "I will give you fifty dark gray horses with dappled red ears, perfect in every way—sharp-eared, broad-chested, wide-nostriled, slender-footed, strong, keen, tall, swift, steady, and yokable—and fifty enameled bridles to go with them." The king agreed to match this.

They played chess and the king won. Midir walked away and was not seen again that day or night. The next day, at dawn, at the third hour, Midir appeared with the horses as promised. The king was impressed and agreed to play again. This time the stake was fifty fiery boars—curly-haired, dappled, light gray underneath and dark gray above, with horses' hooves on them and with a blackthorn vat that could hold them all. Besides that, fifty gold-hilted swords; fifty white red-eared cows and fifty white red-eared calves; fifty gray red-headed wethers, three-headed and three-horned; plus fifty ivory-hilted blades and fifty shining cloaks.

Again Echu won, and again the stake was delivered to him as promised.

The king's foster father took him aside and questioned him about the young warrior. "You must be careful," he said, "for this is no ordinary man you are playing with."

So the next time, Echu set what he thought to be impossible tasks as the stake: Mide was to be cleared of stones, the marshland drained, and a causeway laid; also a whole area was to be forested.

Midir looked thoughtful and said that Echu was asking too much of him—but the king refused to reduce the stake. Midir then agreed that he would accept it as long as no one spied on him if he had to do what was requested.

The king won again, and Midir disappeared as before. Breaking their agreement, Echu sent his steward to watch how Midir fulfilled his promise. He reported back that Midir had sat on a mound of cloaks while thousands of the Sidh had done the task. He also reported that oxen were used in the work, yoked over their shoulders rather than over their heads as was customary in Eriu.

Midir was angry with Echu but said that he would forgive him if he played once more with him—this time the stake to be whatever the winner named. Echu accepted.

But this time Midir won and he asked for his arms around the queen and a kiss from her.

At this Echu fell silent, but he had given his word.

"Return a month from today, and you will have that," he said.

When the month was out he had Temuir surrounded with fighting men to keep Midir out, but Midir nonetheless appeared before them in the center chamber of their home, though all the doors were locked.

At the sight of him Etain trembled, for she realized now how her husband had been tricked . . . and why.

Midir looked at Echu. "I have come for that which was promised me," he said quietly. Echu did not protest.

And then Midir looked at Etain.

"I have come for you," he said.

"What is this?" said Echu sharply. "I promised you one kiss. No more."

"Etain herself promised me she would come with me," the young warrior then said.

Echu looked at Etain, shocked.

"It is no dishonor to her or to me, my lord. She agreed to come with me only if you would give her to me. I have wooed her with priceless gifts, for you knew full well I could have beaten you at any time if I had wished. I have won the right to her."

"What do you say, lady?" asked Echu sternly, looking at Etain.

"I will not go with him, my lord, unless you sell me to him."

"That I will never do!"

Midir bowed. "At least, for your honor, you should let me have the kiss."

Echu agreed. "One kiss and one kiss only—here in the center of the chamber, on this table, where all my men can see that you do her no harm."

The two were placed on the table. Midir shifted his weapon to his left hand and put his right arm around Etain. He held her close and pressed his lips upon her lips. It seemed to her that she had long dreamed of such a kiss.

When the kiss ended and she opened her eyes, Echu and the hall full of rough warriors were gone and she was in a place of extraordinary beauty . . . a place of crystal walls and satin cushions, of exquisite flowers and shimmering light. Before her stood Midir.

To those in Echu's hall it had appeared that as Midir put his arm around Etain they had started to float up from the table and through the central smoke hole. Shouting with rage, Echu and his men had rushed outside to see if they could catch them. But there was no sign of them.

All they could see were two white swans, linked with a golden chain, flying away together. . . .

──── The Second Etain ────

When Etain arrived to live with Midir in the magical land of the Sidh, she was already pregnant with her husband Echu's child, and she gave birth on the first of May. The child grew to be as beautiful as her mother and, on Midir's request, was also called Etain. Mother and daughter were very close, and although Etain the Elder was very happy in the land of the Sidh and had almost forgotten that other life she had lived among the mortals, she occasionally liked nothing better than to sit with her daughter by a silver stream and tell her tales of the world she had once known. The young Etain listened, fascinated by the stories of the great feis at Temuir and the gossip of the court, by the stories of love and hate and vengeance. She began to feel that her life was dull in comparison. Everything was beautiful and harmonious in the land of the Sidh, but there was no challenge . . . no feeling that one had achieved something when one had overcome a difficulty or a suffering. Without knowing it, Etain the Elder must have been yearning for something in the old life too, for her tales made strife and rivalry more attractive than she intended. The young girl began to plead with Midir, who she thought was her father, to let her visit the land in which her mother had once lived.

Midir did not refuse and he did not agree. He said: "One day."

Meanwhile in Eriu, Echu had not rested since Etain was taken from him. It was believed that the great grassy mounds found throughout the land were hollow, and through them one could reach the mysterious land of the Sidh. Angrily Echu set his men to digging them up one by one, becoming more and more enraged as the cunning Sidh used their magical wiles to strew his path with old bones and broken shards of pottery. At last, seeing that he would not give up until he had destroyed all their mounds, a messenger came to Echu and told him where he would find Midir, the king of the Sidh, and Etain, his wife.

Echu and his men began to dig at once at the great mound of Bri Leith, but every morning they found the earth they had dug the day before had been put back during the night, and they could make no progress. Once they saw two white ravens coming from the mound, and once they saw two hounds, white with red ears, called Scleth and Samair. But this was all.

At the end of a fruitless year and three months, Echu returned to the mound of Ban Find, where he had been given the message about Midir, and demanded some help. If they did not help him find his wife, he said, he would tear down every mound in Eriu. He was told that he should return to his digging at Bri Leith, but this time he should take with him blind dogs and blind cats to stand guard at night over the earth he had removed in the day.

This he did, and on the third night he saw Midir coming toward him.

"I won your wife fairly—why do you persecute me and my people?" he demanded of Echu.

"I do not consider that she was fairly won, and I shall not leave a mound standing if I do not have her at my side again," Echu replied.

"Go home then," said Midir, "and by the third hour tomorrow Etain will be with you. If I do this, swear that you will injure me and my people no more."

"I swear," said Echu.

✧

83

At the third hour of the following day Echu was on the hill of Temuir, anxiously scanning the plains around to see if Midir would keep his word. A white mist began to flow over the plains and Echu's hand tightened on the hilt of his sword. What trick was this? But when the mist cleared there were fifty young women standing before him—each the exact likeness of Etain. In the midst of them was a gray hag as thin as a stick. She came before Echu. "You have destroyed our mounds and driven us out of our homes," she said. "For this your blood will pay. You have Etain before you. Take her and leave us in peace."

Echu was at a loss to know which of the fifty young women was his wife. They were all young and he was now old, but in the land of the Sidh he knew that time passed differently. It was quite possible Etain had retained her youth. He decided that as his wife had been particularly graceful and skillful in serving the wine to his guests, he would arrange a feast at Temuir and test all the young women. One stood out among the others, and it was this one he chose. He was sure she was his wife, but when he looked into her eyes he was troubled. He saw no recognition there. His companions reminded him that Etain had been living in the land of the Sidh for a long time, and who knew what magical spells Midir had placed on her to keep her there and make her forget her former life.

In the night, with Etain in his arms, he soon forgot his qualms. It was as though they were making love for the first time and Echu smiled to think of Etain as she had come to him from her father's house all those years before and now—in his old age—he had the pleasure of her youth all over again.

Etain seemed delighted with everything she saw—and her husband began to feel young again.

One day, in the chamber at the center of the house where Midir had stolen Etain from him, Echu was suddenly faced by Midir again.

"Well, Echu," said Midir, "it seems I wronged you by taking your wife, and you wronged me by imposing such difficult tasks on me when we played chess and by destroying the mounds of the Sidh. Shall we agree that all is equal now?"

"I will, if you will," said Echu.

"I will," said Midir, and smiled.

"I am content then and will hold nothing against you."

Midir turned to go, but before he did he looked back at Echu—and his eyes sparkled mockingly.

"Your wife was pregnant when I took her from you," he said. "It is your daughter Etain you now have as wife. Your wife is with me and you have now let her go a second time."

With that he vanished.

Horrified, Echu looked at Etain, his daughter-wife. She was as fair as her mother and she was pregnant, the child—his child—soon to be born. He had sworn to hold nothing against Midir and he dared not go back on his word . . . but he was sick in his heart to think that he had lain with his own daughter. He put her aside and refused to see her again. He told his retainers that when the infant was born it was to be destroyed.

In vain Etain wept and pleaded, bewildered by the king's sudden harshness. Now she was faced with the cruelty and injustice of the mortal world that she had thought so interesting from the safety of her home in the shining lands of the Sidh. She gave birth prematurely and suffered the agony of watching her babe snatched from her by rough and hard-faced men. Her women, frightened as they were by the sudden change in the king's attitude toward his wife, still managed to dress the girl-child in fine clothes with the name "Etain" embroidered in gold over her breast.

——— The Third Etain ———

The men set off for the wilderness with the child, but they stopped on the way at the home of Findlám, a herdsman. Finding no one there, and the child cooing and smiling at them, they resolved to go no further. They pushed her hastily down among the puppies of a bitch that was guarding the hearth, and they left, hoping that in this way they would have at least partially discharged their duty to their king.

Findlám and his wife found her there and reared her as their own. Like her mother and her grandmother, her beauty became legendary, and her skill at embroidery was famed throughout the land.

Echu never recovered. It was as though the light had gone out of the king's house at Temuir. There were no more feasts until the time of his death.

Etain herself mourned her child so deeply that her life became as dry as desert sand, and her heart withered. As gray and thin as the hag who had brought her to Echu, Etain tried everything she knew to get back to the land of the Sidh.

But the mounds were closed tight against the mortals at this time, and death claimed her, too.

One day the king Eterscélae heard of the beauty of the third Etain, and she was fetched to be his bride.

Etain had grown up in isolation in the forests and fields around her foster parents' home and knew nothing of the sophisticated world of the court. Waiting in her chamber the night before she was to lie with Eterscélae, she wondered what it would be like. The only knowledge she had of the mating act was what she had seen between birds and animals. She touched her own body, wondering how it would be with a man. Her husband was not uncomely—but he was not how she had dreamed of him.

The lamp was burning low, but she did not want to snuff it out. She was frightened of this new life—frightened that she would not be able to do what the king expected of her.

Suddenly there was a rustle above her, and she lifted the lamp in alarm, staring into the shadows beyond its reach. It seemed to her a white bird was fluttering above her and, as she watched, its feathers began to float down around her. She reached up a hand to it, thinking that it had been wounded in some way.

"You too," she whispered, "cooped up in this alien place. We should be out in the forests," she continued, thinking of the times she had been resting on some mossy bank beside a stream, sunlight shafting through tall trees, the birds singing all around her—some eating from her hand, some perching on her shoulder.

He did not come to her hand but landed beside her on the bed. She stroked his down-soft head.

The lamp gave its last flicker and the flame went out. Only the faint light of the moon illuminated the chamber now, a pale glow through the window slits.

Etain's body began to feel good, as though the bird was stroking her with his feathers. She sighed and shut her eyes—glad of the feeling, not wanting it to cease. The stroking became stronger, as though the feathers had become hands. She stirred and moved under the touch, afraid to open her eyes and dispel the illusion. She wondered if she were dreaming. But her body told her she was not, and she knew at last what it was like to be loved by a man.

At the end, she opened her eyes. At her side lay a silver being, a man of shining skin, his hair as white as the bird's feathers, but his limbs unmistakably those of a young prince.

He put his finger on her lips to stop the questions that sprang to them. His other hand rested on her womb.

"You will bear my child," he said softly. "He will be one of the greatest kings Eriu will ever know. I leave him with three birth-gifts: the gift of hearing what is not usually heard; the gift of seeing what is not usually seen; and the gift of wise judgment. He will rule with justice and love—and there will be more weeping for him at his death than there will be at the death of any other king."

"Will he die young?" she whispered, sensing the sorrow in his voice when he talked about their son's death.

He did not answer but stooped and kissed her.

"I must go, my love," he said softly. "I will be with you, as I have been with you for long ages—but you will not see me in the future, as you have not seen me in the past. The boy will have gessa upon him for your father's sins. If he does not break them, he will live long."

"What are they—these gessa—these bonds?"

He was already fading from her sight as his voice spelled out the list: "He must not shoot birds. He must not go right-handwise around Temuir and left-handwise around Brega. He is to stay in Temuir every ninth night. He is not to admit to the house where he is staying a single man or a single woman after sunset. . . ."

The list seemed endless.

My father's sins must have been great indeed to bind his grandson with such gessa, Etain thought sadly. But she was glad she was to have a son—and glad that it would be the son of the shining being who had given her such pleasure and taught her so much of loving.

The dawn was coming. She must prepare herself for her wedding to the king.

When the child of that night was born he was called Conare, son of Eterscélae. He was one of the greatest and most loved and honored heroes of all Eriu. But it was he who broke his gessa and was slaughtered at Da Derga's Hostel, thus fulfilling another of Midir's prophecies to Etain.

——— Commentary ———

The fact that there are three Etains in this story—mother, daughter, and granddaughter—echoes the triple-goddess theme that runs throughout ancient Celtic religious mythology.

The one thing the three Etains all have in common is a fertile, rejuvenating, life-giving quality.

Echu originally looks for a woman to take the part of the earth goddess in a fertility ritual. He thinks he has found an ordinary woman, if an extraordinarily beautiful one, but he has actually found the goddess herself—albeit that she herself is unaware of it.

Everything about Etain reinforces the impression that she is an earth goddess, that marriage with her will bring about the burgeoning of the kingdom. She is in green—the color of vegetation. Her tunic is embroidered in red and gold. At that time red was the color associated with death and the red in her tunic hints that Etain is connected with the cycle of life and death. Her mantle is purple—the color of royalty. Her hair is gold and strung with golden balls—does this express her ancient links with the sun goddess of the Danann tribe? Etain combs her hair with a silver comb—the feminine, intuitive, lunar aspect is taming the fiery, masculine, solar energy. She has blue eyes, and blue is associated with wisdom, truth, revelation. Eyes are, of course, the seeing aspect of a person. Among the Druids blue was associated with bards and poets, the most honored of people.

Other images used for Etain build the picture of a nature spirit, an earth goddess: the hyacinth, the blue-black of a beetle's shell, the bower of ferns and mosses, the spring of water . . . even the silver basin with the design of four birds is a very evocative image. It is a container of clear, precious, potent, and life-giving liquid. The Christians would associate it with the chalice or the font; the pre-Christians, with the cauldron of plenty, immortality, and rebirth owned by the Dagda and Danu and Etain's Welsh counterpart, Ceridwen.

The second Etain comes to the old King Echu and gives him a new lease on life. She is chosen from the fifty Etains he is offered because of her grace and skill at serving wine.

The third Etain is a creature of the forests and the fields, trapped in surroundings unfamiliar to her. Her love is given to a bird of the air, and their child is the "just king" embodying the best of both worlds but sadly crippled by family karma which even he cannot rise above. He is slain at last at Da Derga's Hostel in one of the greatest battles between good and evil described in Celtic legend.

The other major theme in the story of the three Etains is Echu's search for the teaching and the rewards of the higher realms. He is a kind of Everyman, or, in Hindu terms, Atman, reaching after something he has great difficulty attaining—even with the help of Etain. Indeed, I'm not sure he does attain it!

There is a triune aspect to King Echu (as there is to Etain)—though one of them is hardly touched on at all. Like Bran in the *Mabinogion*, Echu has two brothers who appear to be different aspects of himself. Ailill Angubae probably represents that part of Echu's soul that is hungering for the upper world. The Druid doctor knows at once that Ailill's malady is no ordinary illness.

Echu makes a mistake in leaving the up-reaching part of himself while he rides off to attend to his daily business. In this way he has cut off and isolated a part of himself—relegating it to the care of the goddess—when he should have kept himself as a whole in his search for his higher self.

Etain tends Ailill. She bathes and feeds him; that is, as goddess she purifies him and gives him spiritual nourishment. But he wants more.

Out of compassion Etain arranges to meet him outside the palace on a hill—a holy hill removed from the hurly-burly of life. She is detached, godlike. She is only concerned about doing what is right for Echu.

Ailill sleeps not only because Midir has put a spell on him but because he is not ready to enter the upper world yet. His flesh is too weak; he becomes drowsy; he sleeps. His obsession with Etain (the goddess divorced from the rest of life) has made him ill.

Even without understanding Midir's prophetic speech about the first Etain, it is clear her life has an extension beyond the visible, affecting people's lives profoundly for good or ill whether she wills it or not. It is also possible her long exile from the other realms means that she also is in a process of trial and training to regain her original status.

If we follow the theme of Echu's search, we come across several interesting points. Echu originally sought Etain, not because he felt any great burning need for her, but because his companions persuaded him. The motivation was not his own. He just felt it was the expected thing to do. As Ailill, he seeks her too fervently, too one-sidedly, too sentimentally. Again, his motivation is wrong.

Later, Echu loses even what he has of her because his greed for material goods from the Other World gets the better of him. I'm reminded of Christ's words about the futility of gaining the whole world if one loses one's soul in the process.

Only after he has lost Etain does Echu realize her true value, and he seeks her passionately—but still in the wrong way, for he is impatient and uses force to obtain his ends. Thus he never attains her and is fobbed off with a substitute who, in the end, brings about his downfall.

Midir wins her with skill, with intelligence, with persuasion—but also with her permission.

Note that the first Etain, as an Other World being trapped temporarily in the world of humans, frequently has to choose between illusion and reality. Twice she is deceived by thinking Midir is Ailill—but her pureness of heart and motive enables her the third time to challenge the illusion and Midir is forced to reveal himself.

Note that Midir does not kidnap Etain as he quite easily could. He wants her to choose to return to him, and he wants Echu to choose to give her up.

Etain cannot leave Echu because she feels she has a commitment to him. His soul is a noble one, and while he needs her and wants her she must stay with him and help him. If he willingly gives her up, however, she is free to go. Remember, if Etain represents the higher realms, it means that if Echu turns his back on those realms, his guide will leave him.

Midir can appear and disappear at will. Echu should have been more wary of him from the start. Some authorities give the name of the board game the two men play as "fidchell," not chess. Fidchell is very similar to chess: the game of life, the struggle between opposites, the soul the real stake. A board game has rules—like life—but within the confines of those rules you are free to make any move you like.

Midir is clever and devious, but if Echu had kept his wits about him, he would not have been tricked. Echu was even warned against

Midir by his foster father, but his greed for what he could get blinded him. His downfall was the result of his own foolishness in accepting an open-ended stake—a common theme, as we have seen, in Celtic mythology.

Echu is a pleasant and an honorable man. He starts playing with Midir in a relaxed and amiable mood, but as he wins more and more, he grows greedy. The hero's fatal flaw! Then he breaks a promise. He has been forbidden to watch Midir at his work. Like Adam and Eve, he disobeys, and by so doing he, makes Midir angry and lays himself open to losing Etain. Midir points out that it is only because Echu was unfair in his demands and dishonorable in the matter of the spying that he, Midir, feels justified in using any means he can to take Etain. Echu has, in a sense, given up his right to Etain by his behavior. His lower self has cost him his higher self.

The stakes are interesting in themselves. At first Echu's winnings are more or less ordinary (of the earth realm). The horses are magnificent, but they are real horses. The second stake is much more unusual and complex. We are now into the supernatural. Boars in Celtic legend are animals of great magic power. Blackthorn is associated with harsh initiative tests. Other World animals nearly always have red ears. The refrain of fifty and of three gives yet another clue that these are supernatural creatures—"three-headed and three-horned." If Echu had been content at this point, maybe the story would have ended differently. But he goes on. He tries to obtain forbidden knowledge he is not yet ready for. Then he loses the last game.

Realizing he has been tricked, Echu tries to trick back. He asks for a month and a day in which to pay, and then he does everything in his power to prevent Midir from coming to claim his prize. A kiss doesn't sound like too much in ordinary terms, but Echu has realized whom he has been playing with—and a kiss in legends and fairy tales is not to be underestimated. Remember the kiss that woke the sleeping beauty and the kiss that turned the frog into a prince?

Midir outwits him and, because he feels Echu has not played fair, takes Etain away in addition to taking his one kiss.

Throughout the story, as always in Celtic myth, every detail builds up a vivid and natural picture and yet at the same time points to an underlying meaning.

Water is often used as a symbol for the threshold between the worlds.

Midir encounters Etain on the banks of a river; later, Echu encounters her at a spring. The river suggests a long association between Midir and Etain; the spring, the beginning of a new one between Echu and Etain.

Like a refrain, gold is repeated again and again in the description of Midir. We cannot miss that he is associated with the sun, with light, with the Other World.

Midir's five-pronged spear is mentioned very specifically. Five is the numeric symbol for the microcosm: the four directions and the one conscious being who is at the center of them. His five-pronged spear is striped with gold, his five-fingered hand is ringed with gold.

Birds are usually the messengers of the gods, and the Tuatha often appear as birds in their dealings with mortals—as we see when Midir takes the first Etain away from Echu in the form of a swan, linked as we suspect they have always been, by a golden chain. The third Etain is impregnated by a being who comes to her first in the form of a bird. The four birds of the silver basin are ready to fly off in the four cardinal directions, or, as aspects of the soul, to the four realms.

The four realms are: *The underworld* (the subconscious), inhabited mythologically by demons, goblins, and mischievous spirits; *the mortal world* (the conscious), inhabited by humans and animals; *the upper world* (the supra-conscious), inhabited by the Tuatha de Danann (to which Midir and Etain belong) and the minor Celtic gods; and finally the world or realm beyond the upper world—beyond consciousness as we know it—inhabited by the very high spirits, the major gods of the Celtic, and other pantheons.

We now turn to the second Etain, daughter of a goddess and a mortal man. Again we have a woman torn between two worlds. While in the mortal realm her mother longed to return to Midir and the upper realms—but the daughter is curious about the mortal world and longs to experience it.

In seeking his wife Echu digs up the sacred mounds of the Tuatha and angers the whole tribe of magical beings—his third fatal mistake. Supernatural signs abound: the numbers three and fifty, *white* ravens, and hounds with *red* ears.

I wondered about the significance of blind dogs and cats, and I came up with this theory. Dogs are used for the hunting of souls in many mythologies, including the Celtic. Cats were feared by the ancient Celts as carriers of dark supernatural power. In this case, the blind animals cannot be deceived by illusion and so would mount an efficient and fearsome guard. Their psychic powers would enable them to be aware of what is really going on.

The hag that brings the young maidens to Echu is the third aspect of the triple goddess (maiden/mother/hag). Perhaps it is the first Etain herself, because in earth terms she would now be an old woman, though in Midir's country she is still young.

Echu faces another test—one that is used a great deal in Celtic legend. He must choose his beloved out of a group of identical young women: the test of illusion and reality. Remember, Etain passed this test when on the third night she challenged Midir in the guise of Ailill. Echu fails the test because he uses as his criterion something very superficial and worldly—his former wife's ability to serve wine well to his guests.

That the second Etain feels no remorse at the deception may partially account for her eventual punishment.

Midir has tricked Echu once more into granting him Etain. He has her now—finally and completely. If Echu had been wary, he would not have been so caught. At last, a broken man, Echu faces all that he has done wrong to bring him to this point.

The daughter and the granddaughter are punished for Echu's mistakes. The granddaughter is saved, as so often happens in myth, by the compassion of those who have been ordered to murder her. She grows up beautiful and happy—but still tragically carrying the seed of her grandfather's terrible feud with the Other World.

Another frequently recurring theme in world mythology (and no less in Celtic mythology) is infant exile. A child is cruelly taken or driven away from its parents, it suffers, it is rescued and grows up incognito, then it returns and takes its rightful place. Does this represent our exile on earth from the glories of the higher realms?

The fact that the three women are all called Etain indicates that they are all part of the one life thread, tangled in a long and inexorable destiny. The events that happen to the son of the third Etain are prophesied by Midir to the first Etain when she is a young girl bathing in the river.

It is very possible that the transformations of the first Etain refer to her reincarnation through various lifetimes. Certainly she passed through many forms through many centuries, and the butterfly is often used as the symbol for rebirth and reincarnation.

The tempests placed on Etain are produced by a jealous rival to drive her away from Midir. In the realm immediately above our own, there is evidently still strife and conflict, love and hate. Etain is trapped in one of her forms by a very strong and very malevolent magic. It is perhaps only at the interface of the two worlds that these magical things can happen. When the two worlds mix, there is a disturbance in the order of things that makes both more vulnerable to interference from the other. Midir's jealous lover is a Druid of this world, not a member of his own realm. She has been allowed into the other realm still carrying her bag of tricks from this. Etain is tossed hither and thither between the realms and can alight nowhere. The earth at this time must have suffered almost as much as the earth goddess herself.

The first Etain is finally freed from her life as a butterfly by being accidentally swallowed by the wife of Etar in a draft of ale. Nine months later she is brought to birth. This theme of conception by swallowing is a fairly common one in Celtic mythology. It could be a remnant from very ancient times when the role of the father in conception was not fully understood—but I think it is used symbolically to indicate that the child has Other World connections and is passing through a process of rebirth. In Taliesin's case he was born as a mortal and then, by swallowing the magic fluid from Ceridwen's cauldron of knowledge, he became capable of shape-changing to flee from her wrath. He was finally trapped as a grain of wheat and swallowed by her as a hen. She then, as woman, gave birth to him. This second birth transformed him from an ordinary village boy to an extraordinary poet and seer.

Without Etain, both Echu and Midir are lesser beings. The pursuit of what she represents is of great importance to the evolution of both their souls, and the manner of the pursuit is as crucial as the eventual goal.

Sources used:
Gantz, Jeffrey. *Early Irish Myths and Sagas*. New York: Penguin Books, 1981.

Rolleston, T. W. *Myths and Legends of the Celtic Race*. London: Harrap & Co., 1917.

Emer and the Women Who Loved Cuchulain

——— Emer ———

"**I** do not believe anyone is as handsome, as brave and as wise as you say," Emer said to her companions. They were in the Garden of Lugh, basking in the sunshine and eating apples. For more than a month she had been bombarded with tales of the extraordinary youth, the son of Dechtire, King Conchubar's sister. It seemed that every young girl and every woman in the country was dreaming of no one else—and husbands and fathers and young lovers had become anxious and started looking out for a suitable wife for him so that their wives and daughters and sweethearts would give up hope of having him as lover or husband.

Emer had seen Cuchulain once in a dream. He had been rolling a burning wheel ahead of himself through a watery marsh, and wherever the wheel touched, the marsh had dried up so that Cuchulain could walk on dry land.

"It is said that he is the son of the sun, of Lugh the Long Hand," Emer's companions told her, "though he is called son of Dechtire and Sualtim."

Emer shrugged, feigning disinterest. "He is a green boy. If I wed, it will be to a man who can match me in every way. I am tired of boasting youths and their tedious feats of arms."

Cuchulain too was tired of the fair and beautiful young girls his companions brought to his attention. Beauty was important—but he wanted a woman who could match him wit for wit, skill for skill. He had seen such a young girl once, daughter of Forgall Manach the Wily, who was nephew to the Formorian king Tethra, and he determined to seek her out.

Cuchulain found Emer in a green field surrounded by the young daughters of her father's dun. She was teaching them embroidery, for there was no one in the country more skilled with the needle than Emer. Cuchulain was in his richest clothes—his five-folded crimson tunic, his white shirt embroidered with red-gold, and his cloak pinned with a great circular golden brooch. Fiall, Emer's elder sister, came forward to greet him, and they joined Emer and the maidens.

After the greeting, Emer asked him where he had come from. He answered that he had come from Intide Emna. Now this was a riddle, for there was no such place as Intide Emna. He spoke in code to test her wits—and meant that he came from Emain Macha, which in the ancient days was called Intide Emna. She then asked him where he had slept, and again he replied with a riddle: "In the house of the man who tends the cattle of the plain of Tethra." By this he meant in the house of a fisherman—because fish are the cattle of the sea—and the plain of Tethra is the sea that flows between Eriu and the islands inhabited by the Formorians. And so it went on—to every question he replied obliquely, testing her knowledge of the ancient times and seeing how quickly she grasped his meaning.

Smiling quietly, Emer answered riddle with riddle, and her companions looked from one to the other in puzzlement, left far behind by the sparkling wits of Emer and Cuchulain. Realizing that he was trying to court her, she let him know that she was guarded by many champions who would not let her be taken away against the will of Forgall, her father "the dark king," and, as for herself, she would not be easily won. She also pointed out that her sister, Fiall, was the elder and should be married before her. Cuchulain made it quite clear that it was Emer and not Fiall he wanted and that he was a worthy suitor for he had not been reared at any small hearth but by his uncle, King Conchubar himself, at court among "chariot chiefs and heroes, jesters and Druids, poets and learned people." Emer left him in no doubt that she too had had no ordinary upbringing and could match him in learning and all the fine virtues.

At last the sight of her white breasts above her dress was too much for Cuchulain, and he pressed her to be his wife.

"The man I marry must be the greatest champion Eriu has ever had. He must be capable of protecting me from every danger," replied Emer.

"You are too young," she said—and Cuchulain reddened with anger for he had already performed grander and more dangerous feats of arms than any man at his uncle's court.

But Emer, still in riddles, told him what feats he would be expected to perform if she were to consider him as husband—and he knew that for these he was not yet ready.

As Cuchulain rode away in his chariot, he flung up his spear, whirled it and caught it, and whirled it and caught it again—so fast that it seemed as though there was a ball of light whirling above his head.

Emer's companions gasped and pointed and chattered excitedly, but Emer only smiled quietly to herself and turned away.

That night when Emer's father returned to his dun he heard the talk about the handsome youth who had spoken so long in riddles to his daughter in the Garden of Lugh. Forgall frowned. His daughter was young, and he was not prepared to part with her yet—especially not to "that mad boy" from Emain Macha.

Forgall disguised himself as a foreigner and went to Emain. There he presented gifts to Conchubar of gold and wine from Gaul and was royally entertained. On the third day he was listening to the praise of Cuchulain and showed great interest in the youth. "It seems to me," he said, "he could be a great champion indeed if he were to finish his training with Scathach in Alban."

Now Scathach was a woman warrior in the Island of Shadows, whose training for warriors was famous throughout the world. Men came from further afield than Gaul to train with her, and if they passed her rigorous tests they were more feared than any other fighting men.

Forgall knew the way to her was dangerous and dangerous was her training. Many they were who set out but did not return. He hoped, seeing how young Cuchulain looked, that he would be one not to return.

Cuchulain, of course, was eager to set out at once—thinking that this would give him the training that would please Emer. He paid another visit to her in secret to tell her what he intended to do. She told him it was her father who had suggested Scathach, because he was hoping Cuchulain would not return. But it was clear to Cuchulain now that Emer loved him as much as he loved her, and he was determined to be worthy of her and to confound her father.

Cuchulain's journey to find Scathach was full of strange and magical happenings. Some filled him with fear and some with wonder—but in each case he acquitted himself with honor.

While Cuchulain was gone, Lugaid, the king of Munster, let it be known that he was looking for a wife, and Forgall Manach at once invited him to his dun and promised him his daughter Emer.

The king, with his twelve chariot chiefs and his richly bedecked entourage, arrived for the wedding, and everything was ready for him—except Emer.

Emer was brought forward, and instead of bowing meekly as her father intended, she spoke up clearly and boldly.

"My lord," she said, "my father has misled you, I think. I have promised my love to Cuchulain, and we are to be wed on his return from the Island of Shadows and the training grounds of Scathach. No honorable man would make me break my vow to Cuchulain."

No man would, thought Lugaid, for Cuchulain's reputation was frightening enough as it was. Lugaid did not want to face him after his time with Scathach.

Forgall said at once that he was unaware of his daughter's promise to Cuchulain, but, at any rate, if they had taken vows they were surely no more than the shallow promises of children and were not to be taken seriously.

Lugaid looked thoughtfully at Emer. She was standing straight as a healthy oak, her clear eyes looking directly into his own. She was no child to make sentimental promises that could easily be broken.

She was a young woman who knew exactly what she had done and exactly what she intended to do.

"My lord," Lugaid said to Forgall, "your daughter is indeed the most beautiful and talented young woman in Eriu—but if the Hound of Culain has her love, it were better that she married the Hound of Culain."

"Every young girl loves Cuchulain," spluttered Forgall. "Must all fathers keep their daughters unwed so that they can dream about Cuchulain?"

"No, father," answered Emer calmly. "Only you—for I have the love of Cuchulain in return."

Lugaid smiled ruefully and rubbed his chin. He made himself a silent promise: If Cuchulain met his death at any time, he would be back for this strong and spirited lady.

When Cuchulain returned at last from Scathach, he made straight to see Emer. But Forgall, hearing of his return, put a strong guard around the dun to hold him off.

"Dream as much as you like," he said to his daughter. "But you will marry a king of my choosing."

"I will marry Cuchulain—or no one," she replied.

But Cuchulain was kept from her for a long time. At last he could bear it no longer and prepared his scythe chariot and all his weapons.

This time Cuchulain made great slaughter of the guards outside the dun and then gave the hero's great salmon leap taught him by Scathach, which took him over the three walls and into the inner court. There he was attacked by three groups of nine, and in each group he killed eight, thereby leaving the leaders of each group, the three brothers of Emer, alive.

Forgall tried leaping from the court to escape Cuchulain, whose fury was now fairly roused—but he fell and met his death.

Cuchulain took Emer by the arm and they ran from the fort. But their troubles were not over, for Scanmead, Forgall's sister, came after them with her army, and at every ford they crossed they had to fight a battle.

At last they reached Emain Macha, exhausted, bloodied—but victorious.

When Cuchulain and Emer were married, the young warrior was made leader of the young men of Ulster—with warriors, praise poets, satirists, musicians, and jesters in his entourage. They lived at first at Conchubar's court, a rich and sumptuous place. Three great houses were there: the Assembly House of Ulster; the House of the Red Branch, where the warriors feasted and challenged each other and where the walls were hung with the weapons and the heads of defeated enemies; and the Speckled House, so named for the colorful gleaming and sparkling of all the warriors' weapons and accoutrements that hung there.

Emer found it a most interesting and stimulating place to live. Visitors from other countries and kingdoms were frequently entertained, and learned people and Druids gathered there for discussions. There were poets in their cloaks of shining feathers and the best trumpeters and harpers to be found.

One day Bricriu of the Bitter Tongue set about some mischief. He built a house as grand as the House of the Red Branch and invited the heroes of Conchubar's court and their wives to a great feast. Like the great drinking hall at Emain Macha, it had nine divisions from the hearth to the outer walls, each thirty feet high and faced with bronze overlaid with gold. Conchubar's golden seat was placed higher than all the others and was studded with precious gems; it was surrounded by twelve seats for the twelve chief heroes of the Red Branch. Knowing that he was out of favor with the court because of his sly and bitter tongue and the trouble he had so often made between the heroes, Bricriu built a little parlor for himself where he could observe without being observed.

The men were wary of the invitation because, as Fergus, son of Rogh, said, Bricriu had a way of stirring up trouble even between friends that might mean the death of more than one of them before the feast was over. Bricriu then let it be known that if they did not come, he would stir up trouble anyway—on such a scale that not one of them would be safe from any other.

The men agreed at last it would be politic to go, but they made the stipulation that Bricriu was to lay out the feast and then leave. Eight swordsmen were to be appointed to see that he did so.

Even so, Bricriu managed to have his fun. Before the feast, he took aside the three best warriors of Emain Macha—Laeghaire, Conall, and Cuchulain in turn—and suggested to each that it was only right that the champion's portion at his feast should fall to him. While the feast was being laid, music was played and all was well, but as Bricriu left the hall as he agreed to do, he called back over his shoulder: "Let the champion's portion go to the best hero of Ulster." Then each of the three men claimed it and before long were fighting for it—their friends and supporters soon joining in. Bricriu in his parlor chuckled, delighted with the game, but Conchubar was furious and ordered them to stop. It was agreed at last that the champion's portion for this feast alone should be divided up and that afterward the three men should go to Cruachan and ask Ailell of Connacht to decide impartially which of the three was indeed the champion of Ulster.

This furor having died down, Bricriu set about stirring up another among the women. They had left the hall earlier than the men and were on their way back to their quarters, laughing and gossiping over the events of the evening, when Bricriu managed to intercept each of the three wives of the three chief heroes. Using honey-tongued flattery and guile, Bricriu persuaded each in turn that she was the first lady among them all, and as such should enter the hall before all the others.

"Emer of the Beautiful Hair," he said, "you are married to the finest man in Eriu and he is justly proud of you. You are first among the women in beauty, in wisdom, in youth. There is no one to outshine you. You should be the one to walk through the great door into the feasting hall—and all following you."

The women began to walk back toward the feasting hall, quietly and sedately at first, but then—seeing that the others might be closer to the door than themselves—stepping faster. The walk became a run and the earth fairly shook as the women raced toward the door, each determined to be the first one through it.

The men inside were soon aware of what was happening and each of the three heroes rose and rushed to the door to open it for their wives. Then there was nearly bloodshed again, but Conchubar intervened and commanded that the door remain shut. "Let the women have a war of words," he said, "and let the winner come first into the hall."

Then each of the women spoke: Fedelm of the Fresh Heart, wife of Laeghaire; Lendabair, wife of Conall; and lastly Emer, wife of

Cuchulain. Each claimed beauty, wisdom, and the courage of their husbands—but Emer spoke longer and more fluently, claiming that there was not a man in Eriu who did not want her, yet she had chosen Cuchulain for his courage, his wisdom, his beauty, his extraordinary skill in feats of arms. Like the finest poet, her words rolled over the listeners, charming them into silence.

Laeghaire and Conall made a rush for the wall and tried to smash through it to let their wives in, but Cuchulain set his shoulder against it and lifted the whole side of the house up so that Emer and her women could duck under it and be first in the hall. When he dropped it again, Bricriu and his wife, who had been lurking in their parlor watching the whole thing, were flung down among the dogs and scraps at the heroe's feet.

Now for all the remaining years of Cuchulain's short and eventful life, Emer was the wife of Cuchulain and he loved and honored her. Their home was at Dundealgan, and they shared their time—when Cuchulain was not away fighting—between this fair home and the mighty court of Conchubar at Emain Macha.

But Cuchulain was handsome and a great hero to the women of Eriu, and many besides Emer loved him, and sometimes other women besides Emer shared his bed. Emer, on the whole, took it as a compliment that he was so desirable to women, and yet, however they enticed him from her side, he always returned and gave her his deepest love. Queen Cathrach Catuchenn of Spain was one who abandoned her country and came to live in Eriu for love of Cuchulain. She died fighting among Conchubar's warriors. Blanad, daughter of Midhir, married to Curoi, son of Daire, secretly arranged for Cuchulain to take her from her husband's dun, but the plan went wrong and in the subsequent violence Curoi was killed. To avenge him his poet followed the fleeing lovers, caught Blanad in his arms, and flung himself and her to their deaths off a cliff.

Eithne Inguba

Then there was Eithne Inguba, with whom Cuchulain had a long relationship. It was to please her he shot at the two magical birds that appeared on the lake at Muirthemne, as a consequence of which he all but wasted away.

This is what happened. One day during the celebration of Samhain, when all the chiefs and heroes of Ulster and their wives were gathered on the plain of Muirthemne, a flock of beautiful and unusual birds flew over their heads and settled on the water of the lake. The men were busy boasting of their triumphs and counting out the tongues of their enemies they had collected in their pouches, while the women were taking the air and amusing themselves beside the lake. The flock of birds excited the women greatly, and all were eager to have the feathers for the shoulders of their cloaks. Levercham went at once to Cuchulain and told him that the women wanted the birds and that she had been sent to ask him to come and catch them. He was annoyed at the interruption and roughly pushed Levercham aside.

"Do the women of Ulster think that I have nothing better to do than catch birds?" he snapped, returning to his count of tongues. Then Levercham mentioned that Eithne Inguba was particularly anxious for him to come to help them—and for her sake he agreed at last.

Impatiently Cuchulain flashed out with his sword and so maimed the birds that the women could easily catch them. Each woman in the end had two birds—except Eithne Inguba, who had none. Cuchulain, seeing her angry and disappointed face, promised that the very next birds of any beauty that came to Muirthemne he would catch for her—and her birds would be better and different from all the others.

Not long after that they saw two birds of greater beauty than the earlier flock, flying low over the lake, linked together by a red-gold chain. Their singing was so sweet that almost all who heard it fell asleep. Only Cuchulain, Laeg—his charioteer—and Eithne stayed awake. Cuchulain at once set his sling, but Eithne said: "See the chain? There is enchantment on those birds. Leave them well alone." But Cuchulain would not listen and shot the first stone. It missed. He shot another—and again missed. He was astonished and angry now for he had never been known to miss a target. Eithne pleaded once more that he should leave them alone, but nothing would deter him from trying again. This time he flung his javelin-spear, which passed through the wing feathers of one of the birds but did no damage. The two birds flew off, unharmed, over the shining water.

Cuchulain walked away from Eithne, shamed and angry. Laeg, his companion in all his victories, and Eithne, his lover, knew him well enough not to intrude on him at this time. He walked until he came to a standing stone and there he sat down with his back against it. Within moments he was fast asleep.

———— Fand ————

It seemed to Cuchulain that in his dream two women approached him, one in a green cloak and the other in a five-folded crimson cloak. They stood before him and they smiled. Then the one in the green cloak began to beat him with a whip, while the other watched. When the first one was tired, the other stepped forward and continued the beating. Then they left.

Cuchulain was found by his friends slumped beside the stone, dazed and incoherent. When they could not rouse him, they spoke of taking him home to Emer, but he babbled that he must be taken to Emain Macha with Eithne Inguba, and so it was to Emain Macha he was taken. He lay there for a year, gradually wasting away, while Emer knew nothing of his plight.

The time of Samhain came around again. Cuchulain's friends were gathered at his bedside, Eithne at the foot, when a stranger entered the chamber. He was a man of great stature and presence. He told them that he was Angus, son of Āed Abrat, and that his sister, Fand, was pining for love of Cuchulain. If Cuchulain would come to her, he would soon be cured of his wasting sickness. On Āed Abrat's departure he said that Li Ban, his other sister, would soon come for Cuchulain.

Then Cuchulain sat up and found his voice again and told them about the vision he had had the previous year after he had shot at the two birds. It was agreed that he should return to the same standing stone against which he had sat when he had had the dream.

There, once again, he met the woman in the green cloak.

"I am Li Ban, daughter of Āed Abrat," she said. "I have come to tell you of the love my sister Fand has for you. Her husband, Manannan of the Sea, son of Llyr, has left her and she can think of no one but you, night and day. My husband, Labraid Luathlam ar Cladeb, says he will send Fand to you in exchange for one day's fighting against his enemies."

"I am weak from the sickness you put upon me and cannot fight," Cuchulain said.

"You will be healed."

"Where is this land you speak of? Where is this Labraid Luathlam ar Cladeb who wants me to fight for him?"

"It is far and yet not far. He is visible yet not visible."

"Take my charioteer, Laeg, and let him bring me a report of the land of this man. Let him tell me about this woman—this daughter of Āed Abrat who is your sister."

So Li Ban and Laeg departed in a boat across the lake and came to an island that could not be seen from the shore.

"Do not try to leave this place," Li Ban said to Laeg, "unless you are under the protection of a woman."

Laeg looked around nervously. "I wish Cuchulain were here instead of me," he said.

"I too wish that," said Li Ban.

On the green mound of the island they found a doorway, and at the doorway stood a man. Li Ban asked where her husband was, and she was told that he was gathering his hosts for battle. Then they entered a great house, and Laeg found himself surrounded by women. They passed through them to an inner chamber where they found Fand herself, as clear and pure as a tear in the eye, more beautiful than any woman of the mortal world.

But before they could speak to her they heard Labraid's chariot approaching, and Li Ban took Laeg to meet him. She greeted him with three poems of praise, but he chided her, saying he was not proud nor arrogant and needed no such speeches of adulation.

"This is Laeg, charioteer of Cuchulain," Li Ban then said.

"Ah, Laeg, charioteer and companion of the Golden Hound of Culain! Will he come, do you think, to lend us his strength?"

"I will bear the tale of all that I have seen," Laeg said. "I think Cuchulain will come."

Then Laeg returned to Emain Macha under the protection of Li Ban and told Cuchulain everything. He tried to rouse him from his bed by telling him of Fand's beauty and the need of her brother for his strong arm. But still Cuchulain did not rise. He asked Laeg to go to Dundealgan to tell Emer how he had almost been destroyed by two women of the Sidh and to ask her to come and visit him.

On hearing what had happened and that Cuchulain had not been on Conchubar's business all this time but lying ill and near to death at Emain Macha, Emer was furious—both that she had not been sent for before and because none of the great heroes of Ulster had lifted a hand to help him. "If Fergus or if Conall or if any of the others had been in a similar plight, Cuchulain would not have rested a moment until he had helped and saved him," she said. "And as for you, Laeg," she snapped, "how could you go into the country of the Sidh and return without a magical cure for your lord? For more than a year," she continued angrily, "I have been without a man in my bed, without a man's pleasing conversation—and all this time I could have been with him if you had brought me this news earlier."

Then Emer went at once to Emain Macha and stood beside Cuchulain's bed.

"Shame on you," she said to her husband. "How could you let this happen to you? Rise up, warrior of the Ulaid—weakness is next to death! Rise up and take your place among the wonders of the world . . . take your shining spear, your sword, your shield."

She shook him by the shoulders and he rubbed his eyes and passed his hands over his face and gave a great sigh. Then he rose and took up his spear, his sword, and his long shield with its boss of bright gold and rim of silver.

Cuchulain returned to the stone of vision, and there Li Ban approached him once again and invited him to return with her to the Sidh. But he wanted to hear more about Labraid, her husband, before he decided. She told him of the shining lake, the island, the house with pillars of silver and crystal, and the king whose own people lived in peace—yet who had an enemy against which he needed the help of Cuchulain.

But still Cuchulain hesitated and made the excuse that he would not go on the invitation of an intermediary, particularly not of Li Ban. He insisted that Laeg should return with her and make sure it was genuinely Labraid himself who was asking for his help.

Then Laeg went again and brought back a description of the Sidh hosts eagerly gathered for battle. He described Labraid himself, with his yellow hair tied at the back with a golden apple, with his eyes shining with eagerness to be started. He described the house full of royal guests, brightly colored mantles with pins of gold, bedposts of bronze, pillars of white and gold, precious gems lighting the place like candles. At the west door the horses were waiting, gray and chestnut with shining manes. At the east door grew three trees of gleaming crystal from which could be heard the sweet and enchanting singing of birds. There was a tree at the entrance to the court and another of silver that turned the color of gold in the setting sun. There was an orchard with three score trees laden with fruit, there was a well, and there was a vat of mead that never emptied . . . .

In the house, Laeg was taken to see Fand of the golden hair and found her the fairest of women, her beauty enhanced by her intelligence and charm. She spoke to him, regretting that he was not the one for whom she was looking. She confessed that she was waiting for Cuchulain. Everywhere he looked, Laeg told his lord, there were musicians and women more beautiful than he could imagine—even more beautiful than Emer and Eithne Inguba—yet none as beautiful as Fand.

Then Cuchulain agreed to go to Labraid—and Emer agreed to let him go, for she knew that the spell that bound him could only be released by the one who had cast it. Together Laeg and Cuchulain set off in the chariot across the waters of the clear lake. There they were welcomed by Labraid.

Impatient to do what he had come to do, Cuchulain insisted on being shown the fighting men he could call upon. Labraid took him before his host.

Above Cuchulain's head hovered two Druidic ravens. The host of Echu Luil, Labraid's enemy, seeing this, hunted the ravens and drove them away.

Cuchulain then sent Labraid himself away and set about the task he had undertaken.

At dawn one morning Echu Luil was washing his hands at a spring when Cuchulain came upon him and speared him through the shoulder. Instantly Echu Luil's men attacked, and Cuchulain, with his battle fury upon him, laid about him. There were so many killed that at last Labraid pleaded with Cuchulain to desist—but he would not.

Laeg advised Labraid that when Cuchulain was in his battle fury it was difficult for him to stop, and he suggested that they should prepare three vats of cold water. Cuchulain was then plunged into them one by one. The first boiled as his body touched it; the second was so hot no one else could touch it; but by the time he was put into the third vat he had begun to cool down.

Fand looked at Cuchulain, and she saw a stately chariot-warrior, a fair young man, nobler than a king. His ways were not the ways of the Sidh, his song was not their song—but her heart raced for him and she longed to be with him. Then he displayed feats of skill for her—juggling fifty golden apples in the air, flashing and tossing his red sword and spear. Fand's eyes shone to see him use so precious and delicate a skill with limbs so rough and hard.

Then the stately Li Ban praised him and thanked him, quietly leading him on to tell Fand what he had done.

Cuchulain described how he had cast his spear into the mist and was not aware whether it had reached its mark or not. He could scarcely remember anything of the battle—only that from every direction the shining hosts had come and he in his battle fury had fought against them.

Cuchulain stayed then with Fand in the country of the Sidh, and it seemed to him each day was more pleasant than the last. Her beauty appeared ever-changing, their loving ever-new. But after a while memories of his other life began to intrude.

"Stay with me," Fand pleaded. "No time is passing in the mortal world. No one will miss you."

But it seemed to him that—though Fand was beyond all his dreams of what a woman should be—he was missing something. He began to be restless and moody. The exquisite life of the Sidh was not for him.

Fand, seeing that she could no longer hold him, suggested that she should follow him to his world and that they should meet there and continue their companionship. This idea pleased him and a trysting place was arranged.

There they met among strong oak trees and rugged hills. There they made love on a hard wooden bed or on a carpet of sweet hay. But when Fand's birds sang to him, Cuchulain felt he was back among the elegance and the comfort of her castle, and the chamber was lit by precious gems instead of by mutton-fat candles.

It was not long before Emer found out about the meetings of Cuchulain and Fand and was angry. She had never been jealous of the women her husband had made love to before, because she knew they were no threat to her. But Fand—Fand was different. She had enchantments far beyond any Emer could command, and she might draw Cuchulain away from the mortal world altogether so that he would be lost to Emer and the heroes of the Ulaid forever.

One day Fand was lying with Cuchulain when, over his shoulder, she saw Emer approaching, armed with knives and with fifty of her women marching angrily behind her.

"My love, see where Emer, daughter of Forgall, comes, armed like a warrior?" she said to Cuchulain.

Surprised, he looked around and saw that she was right.

At once Cuchulain dressed himself and lifted Fand up onto his chariot.

"Have no fear," he said. "Emer will not touch you under my protection."

"Will I not?" cried Emer fiercely. "Cuchulain, stand and fight me, for the sun will not go down this day but I will part you from Fand forever!"

"Stand aside, woman, for I love you and I will not harm you—but I have sworn to defend Fand against the dangers of our world. What do you hope to do against me with that puny knife and those untrained women?"

Emer shook her knife angrily.

"I am Forgall's daughter, and I am used to fighting for what I want," she said coldly. "Stand down, I say!"

"Why do you want to part me from this woman? She is worthy of a king."

"She may be so—but so am I. You leave me for her only because the unknown seems more exciting than the known. We were good lovers once and could be so again. Give her up, my husband!"

Cuchulain looked from one to the other, and his face was sad and dark. He loved them both.

Fand stepped forward and looked deeply into his eyes—and then she turned to Emer.

"He will leave me," she said sadly, "for you have the greater claim."

"I do not want him if he comes by claim and not by love. Rather he stay with you, if it is your love that gives him greater pleasure."

"It is I who must go," Fand said gently, tears coming to her eyes.

Cuchulain meanwhile was sunk into a melancholy reverie and heard nothing of the women's argument. It was as though time had stopped.

Between the moments where there was no time, Manannan of the Sea appeared to Fand. No one else could see him—only she.

"We loved once, my lady," he said quietly. "We could love again. Will you leave this land of sorrow and return with me to the golden land?"

Fand took his hand, but her head was turned to Cuchulain and it seemed to her she suffered now as mortals suffer.

She looked at Emer. If she had to leave him, at least she left him in worthy hands.

"Ah, Emer," she whispered, "there is no one else to whom I would release him. Take good care of him."

And then, because she wanted to make it clear that she had left of her own free will, Fand raised her hand in farewell to Emer, and those that were gathered there saw her walk away with Manannan of the Sea.

"What is this?" cried Cuchulain, suddenly realizing that he was losing Fand. He tried to rush after her, but Manannan of the Sea had shaken out his shining cloak between them, and he could see her no more.

Bitterly, Cuchulain turned his back on Emer and on all who were there and strode off into the mountains. There he stayed by himself, rarely eating or drinking or sleeping, wild-eyed among the bleak rocks and windy crags.

Emer went to Conchubar and told him all that had happened, and the king sent men to try to bring Cuchulain back. But he would not come and attacked all who approached. Conchubar then sent poets to sing to him of his heroic deeds and how much his companions in arms needed him, but Cuchulain would not listen and threw stones at them. Then Druids were sent who used powerful enchantments. When he was bound and helpless at their feet and pleading for a drink, they gave him a drink of forgetfulness so that his love for Fand would never trouble him again.

Cuchulain returned to Emer as though nothing had happened, but she could not forget that he had loved Fand as much as he loved her and that he had not been able to choose between them. When they made love it seemed to her that she saw, standing beside the bed, the silver shadow of Fand; and when she walked in the woods it was the faint and mocking call of the enchanted birds she heard. As Cuchulain grew stronger and the shadows of his exile in the mountains fainter, Emer grew thinner and paler—until at last her women spoke to Levercham and Levercham to Conchubar. One feast night at Emain Macha, the king's chief Druid poured wine into Cuchulain's golden cup and offered it to Emer. By the time she had drained the liquid and reached the bird of precious gems decorating the bottom, she too had forgotten Fand.

—— Aoife ——

When Cuchulain was a youth, while he was in training with Scathach on the Island of Shadows, he had fought a battle on Scathach's behalf against her great enemy, another formidable woman warrior, Aoife. In the battle Cuchulain had almost been defeated—but in the end he had captured Aoife and destroyed her champions.

After the peace was made between Scathach and Aoife, the warrior queen seduced Cuchulain and took him as her lover. He lived with her a year, learning from her as much as he had ever learned from Scathach—and more besides in the art of lovemaking.

When it was time for him to return to Eriu, Aoife was with child. Cuchulain gave her a golden ring of his own and told her that whenever she wished she could send their child to him in Eriu. He would know him by the ring.

The years went by and Cuchulain's son grew to be as extraordinary and as formidable a fighter as his father and his mother. Whenever he asked about his father, Aoife would promise that one day he would return to them—for she firmly believed that he would.

But one day Aoife heard that Cuchulain had married Emer and had no intention of returning to the Island of Shadows. She was angry and brooded on how she could take vengeance. Her eye fell on Conlaoch, their son, and she thought of a way of hurting Cuchulain.

When Conlaoch was grown to be ten years old—about the age Cuchulain himself had first started showing his amazing prowess as a fighter—Aoife called him to her and told him that he was to go to Eriu to see his father. "But I put three geiss on you, my son," she said, "for your own protection. One is that you tell no one your name. The second is that you never give way to any living person. The third is that you never refuse a challenge no matter how great the champion who delivers it."

And with these geiss upon him Conlaoch set off across the sea to Eriu. His boat came in on Baile's Strand near Dundealgan. It was at this time that Conchubar was holding court in that district and word came to him that a foreign ship had arrived, and a young lad was there armed as if for battle, with armed men behind him.

Conchubar sent a messenger at once to inquire his name and business. But the youth refused to divulge his name and boasted that no one would get it from him nor would he stand down for anyone.

Conall then went to him and, on the boy's repeated refusal to state his name and business and his scornful boast that he would give way to no man, Conall attacked him. The two fought furiously until the great Conall was worsted and had to retreat.

On receipt of this news Cuchulain stormed out to deal with the arrogant youngster.

Again Conlaoch's name was demanded and again he refused to give it. Cuchulain challenged him to fight.

At that moment Emer, who had come with others to see the extraordinary child who had defeated one of their greatest heroes, called out to Cuchulain: "Stay your hand, my lord. There is something not right here." She was looking at the boy, and to her he seemed in every feature to be a younger version of her own husband . . . the same beauty . . . the same fierce light of battle fury playing around his head.

But Conlaoch was already stabbing at Cuchulain with his sword.

Hesitating at Emer's call, Cuchulain put up his shield.

"Is it possible he is your son?" she cried. But the sound of her voice did not reach Cuchulain, who was hard pressed by the swiftness and violence of the child's attack. The hesitation cost him the advantage, and he found himself giving ground. This made him angry, for he was determined not to be shamed as Conall had been shamed. Cuchulain seized the deadly notched spear Scathach had given him— the one he rarely used, for its thrust was cruel and fatal, beyond any other known to man. As he raised it, Conlaoch recognized it and with it his father. His own spear hand was raised already, but he sent his weapon wide so that it whistled past Cuchulain's fierce head. He was not so fortunate himself, for Cuchulain in his rage threw the gae bolge—Scathach's hateful weapon—and his aim was true.

Cuchulain stood over him as he fell.

"Now, boy, tell me your name?" he demanded triumphantly.

"Can you not see?" Emer cried, rushing to his side. "The boy is your son!"

Cuchulain looked down and saw his own ring on the lad's hand. He knelt beside him and took him in his arms.

"Why did you not tell me, child?" he moaned. "I would not have fought you for the world!"

"My mother," whispered the boy, "my mother put me under geiss not to reveal my name to anyone and to accept every challenge."

"Your mother knew it would come to this," Cuchulain said bitterly.

The boy nodded, scarcely able to speak for the agony of Scathach's venomous metal in his body.

"A curse be on your mother," muttered Cuchulain.

"A curse be on her," the boy whispered, "but oh, Cuchulain of the bright blade, why did you not suspect when I threw my spear wide of you?"

Cuchulain looked into the boy's tormented eyes and his own filled with such pain Emer's heart almost broke to see it. For all their loving she had borne him no child.

Cuchulain lifted his sword and plunged it into the boy's heart to prevent the long, slow suffering of the gae bolge. And then he stood astride him, raised his mighty arms to the sky, and howled his curses at Aoife that she should have brought this about.

"If he had lived, the two of us would have stood together against the enemies of Ulster—and no army in the world would have been able to defeat us. I am a raven that has lost its home. I am without a son, without a brother. I have no one to stand at my side. I have no one to carry on my strength and my name!"

Conchubar, seeing where his grief and his anger were leading, called Cathbad the Druid quickly to his side.

"If he cannot work off his anger," he whispered, "he will be a danger to all of us. See what you can do."

And so Cathbad cast a spell and Cuchulain left Conlaoch and rushed toward the strand. There for three days and three nights he fought against the waves as though they were incoming hosts. At last, spent and weary, his anger gone and only the sorrow remaining, Cuchulain allowed himself to be gathered into Emer's arms.

In all the time Cuchulain had been defending Ulster against its enemies; in all the time he had challenged and fought for the sheer joy of the battle; in all the time he had boasted and killed and taken other men's wives—he had stored up against himself a host of people out for revenge.

During the Battle for the Brown Bull of Cuailnge, he had single-handedly destroyed most of Maeve's own best fighting men and many of her allies. Among these were Calatin and his sons.

Calatin had left behind a pregnant wife, and when she came to term she was delivered of three daughters on the same day, each with only one eye. Maeve visited her and took away the three girls to foster and care for. When they were grown Maeve stirred up resentment in them against Cuchulain, who had killed their father and their brothers, and she suggested that they should travel the world in search of knowledge and enchantments and spells so that one day they would have the power to avenge their father. Maeve provided them with the means to travel and protection—and sent them off. For many years they sojourned in countries that were noted for their use of magic—Alban, Finland, Egypt, far Asia. . . . When they returned to Maeve they were formidable opponents for Cuchulain.

Then Maeve set about stirring up everyone who had lost someone to Cuchulain and raised a great host to march against him. She knew that at this time the men of Ulster would be suffering again from the weakening spell Macha had cast upon them and would not be likely to be able to help him.

Conchubar, hearing of the approach of the host and of its purpose, sent Levercham to Dundealgan to fetch Cuchulain. He knew they must make some plan to delay the battle until the men of Ulster were ready to fight with him.

Levercham found Cuchulain at Baile's Strand. Since he had been the cause of his son's death he had been sad and morose, finding nothing to interest or arouse him. Levercham delivered Conchubar's message—but Cuchulain said he would rather stay and defend his own place by himself than go and hide from his enemies at Emain Macha.

Levercham took Emer aside and explained what was happening.

She at once bustled about, sending the cattle and servants to the mountains in the north and putting her house in order to leave. She insisted Cuchulain should accompany her to Emain Macha.

Conchubar instructed Cathbad and the learned men and women to keep watch over Cuchulain and see that he did not leave the shelter of the fort—for if he fell to Maeve's host, Ulster would be left defenseless. Cuchulain was royally entertained with feasting and song in a fair and sunny house.

Maeve's host marched on Dundealgan but found that it was deserted.

As soon as the three daughters of Calatin saw that he had slipped from their grasp, they flew by enchantment to Emain Macha and settled unnoticed on the lawn in front of Cuchulain's sunny bower. By tossing about little tufts of grass, fallen oak leaves, and twigs, they gave the illusion of an army attacking the fort. Cuchulain started up when he heard the battle shouts and screams, the clash of iron weapons. He put his hand on his sword and his face began to redden with battle fever. Geanann, son of Cathbad, who was on watch with Emer at that time, rushed forward to hold Cuchulain back while Emer tried to persuade him that he was imagining the sounds of battle—that no one else could hear them. "It is enchantment, my bright lord, put on you by Maeve and the daughters of Calatin. Pay no heed to it."

Hearing the commotion, others rushed into the chamber and, one by one, confirmed that Geanann and Emer were right—there *was* no battle.

The next day Cathbad himself was on watch when the three daughters of Calatin spoke their words of power. This time, though Cuchulain half-knew he was bewitched, he still tried to free himself from the restraining hands of his friends. This day, not only did he see and hear a great battle, but he heard the sweet, sad music of the Sidh and believed that this was to warn him that his strength and his life would soon be at an end.

Cathbad told him that if he would only stay quietly there for three days, the danger would be over—the enchantment would lose its power, and the hosts of Ulster would be ready to stand beside him in the battle with Maeve and the daughters of Calatin.

The next day Conchubar suggested that they take Cuchulain away from Emain Macha to Glean-na-Bodhar, known as the Deaf Valley, because no sounds from outside ever penetrated it. He suggested they sing and make music there so that Cuchulain would be doubly sure not to hear anything of the noise of battle if the three daughters of Calatin created their illusions again. But Cuchulain refused to go and said he would stay where he was. This time not even Emer could persuade him to leave.

——— Niamh ———

Then Emer went aside and thought about her love for Cuchulain, how it was more important to her than anything else in the world that she keep him safe. She knew that he looked at Niamh, Celthair's daughter, a great deal, and she suspected that they were, or had been, lovers. Let Niamh take him to the valley, she thought. It will be difficult for him to refuse her. And she arranged with Cathbad that he should invite Cuchulain to a feast in a house he had in the valley. But again Cuchulain refused to rise from his bed.

"Listen to me, little hound," Emer said. "I have asked very little of you in all the time we have been together—and I have never stood in your way. But this time I ask a great favor of you. Go with Cathbad, for he is an old and trusted friend—a man of honor and a man of power. It would be churlish of you to refuse his hospitality."

But still Cuchulain refused, believing that his enemies would name him coward if he ran away from them.

Then Emer left the room, and Niamh came to him in robes as light as thistledown. She took him in her arms and made love to him. On the third deep kiss she made him promise that he would not go into battle without her permission. Roused by her touches and forgetful of all else, he promised.

And so it was that he went with her to Glean-na-Bodhar.

Once there, Cuchulain began to grumble that he hated the place and wanted to leave, but Niamh held him to his promise, and Cathbad held him to the feast. They unyoked the horses from the chariots and put them out to graze. They played music and they sang songs—and the feasting began. All were trying to bring pleasure to the dark and brooding heart of Cuchulain.

Meanwhile, the three daughters of Calatin noticed that Cuchulain was no longer at Emain Macha and they began to search the whole kingdom for him, flying over forests and fields and forts. Then at last, in one deep and secluded gorge, they spied Cuchulain's horses out to graze, the gray of Macha and the black Sanglain, with Laeg, his charioteer, beside them.

They alighted not far from the house of Cathbad and began again to create the illusion of a battle. Cuchulain seized his weapons, but once again he was restrained by his friends.

When the three daughters of Calatin saw that once again they had been foiled, one of them—Badb by name—told her sisters that she was going down to talk with Cuchulain, even if it meant her death.

She left them to make the sounds of battle in the air, and she went down to the house. There she put on the appearance of one of Niamh's women and called her out of the feast hall as though she had special and urgent news for her. Feigning extreme agitation, she led her off down the valley as though to show her something.

Niamh followed trustingly—until suddenly she found herself lost in a thick mist and her guide nowhere to be seen.

Badb took on the shape of Niamh and approached Cuchulain in the hall.

"Rise up, Cuchulain," she called out. "Dundealgan and Muirthemne are destroyed, and the men of Connacht are trampling on Emain Macha. It is time for you to go now and do great deeds and save your companions from dishonor and death."

Then—because he had given Niamh his word that he would not fight without her permission and now she had granted it—he seized his weapons, and no one could hold him.

"It is enchantment!" Cathbad cried. "See how she skulks away. That is not Niamh! If you can just hold out one more day. . . ."

But Cuchulain would not. He could see the whole of Emain Macha in flames and Conchubar and all his court put to the sword—and all because he was not there to defend them. He commanded Laeg to make his chariot ready, and when his loyal companion protested he seized the horses' bridles himself and tried to yoke them. But it seemed the gray of Macha and the black Sanglain sensed that there was something very wrong and they, for the first time in his service, trampled and snorted and tried to break away from him. He had to force them to obey, which they did at last—but others could see the great tears in their eyes.

Cuchulain rode like a storm wind to Emain Macha and drew up before the house of Emer.

"My lord," she cried, "can you not see that you are under enchantment still? Just one more day! Just one more day, my lord!"

But he would not stay.

"My great name will be reduced to dust. I will die unknown and unsung if I fail to meet this challenge. You, my love, who have stood by me through danger after danger, cannot fail me now. If my death is near, let it be met with courage. Let Emer say Cuchulain, the greatest of heroes, loved her—and she was honored by his love."

Emer reached out her arms to protest, but he was already gone.

He stood before his mother, Dechtire, sister of King Conchubar. She looked into his eyes and knew that he had come to say good-bye. She poured a chalice of wine for him and he lifted it to his lips in a silent toast to her.

But the liquid in the cup was blood not wine.

"What is this, mother?" he said sorrowfully. "My mother gives me blood to drink?"

She took the cup from him and poured another. Again the wine was blood when he came to drink. A third cup was the same.

Then they embraced for the last time, and Cuchulain left, his heart heavy with foreboding.

Meanwhile, Cathbad had followed him and came with him now as he turned toward Muirthemne. At the ford they saw a young girl washing clothes, and when they looked closer they saw she was of the Sidh, silver-skinned and golden-haired, and the clothes she was washing were Cuchulain's own. They were red with blood.

"Dear master," Cuchulain then said to Cathbad, "I cannot turn back now. Take my love and greetings to Emer my wife and all my friends. It is not likely that I will see them again. Oh, Laeg," he said sadly to his charioteer, "we are going into shadow and may not return to Emer, as we used to do, with brave tales of adventures in far countries."

Erc, son of Cairbre, was the first to see him coming, his chariot at full tilt, his hair flying out around his head like the sparks of fire from a smith's forge, his sword shining red in his hand. . . .

But this time there were too many even for Cuchulain and, though he slaughtered more than any other man, he was at last fatally wounded—Laeg and his steeds defeated—and alone.

Cuchulain crawled to a standing stone on the west side of the lake and bound himself to it so that he would not die lying down. There he fought his last fight.

It was Lugaid who struck off his head and his right hand and carried them off as spoil. But he did not savor the taste of victory for long, for Conall and the men of Ulster, recovered at last from Macha's weakening spell, came thundering up to avenge Cuchulain's death.

Levercham brought the news to Emer as she sat in her parlor, staring out of the window.

Quietly Emer rose and pinned on her cloak. Then she and the women of Emain Macha went to where Cuchulain was still standing, tied to the tall stone, his head beside him, returned by Conall. The women wept and keened over his death, singing his praises—but Emer took her husband's head in her hands, washed it gently in the shining lake, bound it with clean silk and brought it to her breast like a mother her child. There she rocked it and whispered to it, sighing over the good times they had had together . . . over his strength and his gentleness . . . over his quickness to come to the aid of all who asked him . . . over his beauty and the sweetness of his lovemaking. "I am carried away like a branch on the stream," she said. "There is no life for me without you."

When Conall returned from the vengeance he had wrought on the men of Ireland and had flung down their heads on the lawn at Dundealgan, naming each one and the deeds they had done, it was agreed that it was time now to bury Cuchulain.

"Dig a wide grave, Conall of the Battles," Emer said. "For I will not live after my great love."

And when the grave was dug, she climbed into it beside her husband, laid her lips to his, and died.

It is said by the women of Emain Macha that at certain times Cuchulain can still be seen riding over the plain in his chariot, the music of the Sidh all around him.

Commentary

Although the twelfth century *Book of the Conquests of Ireland* mentions six waves of invaders in ancient times, and writers often refer to them as though they were in separate and almost watertight compartments, there is evidence in the sagas and legends that there was intermarriage and interflow between the different peoples. Emer, for instance, is the daughter of Forgall Manach, who is the nephew of the Formorian sea king Tethra. Her mother is not mentioned, and it would

seem she is no longer alive at the time Emer meets Cuchulain—for it is
her aunt, Forgall's sister, who pursues them when they elope. I assume
that her mother was of the currently dominant race, the Milesians
(Gaels), for there is no suggestion of Emer herself being a Formorian.

Cuchulain, the Ulaid's greatest hero and Emer's husband, is the son
of Dechtire, sister to the Ulster king and therefore presumably of the
ruling race; but she was abducted and seduced by Lugh—an Other
World being associated with the sun, who is said to have driven the
Formorians from the country. At the same time, Cuchulain is the
grandson of one of their most fearsome leaders, Balor. Cuchulain
therefore has Formorian as well as Other World blood in him—and
it is probably for this reason he does not fall under the spell of Macha's
curse on the men of Ulster and can fight on while they are lying as
weak as women about to give birth.

On one level this is a most moving and very human love story. Emer
is not married off by her father but chooses her own mate, who must
pass stringent tests before he is worthy of her. I find it touching that
Emer will not marry Cuchulain at first because he is not man enough
for her, and then at the end, when she has been through every suffering with him and their love is mature and deep, she takes his head in
her arms and rocks it like an infant at her breast. Throughout the
saga, Cuchulain the great hero, for all his mighty "macho" deeds, is
childlike compared to Emer.

There are many stories, then as now, of lives ruined because of jealousy. I find Emer's attitude toward Cuchulain admirable. She loves
him beyond life itself, yet she does not waste their time together fret-
ting about the other women in his life. She knows him. She knows
him well. He is pursued by women wherever he goes, like all handsome and glamorous heroes. She is secure in her own estimation of
herself and understanding of him. There is no one who can jeopar-
dize his love for her. He plays, he boasts, he fights. But the home he
comes to is always hers. She lives at Dundealgan, a rich and respected
woman with herds of cattle and a host of servants. She goes to court
when she feels like it or she entertains the court in her own house.
She rules her own domain. She makes her own decisions—and often
those of her husband.

Only once does Cuchulain fail to return to Emer after an important adventure, and that is after his experience with Li Ban and Fand.
He insists on being taken back to Emain Macha instead of to

120

Dundealgan. I get the impression it is not because he loves Eithne Inguba more but because he does not want Emer, his greatest love, to see him in the degradingly weak state he was in. Emer was proud of his strength and proud that she could match it. What would she say if she saw him helpless? He underestimates her, of course. It is Eithne who sits helplessly by and can do nothing for him and Emer, when she finds out at last, who raises him up by her sheer faith in him.

The only meetings with a woman Cuchulain seems to deliberately keep from Emer are those with Fand on his return from the land of the Sidh. Emer hears about it. She is angry—partly because for once he has not been open and honest with her and partly because she can see that Fand poses a different and more dangerous threat to their love.

The contrast between Emer and Fand is a very important one if we are looking below the surface of the story. Emer is of the earth—healthy, strong, intelligent, vigorous. Her love for Cuchulain is the best of human love. Fand is of the Other World. She sends for him; that is, he experiences a call. He tries to resist and fights it by becoming ill. His first close encounter with Fand and what she stands for is when he tries to shoot down the two magical birds over the lake. The flock of birds, which the women want for nothing better than to adorn themselves, are the magical birds of the land of the Sidh, the ones Laeg later hears singing in the three crystal trees at the eastern (dawn) entrance to the Other World.

Up to this time Cuchulain has been a very physical hero—a kind of Rambo. When you read the stories in which he is featured, more often than not he is single-handedly slaughtering vast numbers of enemies. But there is another thread that runs through his story. Cuchulain seeks a woman to wed who is not just physically beautiful but, more important, intelligent and wise. His father is not Sualtim, his mother's husband, but Lugh, the god of light. Cuchulain rolls a wheel of fire through the marsh and dries it up—he is the son of the sun.

Cuchulain is a hero of the Celts because he defeats his enemies; the greatest virtue to the Celts at this time was prowess in battle. But the Celts also believed in immortality—so to them the killing was not so much the ending of lives but the testing of one man against another, after which the loser was translated to another realm. When Emer climbs into Cuchulain's grave she is ensuring that she will be going with him to wherever he is going.

When Cuchulain has passed all the tests of physical strength and courage it is possible to have, he is drawn into the testing of his deeper nature. Note that this testing occurs at Samhain, on November 1, our All Saints' Day, the time when the door between the worlds is open and encounters between this world and the Other World are possible and frequent.

The magical birds, the messengers from the high realms, skim across the water. Water, as always in myth, is associated with the crossing from one reality to another. Instead of recognizing the birds for what they are, Cuchulain maims them to satisfy the vanity of the women. Truths are brought down from the higher realms, distorted, misused, and made the cause of strife. Eithne Inguba is angry and dissatisfied because she is given no feathers so Cuchulain promises to shoot down more birds for her. He is warned that these are more than just birds—but he fails to listen. He does what he is used to doing—he attacks. But this testing is on a different level, and he cannot win with the weapons he has used before. He is out of his depth; he is confused and feels himself to be shamed. If he only knew it, he is about to enter a new and very important phase—an air lock, as it were, between the realms. Cuchulain walks away, shocked that all the skills he had relied on before have failed him, not knowing how else to conduct himself. He sits down, alone, with his back to a standing stone.

The stone circles and standing stones of Ireland and Britain belong to the long ages before the Celts. They were to the Celts, as they are to us, mysterious and powerful objects. It is significant that at this moment, when he first begins to question his old way of life and see the glimmering of a new one, it is to a standing stone (or "pillar stone") he comes. Similarly, at his death, Cuchulain binds himself to a standing stone.

Cuchulain has been forced, by his failure to achieve something he thought he was quite capable of achieving, into questioning himself and the reality around him. He shuts his eyes. He shuts out the mundane world he knows. The energy of the stone-symbol at his back loosens his ties with the reality he has known and frees him to experience a different reality. His first encounter with this different reality is a painful one—as it almost always is. Two spirit-women, one in the color of life and the other in the color of death (for red is associated with death in the Celtic mind), greet him, smiling. Then they take turns beating him until he is too weak to move or speak. They are breaking down his old self before the new one can take over.

When they have done what they came to do, they leave him. His friends find him—the great Hound of Culain—helpless, almost in a coma. The obvious thing would be to take him back to Emer, but he insists that he is to be taken to Emain Macha—not only because he does not want Emer to see him so weak but because Emer belongs to that part of him which is now being broken down, and he is not allowed to go back to her yet. It is as though he has to face this alone—without her help.

The next time the doors are open between the worlds, the next Samhain, Cuchulain receives a direct call to leave this world—to take up the cause of an Other World king and accept the love of his higher self, his spirit-destiny, Fand.

That he has been ill for a year is an indication of just how unready Cuchulain is for this. Even now he won't go with the shining Sidh being, but he takes a small step. He returns to the standing stone where he first encountered the women—and there he meets Li Ban again. Note he does not meet Fand, who is the one who is calling him, but her sister, an intermediary. Cuchulain is still not ready and, in fact, sends his own intermediary, his charioteer and faithful friend Laeg, to see how things are. Laeg reports back full of praise for what he has seen.

Laeg has entered the Other World as a lesser mortal than Cuchulain. He is not the one called to great things—but his loyalty, his courage, and his love make him a worthy messenger and intermediary.

At this point Cuchulain can find no more excuses for not embarking on the unfamiliar spiritual adventure. He sends for Emer, half hoping, I suspect, that she will refuse to let him go—thereby freeing him from the guilt of making the wrong decision—half needing her strength and encouragement *to* go.

Emer rouses Cuchulain from his sickbed and forces him to accept whatever challenge he is called upon to face. Emer is the best of Cuchulain: his other half. It is significant that in his death Emer chooses to lie with her lips on his so the two of them can be seen by all around to be the whole they always were.

Full of good intentions, Cuchulain, after his invigorating meeting with Emer, sets off for the stone again and talks with Li Ban. But once again he hesitates to take the final step.

Laeg is dispatched again to the land of the Sidh, this time on the excuse that Cuchulain wants to be *sure* of the invitation.

At last, after Laeg's assurances, Cuchulain enters the other reality, is tested in a symbolic battle, and comes to union with Fand, the purest, most beautiful, most immortal part of the spirit. For a while Cuchulain stays united and in bliss. But he is not ready for an eternity of this, and his old life, his old values, call. Fand will not hold him against his will, and he returns to Emer.

But things are never quite the same between Emer and Cuchulain—perhaps because he has changed. Emer can feel it. Before, when he went off and took other women to bed, she did not mind—because when he made love to her she could feel that he was totally with her. But now part of himself, part of his love, seemed to be missing. She sensed that someone stronger than herself was pulling him away. She knew what Fand was, and she knew she was no ordinary rival. She knew also that if Cuchulain was wavering between the two worlds he was vulnerable and insecure.

Emer and Fand are complementary.

Emer refused to accept Cuchulain as husband until he was worthy of her. He endured the physical rigors and dangers of Scathach's training on the Island of Shadows (present-day Skye) for her sake just as later he had to go through the spiritual training of Fand—the long period of thought forced on him by the inactivity of his wasting sickness.

But Emer is not an abstract concept. She is very much a woman of flesh and blood, who changes, strengthens, and grows through the trials of her own life. The woman who persuades Cuchulain to accept the mysterious Other World invitation and later hands him over to Niamh because she can see this is the only way to save him, is a deeper and more mature person than the young woman who ran to be the first through the door of the feasting hall at Bricriu's house, boasting that all the heroes of Eriu were wanting her.

Emer at once stands for certain aspects of the human being and yet at the same time *is* a human being.

Through most of the saga of Cuchulain, the hero has been fighting foes, drinking, and feasting, while Emer has run her estate and entertained her friends. Their love has been strong and resilient. But as the story draws to its close, much deeper issues emerge. In Cuchulain's encounter with the Other World, he suffers the conflict of being part spirit and part flesh. Here Emer's practical, down-to-earth nature only partially understands what is going on. She fears for his safety—but she also suffers the pangs of jealousy.

As he kills his only son—the son who should have stood shoulder to shoulder with him—Emer fully understands his pain when he turns from her and vents his bitterness on the waves of the sea. They have not had a child between them. That is, though their love makes the two of them a whole, out of that whole there is only a limited progression.

The image of him fighting the waves of the sea is a very poignant one. I see it as the dark night of the soul. The sea is the ocean of consciousness with its depth upon depth. He stands on the shore, fighting his own thoughts, his own doubts and fears and passions.

From this battle Cuchulain never fully recovers. He has great resources as a warrior of worldly battles, but in these nonphysical struggles he has not yet emerged a champion. Emer watches. She can give him her love, but she cannot fight his battles for him.

In the last act Cuchulain is tormented by illusions. Note that the enemies he has made by his own acts gather together against him. This is important. They are not just random opponents. He has brought their vengeance on himself.

Again the women who love Cuchulain try to protect him from his own weakness—that is, his inability to recognize illusion. The intuitive "feminine" side of the psyche sees through illusion more clearly than the intellectual "male" side.

There is something tragically heroic about the way he doggedly goes on to meet certain doom, with every possible omen against him. It is as though he knows he has gone as far as he can go in the worldly sense, but he just cannot make the transition to heroism in the Other Worldly sense without losing his life in the only honorable way he knows.

Emer watches and waits.

Emer finds Cuchulain bound to the standing stone against which he had first encountered Li Ban and Fand. It is on the west of the lake—the side traditionally associated with the going down of the sun and death. His head and his right hand have been chopped off—his worldly intelligence and his fighting arm. She washes his head clear of all its imperfections and takes it to her heart for nurturing. Her strength is still with him and she chooses that her strength will go with him into the Other World. We feel that, with her beside him, finally he will be able to cope with what is beyond. She sees that he has chosen to meet his death at the place where Fand had called him. It is possible he is with Fand even now. But Emer is determined she will not leave his side. She knows she can give him passion and courage and life in a way that the ethereal lady of the Sidh never could.

Together they lie in the one grave. I am surprised that the women who reported seeing him riding his chariot over the plains of Muirthemne as a ghost did not see Emer with him.

Sources used:

Gantz, Jeffrey. *Early Irish Myths and Sagas*. New York: Penguin Books, 1981.

Gregory, Lady Augusta. *Cuchulain of Muirthemne*. Gerrards Cross, U.K.: Colin Smythe, 1970.

Rolleston, T. W. *Myths and Legends of the Celtic Race*. London: Harrap & Co., 1917.

Macha

Macha, the Daughter of Red Hugh

Before Red Hugh, High King of Eriu, died, he arranged that his kingdom should be divided between his two brothers—Dithorba and Cimbaoth. But his daughter, Macha, who had enjoyed his confidence in matters of state for a long time and had sat at his right hand at all great occasions, disputed this.

Macha attacked Dithorba before he could leave his dun and slaughtered him with all his men. She held Cimbaoth at sword point until he agreed to marry her.

For years Macha ruled as Eriu's strong and fearsome queen—but one day it came to her notice that the five sons of Dithorba, now grown to manhood and living in exile in the furthest west regions of the country, were plotting to unseat her. She set off alone in the night on her horse and came upon them in a forest.

Weary from a day of traveling and hunting, the five young men were gathered sleepily around their fire cooking venison. One by one Macha appeared to them, a shadowy female figure beckoning just out of reach of the firelight. One by one they slipped away from their brothers, their weariness forgotten as she drew them deeper into the forest and revealed by moonlight her extraordinary and seductive beauty. One by one the young men made love to her, and when they were savoring the relaxation after climax, she overpowered them and bound them tight and helpless.

When she had all five captured, Macha slung them onto her horse and rode home with them. There the hapless princes were forced to labor for her, building the great ramparts of her fortress—which later became known as Emain Macha, the Brooch of Macha.

——— Macha, ———
Wife of Crunniac, Son of Agnoman

Crunniac's first wife died leaving him with children to rear in a lonely and secluded part of Ulster.

One evening the door opened and a tall, fine-looking woman appeared, and without a word started to sweep the hearth and cook the food for the family's evening meal. Surprised, Crunniac stood aside and let her do what she was doing. After the meal, she put the children to bed as though she were their mother and then drew Crunniac himself to the couch where he was wont to sleep. Thinking that the whole thing was a dream—or possibly that his own wife had returned in spirit form—Crunniac said nothing but allowed himself to be held in her arms. The warmth of her body was unlike that which he would have expected from a ghost, and he was soon enjoying her strong and rhythmic lovemaking.

They lived as man and wife for a long while. He never asked where she had come from, and she never let slip a hint of her past. He prospered and his children thrived.

One day the time for a great feast at the king's house arrived, and Crunniac suggested that they should go to it. Macha refused—but he decided to go without her.

"Take care," she said. "Say nothing about me. Watch your tongue at all times."

"Never fear," he said. "I have kept our secret this long—I will not give it up now."

The celebrations lasted many days, as usual. There were musicians and storytellers from all over the country and feats of arms and races by the score. Crunniac was enjoying himself and drinking more wine than he had drunk in many a long year.

On hearing boasting that the king's two chariot horses were faster than anything in the world, Crunniac drunkenly laughed and said his own wife could outrun them any day. The king took this as an insult and said at once that Crunniac's wife must be brought to run against the horses and that Crunniac himself would be put to death if his had been an idle boast.

Crunniac was held captive while messengers were sent to the remote farm where Macha was peacefully going about her chores—at this time very near to delivering herself of a child.

She greeted the messengers cordially but was shocked to hear how foolish her husband had been.

"As you can see, I am in no fit state to run," she said. "I am heavy with child."

"No matter, lady," they said. "Our instructions are to bring you to the king, and if we fail, we ourselves will be in trouble."

Very unwillingly, Macha went with them and, seeing Crunniac cringing in his bonds, gave him a fierce and angry look. Then she turned to the king and looked him straight in the eye.

"You can see, my lord," she said, "I am near to term. I cannot run. But if you will wait a month or two I would be glad to make good my husband's boast."

"We will not wait, lady," the king said coldly. "Your husband insulted us. He dies if you cannot make good his boast this very day."

Macha turned to the crowds who were pressing in around her and staring and joking at her enormous belly. She saw no pity in any eye.

"Speak for me, men of Ulster," she pleaded. "You can see I am in no fit state to run."

No one spoke for her—but many of the men made jokes about her condition and her figure. Crunniac was in despair, but there was nothing he could do.

Biting her lip then, and holding her head high, Macha walked to the starting place.

"I will race for your life," she said to Crunniac. "But I will not return to your hearth."

The course was explained to her. The two horses were fresh and already champing at the bit to be off.

"Are you ready?" sneered the king.

"I am ready," she said coldly.

The race began. The chosen course was long and hard. Macha outstripped the horses, though sweat and blood poured from her. She won the race, and then, as she reached the finish, she fell down and gave birth to an infant boy and an infant girl—Macha's twins.

With her face distorted with pain and rage she pronounced a curse on the staring faces gathered around her.

"Men of Ulster," she said bitterly, "you have shown me no mercy in the weakness of childbirth. You will suffer the same pain and weakness for five days and four nights whenever you most need your strength—you and your sons and your son's sons until the ninth generation!"

Commentary

There are many stories about Macha, and most of them link her with Badb and the Morrigu as one of the mighty war goddesses of Ireland. She appears as the wife of Nemhedh—the leader of one of the very early Aryan invading forces of Ireland.

Later, when Ireland is invaded by the Tuatha de Danann, Macha, with the Morrigu and Badb, spread a dark and swirling mist to confuse the defending tribes of the Fir Bolg.

Later still, in the mighty northern battle of Magh Tuiredh (or Moytura) fought between the Tuatha and the Formorians, it is said that Macha, as one of Lugh's warlike wives, was slain by Balor of the Evil Eye.

It was Macha's curse that left Cuchulain alone to defend Ulster against the fearful attacks of Maeve in the matter of the Brown Bull of Cuailnge (see "Emer and the Women Who Loved Cuchulain," page 95). And it was Macha's curse that prevented the men of Ulster from coming to his aid when finally, on the plains of Muirthemne, Cuchulain met his lonely death.

Emain Macha, later the royal dun of Conchubar, was at the center of the ancient kingdom of Ulster. One can still see the grassy ring of a great hill fort close to Armagh. It is now called Navan Fort but was once the home of the mighty warriors of the Red Branch—a rival in splendor to Tara of the Kings.

The northern Magh Tuiredh (Moytura), where one of the Machas was slain, is thought to be a plain at Carrowmore, near Sligo, which is full of cairns and burial mounds and standing stones.

As war goddess, Macha was always associated with the pillars, called "mesred machae," on which the heads of slain warriors were displayed. Another grisly name for the heads gathered from the field after a battle was "Macha's acorn crop."

It is in her capacity as a horse goddess that Macha runs the race against the King of Ulster's chariot horses.

Sources used:

Gantz, Jeffrey. *Early Irish Myths and Legends*. New York: Penguin Books, 1981.

Gregory, Lady Augusta. *Cuchulain of Muirthemne*. Gerrards Cross, U.K.: Colin Smythe, 1970.

Rolleston, T. W. *Myths and Legends of the Celtic Race*. London: Harrap & Co., 1917.

Squire, Charles. *Celtic Myth and Legend*. Newcastle Publishing Co., 1975.

The Morrigu

O ne day, long before the coming of the Milesians to Eriu, the Formorians under their formidable leader, Balor of the Evil Eye, landed at Scetne. Lugh of the Tuatha de Danann sent the Dagda to spy on their numbers and to try to delay their attack while he made his own forces ready.

The Dagda came to the camp of the Formorians and won their agreement for a delay, on the understanding that he would have a meal with them. Secretly they had decided to have some sport with him, and, knowing that as earth god one of his magical possessions was a cauldron of food that never emptied, they claimed to have one of their own and challenged him to empty it. If he did not, they said, they would kill him. They plied his huge appetite with broth until at last he fell down in a bloated stupor and slept. When he woke and lurched off back to Lugh, disheveled and chagrined, the Dagda saw a naked woman washing herself in the river, her left foot on one bank and her right on another. This inflamed another of his appetites, and as prodigious as his eating had been at the camp of the Formorians, so was his lovemaking with the woman.

When they drew apart at last and looked at each other, she saw that it was the Dagda who had given her such pleasure, and he saw that it was the Morrigu. They talked, and she listened to his tale of how he had been treated in the Formorian camp.

"I will bring you the heart's blood of those who threatened you," she said. "Yours will be the victory."

Then followed the great battle of Magh Tuiredh. The Morrigu fought with the Tuatha de Danann, and at the battle's end it was the Morrigu who cried out the news that the Formorians had been defeated and the land belonged to Lugh and the Children of Danu. Her voice reverberated through the hills and along the rivers, and there was no one alive in Eriu who did not hear it.

——— The Morrigu and Conare ———

Conare, the just king, son of Etain and a bird spirit, came to Da Derga's Hostel and prepared to rest for the night.

A woman came knocking at the door, leaning against the doorpost and asking for shelter. Long and thin and dark she was—with a gray wool mantle and a gray beard almost to her knees.

"I cannot give you shelter," the young king said, "for I am bound about with gessa, and one of them is that I cannot receive a single man or woman who comes to my door after sunset. You look like a seer—can you see my future?"

"You will not leave this place," she said, "unless your flesh is carried out in the claws of carrion birds."

"That is a dark foretelling, woman. What is your name?"

She gave a twisted smile and a list of different names as long as a long breath lasts.

He ordered his men to take her food outside, but she sneered at him for lack of honor that he should turn an old woman away from shelter in the dark of the night.

Sighing, he allowed her to come in, but he knew and his men knew that, what with breaking the geiss and the doom she pronounced, they had not much hope of getting out of there alive.

Bad omen after bad omen manifested that long and fearful night, culminating in the sight of three naked and bleeding female forms hanging by ropes from the roof beams—the daughters of the Morrigu, slain in every battle and in the thought of every battle.

Inexorably, Conare's doom was played out and the Morrigu's prophecy was fullfilled. The enemies that had been closing in on the hostel all day attacked; none of the heroes he had with him could withstand the onslaught, though they fought bravely and long.

——— The Morrigu and Maeve ———

Now Ailell of Connacht had a white-horned bull that was his pride— and no bull could match it except the Brown Bull of Cuailnge.

One day the Morrigu brought a cow from the Hill of Cruachan to the Brown Bull of Cuailnge, and a marvelous calf was born of the union. But the presence of the calf in his territory enraged Ailell's white-horned bull and he attacked it. The animals fought on the plain of Cruachan, and the bellowing was heard throughout the household of Ailell and Maeve.

"What did the calf bellow?" asked Maeve of her cowherd.

"He boasted of his father, the Brown Bull of Cuailnge, my lady," the cowherd said, "and claimed that if the white-horned bull were to fight his father instead of himself, he would be beaten across the whole plain on every side."

"He bellows that, does he?" said Maeve. "Well, we shall see. I shall not drink wine or ale or lie on feathers until I see those two bulls fighting before my face."

And so it was that the Morrigu ensured there would be a war for the Brown Bull of Cuailnge that would kill many brave heroes.

But the Morrigu's work was not done when she had started the war. She was busy on both sides and even warned the Brown Bull himself of the coming of the hosts, so that he took fifty of his heifers and left the place and hid. It was thought that he had been stolen— and more bloodshed followed.

Many a time the Morrigu was seen as a gray and bony hag, shrieking insults from one army to the other, stirring up anger and hate, and filling all hearts with fear and dread.

The Morrigu and Cuchulain

One night Cuchulain was deep in sleep after the exertions of fighting Maeve's warriors all day. He woke, startled, to hear a great shout. He rushed out of his tent to find Laeg, his charioteer, yoking his horses, claiming that he had also heard the shout. They both thought it had come from the north—so toward the north they set out.

They had not gone far when they came upon a chariot with a great red horse yoked to it, and in it was a tall and striking woman dressed in red, with a red cloak so long that it almost covered the wheels of her chariot and with red eyebrows and flowing red hair. Strapped to her back was a gray spear.

"Greetings, Cuchulain," she said, barring his way.

"Greetings," Cuchulain replied. "What is your name and what is it that you want with me?"

"I am the daughter of a king," she said, "and I have sought you because of your great deeds and because of your great beauty. I offer you my love this night and any night you will have me."

Laeg stared at her. She was of great beauty—gold on her bare arms and at her bare throat. But many women loved Cuchulain. Laeg looked at his master, who could hardly stand for weariness.

"You have chosen a bad time," said Cuchulain. "I am worn out with fighting and am in need of sleep more than of a woman."

"I am no ordinary woman," she said. "I have been helping you against your enemies without your knowing it, and I could continue to help you."

"I need no woman to help me in the work I have to do," said Cuchulain impatiently, "and I have no desire for your loving now or henceforth!"

"If you will not have my love," she said, and her voice now sounded cold and hostile, "you will have my enmity. When you are fighting, I will take the part of your enemy. My spear will be at your back as his spear is at your front. I will come at you in any shape I choose—anytime, anyplace. . . ."

"Come at me now then," Cuchulain cried, and he took his sword and made a leap at the chariot. The iron touched her flesh, but as it did so the woman, the chariot, and the horse disappeared, and all that was there was a screeching black crow winging away with feathers falling from it.

It was then Cuchulain and Laeg realized that the woman was the Morrigu.

The next time Cuchulain saw the Morrigu, though again he did not realize it was she, was when he found an old woman milking a cow with three teats. Thirstily Cuchulain asked for a drink, and she gave him one from one of the teats.

"May good come to you for your kindness," he said.

At once the Morrigu's eye that had been wounded by his sword was healed. Then she gave him a drink from the second and the third teats, and each time his gratitude and his good wishes healed the wounds he had given her.

As Cuchulain walked away the old woman smiled, for she knew that it was only he who could heal the wounds he had given her—and she was now ready for action again.

Near to his death—when the great host of his enemies was gathered on the plains of Muirthemne to destroy him—Cuchulain saw the Morrigu in the shape of a young maiden with golden hair at the ford washing the blood from some clothes. When he saw that they were his own clothes his heart sank low—for he knew it was a presage of his death.

And finally, in his last moments, fatally wounded and bound to the standing stone on the western shore of the lake at Muirthemne, a crow alighted on Cuchulain's shoulder, and his enemies—taking this as a signal from the Morrigu that he was now powerless—closed in and cut off his head.

––––––– Commentary –––––––

These are but a few of the appearances of the Morrigu throughout the ancient Irish sagas. She is always the most fearsome of the three great war goddesses of Ireland. She appears and disappears in many different forms, but more often than not she is seen as a black carrion crow presaging death.

The Morrigu is never far away, though her story is never fully told. It is said that she lived at Tara (Temuir/Teamhair) before it was taken over by the kings. There she had a great spit for turning meat and a son called Mechi, who had three hearts, each of which contained a serpent. Mechi was slain by Mac Cecht, who burned the three hearts and threw the ashes into a nearby stream. The water boiled instantly and dried up, and every living creature in it died. It was said that if Mechi had been allowed to live, the serpents would have devoured Ireland. The pollution of the stream from the ashes of his hearts warns about the contaminating and poisonous destructiveness of war.

The Morrigu was a great one for stirring up trouble—for stealing cattle so that others would be blamed and battles would ensue, for setting friends against friends and enemies against enemies.

The Morrigu's twin appetites for sexual gratification and for bringing about violent death are a travesty of the very necessary and natural forces of creation and destruction that keep the universe functioning, any imbalance of which brings about disaster.

Sources used:

Gantz, Jeffrey. *Early Irish Myths and Sagas.* New York: Penguin Books, 1981.

Gregory, Lady Augusta. *Gods and Fighting Men.* Gerrard Cross, U.K.: Colin Smythe, 1970.

Rolleston, T. W. *Myths and Legends of the Celtic Race.* London: Harrap & Co., 1917.

Deírdre

"In all the tales you tell me, foster mother, there are fair maidens and mighty men, there are hosts and feasts and battles, wooings and weddings—but never have I seen anyone in the world but the gentle hind on the hill and yourself. Where are the country people thus? Where are these great and noisy deeds?"

Deirdre had lived all her fourteen years in a small house thatched with green sods, secluded behind a wall and an orchard of apple trees on a round and wooded hill. Sometimes she had strange dreams and woke crying. There was a tall man with a Druid mark upon his forehead, pointing his finger at her and speaking of the sorrows she would bring about if she were to venture out of her seclusion. Sometimes she dreamed she was on a broad field and around her lay men bleeding and dying. The Druid was standing tall above them, looking into her eyes and accusing her of their deaths.

Each time Deirdre had such a dream she told her foster mother, and each time Levercham took her in her arms and rocked her, kissing her hair and whispering that no harm would come to her as long as she stayed where she was, safe on this round and magic hill among the apple trees.

Deirdre often paced her walled garden restlessly, wondering why so many braved the dangers of the outer world while she was held back from it. When she was a child she had been content, knowing no other life. Levercham, daughter of Aedh, taught her many things— but not enough. When she was on the threshold of womanhood Deirdre was no longer content. Everything that had been devised for her protection she began to resent. "What if I have to face the dangers Levercham has told me about? What if I have to face suffering and death? Is it not my right? Is there a life worth living that is not lived against the challenge of such things?"

One stormy winter's day a hunter went astray from the hunt and found his way into their remote and isolated valley. The wind howled and blew the snow in icy flurries around him. He was tired and desperate and at last sank into the snow, unable to take another step. Half conscious, he had a vision that the snow-covered knoll near him was in fact hollow and within it he could see people gathered around warm hearth fires. He cried out to be let in to the warmth—and he cried out three times.

"What cry is that?" Deirdre asked her foster mother. But Levercham said that it was no more than the cry of a bird in the storm.

At the third cry Deirdre could bear it no longer and drew the bolt back and opened the door. There she found the fainting hunter and took him to the fireside.

For this kindness Deirdre was poorly repaid, for the hunter, astonished at her beauty, carried tales of it back to King Conchubar at Emain Macha. Soon King Conchubar and his companions were rapping at the door of the cottage, and Deirdre's life of isolation was over. She and her foster mother were carried back to Emain Macha, and the grizzled warrior king told the young girl that she was to be his bride.

Excited as she was to be at the court of a great king among fine ladies and young warriors, Deirdre was nervous and unsure of what being the wife of the king would entail. She pleaded for a year in which to prepare herself. The king, most unwillingly, agreed.

One day Deirdre caught sight of the tall Druid priest she had seen in her dreams among the companions of the king, and she shrank away. Cathbad, the Druid, looked at her long and intently. She had grown, as his prophecy to her father had said she would, into the most beautiful young woman the country had ever seen. He remembered his words and sighed. Fedlimid, harper to King Conchubar, had longed for a child but had thought that he and his wife were destined never to have one. He had pressed Cathbad to use his Druid sight to look into the future. Cathbad had seen a daughter for him, but he had said: "Call her name Deirdre, for she will be the mother of many sorrows. She will be the cause of the treachery of kings, and heroes will die for her." There were some who advised Fedlimid at her birth to kill her to prevent this dreadful prophecy from coming true, but Fedlimid thought to avert her destiny another way, by sending her far from the eyes of men and charging Levercham, daughter of Aedh, to watch her closely and never let her out of the remote valley he chose as her prison. But here she was—at the court of Conchubar—and by the expression in her eyes as she looked into his, Deirdre was not unaware of the shadow that hung over her.

Deirdre turned from Cathbad with a shiver and walked away. Why had she left her secret home? She had thought she would be happy to be among the fine people Levercham had told her about, for Levercham was nostalgic and the stories she told were about the life she had once lived and the people she had once known. But Deirdre was not happy. Women who she thought would be her friends turned from her, jealous of her beauty and the way their husbands and lovers looked at her. Men followed her everywhere with their hungry eyes but held back in fear because of the king's interest in her. The king himself? He was not how she had imagined her lover to be. Before the hunter came to her valley she had had a dream of a young man with raven-black hair, fine and strong and kind. She always saw him with two companions, his two brothers it seemed, like him and yet not a match for him. She searched among the young men of Conchubar's court for them—but she did not find them.

One day three young warriors rode through the gate of Emain Macha, and Deirdre knew that she had found the one for whom she had been waiting. The three warriors were the three sons of Usnach— Ainnle, Ardan, and Naoise. Naoise had hair the color of a raven's wing and outshone his brothers and any other men she had seen, as the sun outshines the moon and the stars.

That night they sang at the feasting in Conchubar's great hall, and Deirdre, the harper's daughter, served the wine with the other women and thought it the most beautiful singing she had ever heard. Watching her, Cathbad saw that she never took her eyes from Naoise the whole evening and that when Naoise glanced at her, her cheeks flushed crimson.

It begins, the Druid thought but said nothing.

Conchubar looked at her but noticed nothing.

That night Deirdre went to sleep in the chamber with her foster mother, as she always did, but for the first time she did not chatter about the events of the day as the older woman brushed out her shining hair. She was in bed with the lamp flame blown out before she said a word.

"Mother," she asked, in a very small, quiet voice. "What is it like to go to bed with a man?"

"Hush, child," Levercham replied. "There is time enough for you to find that out on your wedding day."

Deirdre lay in the dark and thought about Naoise. Her body felt different—but she could not have said in what way.

As the days went by, the warriors practiced their skills against each other, some teaching the young lads, others boasting of their deeds around the smith's forge while they waited for their favorite weapons to be honed. Deirdre took every opportunity to be where she could see Naoise and his two brothers. It seemed they were great friends as well as kin, for they were never apart.

Ainnle and Ardan began to notice the way Deirdre and Naoise gazed at each other, and they tried to persuade their brother to leave the court of Conchubar. "No good will come of it," they said. "She is promised to the king and there is nothing you can do."

Naoise was at last persuaded to leave and, very reluctantly, set off early one morning before the rest of the court was awake. They had not gone far when they heard the sound of a rider behind them and waited to see who it was, their hands upon their weapons. It was Deirdre, white on a white horse—with no companions—a traveling cloak over her shoulders.

"Ah, Naoise," she said. "So cruel to leave me."

"Ride on," whispered his brothers on either side. "She is a spirit come to tempt you. This is not Deirdre herself."

But Naoise would not ride on.

"It is not I who is cruel, lady," he said sadly, "but Fate that has given you to King Conchubar."

"If it is my fate to marry the king," she replied, "why do you come to me in my dreams? I saw you before ever I saw you. I loved you before ever I loved you."

"You see—a spirit!" whispered the brothers. "Come, Naoise—no good will come of it if we tarry."

"Go back, lady," said Naoise. "I too have seen you in my dreams. I too have loved you before I have loved you. But for my honor I cannot steal what is the king's."

She tossed her head and looked at him with bright, fierce eyes. "I am no chattel of the king," she said proudly. "No marriage feast has been prepared. I am Deirdre, and I am free to choose the man I go with."

"Nay, lady," protested the brothers. "You will bring harm to Naoise if you will not leave him alone."

Naoise looked at them angrily now.

"Quiet!" he said to them. "This is between Deirdre and myself."

"If it were only so!" whispered Ardan, and he sighed deeply. But the two brothers withdrew a step or two and watched without further word as Naoise and Deirdre embraced and kissed.

Deirdre shut her eyes and knew that from that kiss there was no going back. Naoise knew it too.

Naoise gave his brothers the chance to leave him, but they refused.

"We will go with you. Wherever you go, there we will be to defend you."

They knew they must get as far away as they could from Emain Macha and, their reputations being what they were, they expected and were given sanctuary in many other kingdoms. But Conchubar's reputation being what *it* was, and his anger being insatiable, one by one the kings who sheltered them had to ask them to leave.

The four wandered from place to place throughout Eriu and finally decided to set sail for Alban, where they hoped to be free at last of Conchubar's pursuit.

They stayed for a while on the Island of Shadows, where Scathach, the great female warrior, had her training school. There the three young men polished the skills they already had and learned others that they hitherto had not.

Deirdre gave birth to a child and sent it into the care of Manannan, son of Llyr, because she knew that traveling as they were, with no safe place to lay their heads, the child would have no proper life with them. Scathach took Deirdre when she was strong again and taught her the warrior's salmon leap and many hunting tricks that she had not known before.

"Hard will be your life, Deirdre of Sorrows. Hard you must be to endure it."

"I will endure," said Deirdre. "If I can have the warmth of Naoise at my side at night, I can endure anything."

Scathach looked at her pityingly—for she too had the Druid gift of sight.

There came a time not long after that, when they heard of the approach of some warriors from Conchubar's court come to take their training with Scathach. Though there were now not many men alive who would be a match for the sons of Usnach, the brothers were not of a bloodthirsty turn of mind and would rather avoid a fight than seek it.

They made their way to the mainland of Alban, and there they gradually traveled eastward until they were in the heart of the country, among the great mountains and the glens and far from the reach of Conchubar and his men. There they built sturdy shelters against the weather and lived on the game they could hunt and the fruits of the forest.

Each night Ainnle and Ardan lay down in one shelter and Naoise and Deirdre in the other. Though the life was hard and the meat scarce, Deirdre was happier than she had ever been. Her love for Naoise knew no bounds, and her affection for his brothers was deep and true. When the winter howled down the glen and the icy mists swirled around them, they moved south, sometimes sheltering overnight in nothing more than a depression in the heather, with bracken pulled over their heads, the four of them huddling together for warmth. The rivers were frozen and fish hard to come by. Sometimes they resorted to stealing cattle when the wild game eluded them. This was the beginning of the end for them, for then they themselves were hunted—and in the hunt the beauty of Deirdre was noticed.

It was not long before the king of that area set his heart on having Deirdre for his own. Messengers were sent to her in secret, when she was picking flowers or gathering reeds for thatching, to offer her great riches if she would leave her companions and come to court. She refused scornfully.

At night Deirdre clung fiercely to Naoise, feeling that the world was trying to take him away from her.

"I will never leave you," he whispered, holding her as she liked to be held, touching her as she liked to be touched. "You and I are one. We have endured the raging of a king and of a tempest—nothing will part us!"

But in the evening when the brothers sat beside the fire and sang the old tales of Eriu, Deirdre noticed that there was longing in their voices for their own land, for their friends and family, and for the old and familiar ways. Tears came to her eyes. Was the love she gave him enough to make up to Naoise for all that he had given up for her?

The Pictish king gave up trying to entice Deirdre away with gifts and tried a different tack. He pretended friendship to the brothers, and when they were deep in his debt for the fine house he had built for them and the honors he had heaped upon them at his court, he asked for their help against his enemies. For their honor they could not refuse, and from that time on the three were rarely at home. They were in battle after battle, and their fame as warriors spread far and wide. The king intended Naoise to be killed, but so great were the skills Scathach had taught him, he returned each time unscathed.

Meanwhile Conchubar heard of the feats of the three warriors in the land of Alban—and guessed who they were.

He called the three chief champions of Ulster to him and asked if they would go to Alban and fetch back the sons of Usnach. Conall refused and so did Cuchulain, but Fergus believed that Conchubar had forgiven them and agreed to bring them back under his protection.

Conchubar then charged him that on the way back he was to call at the fort of Borach, for there he had something that had to be done. Fergus agreed and set off.

One day Deirdre and Naoise were playing chess when they heard a great shout along the valley. Naoise instantly pricked up his ears and said he was sure that it was the shout of an Ulsterman.

"No," said Deirdre, her cheeks already paling. "It is the shout of a local warrior calling his companions."

Again Naoise heard the shout and again declared that it was the shout of an Irishman. Again Deirdre denied it and tried to distract him with a kiss.

But when the shout was heard a third time, Ainnle and Ardan came running, and Naoise rose to meet them. He sent them on ahead to greet the man, whom they now believed to be their old companion Fergus, while Naoise stayed behind to comfort Deirdre.

"What is it, my love? Fergus was ever our friend. No harm will come to us through him."

"I had a vision in the night," said Deirdre. "I saw three birds coming to us from Emain Macha with three drops of honey in their beaks. They dropped the honey before us—but when they flew away their beaks were full of our blood."

"A foolish dream. What meaning could it possibly have?"

"Honey-sweet words they bear—promises and sureties—but I know they will be the death of us."

Fergus and his two sons, Iollan of the fair hair and Buinne of the red, arrived, and the three sons of Usnach greeted them warmly. Eagerly they asked for news of home, and eagerly they listened to everything that Fergus and his sons had to say. Deirdre watched with aching heart, sad to think that while she had been so happy in Alban they had been longing all the while to return to Eriu.

"Conchubar has vowed forgiveness and longs to have the strong arms of his foster brothers at his side again," Fergus told them and offered many fair words and promises of protection.

"Do not trust him," Deirdre whispered to Naoise. "I had a dream of the three sons of Usnach in a single grave."

"Not every dream is a prophecy, my love. Lay this one on the wind and let the wind take it way."

"I see treachery and death and Deirdre alone—weeping," she persisted.

"I see home, the hills of my youth, my family and friends all smiling and happy at our return."

Deirdre turned from him, knowing that he would not be content at her side again until he had seen the rolling hills of Eriu and tasted the sweet water of its streams. She looked at the crags of Alban and knew that she would not see the red rowan so richly clad again nor the dainty stepping deer so shy and free. No more would she hear the roar of the cataract in the mountains or hear the wild song of the wind in the high forests. Naoise was her home—and where he was, there she would also be.

Fergus swore that no man would touch them while he was at their side, and this vow by one of the greatest champions of Ulster was enough for the sons of Usnach. They took ship and departed from Alban, Deirdre leaning over the side trying to see the land she had loved for as long as she could—the deep glens, the great mountains—and remembering the joys she had had there with her beloved.

At the fort of Borach they stopped awhile because Fergus had promised he would do this for Conchubar.

But Borach had also made a promise to Conchubar: to keep Fergus back at the fort and to send the others on.

Borach claimed he had prepared a great feast, and Fergus was under obligation to accept it on Conchubar's behalf. To do so would delay the party for longer than they intended, so Borach suggested the sons of Usnach should continue and be joined by Fergus when the feast was over. Fergus was annoyed by the delay but hedged in by his promise to Conchubar that he would do what had to be done at the fort of Borach and his promise that he would return the sons of Usnach and Deirdre to Conchubar without delay.

"I will send my two sons with you," Fergus told them. "Under their protection you will be as safe as under mine."

The sons of Usnach instantly accepted the plan, but Deirdre tried to persuade them against leaving without Fergus. She was sure they were going to their deaths and Fergus was betraying them.

But Naoise would not listen. Fergus was a man of honor, and Naoise trusted him completely. Fergus would not lead them into a trap. If he said Conchubar had forgiven them—Conchubar had. And if they were under his and his family's protection, no one would dare to attack them.

But Deirdre had had a dream in which she had seen Iollan, their protector, without his head and Buinne, their other protector, betraying them.

Naoise grew impatient and told her to forget the mournful shadows that haunted her sleep. He understood her anxiety, he said, but it was groundless.

Seeing that he would not listen to her premonitions, Deirdre tried to persuade Naoise not to go directly to Emain Macha but to divert to the home of Cuchulain, another of his trusted friends. But Naoise was impatient to have everything straightened out between Conchubar and himself and would make no diversions. "Time enough to see Cuchulain later," he said. He totally believed that they were to be welcomed back—and if not, well, they were warriors who could give a good account of themselves no matter who came against them. And, besides, they had the protection of the sons of Fergus and the word of Fergus that they would be safe.

This was the first real quarrel Deirdre and Naoise had had since they had been together, and Deirdre was white with anger and despair.

At last they came to Emain Macha and struck the door of the house of Conchubar.

The doorkeeper challenged them, and they announced who they were. Conchubar sent a message that they would be made welcome in the House of the Red Branch and should go there at once.

There they went, and there for the first time, because of Conchubar's refusal to see them at his own door, they began to wonder if Deirdre had perhaps been right to doubt the offer of forgiveness. Was it only a coincidence that at the House of the Red Branch the heads and weapons of defeated enemies were kept?

Deirdre tried to persuade them to leave at once—but Iollan said they could not, for now it would look like cowardice to do so, and to show doubt of a king's word would be to dishonor both themselves and the king himself.

"We will accept the hospitality of this house and wait and see what happens."

They ate and drank and rested, and Naoise insisted on playing chess with Deirdre to try and take her mind off her fears.

Conchubar, meanwhile, curious to know what the years had done to Deirdre, dispatched her foster mother to the House of the Red Branch to bring back a report. On the way she noticed a troop of warriors, and none of them were Ulstermen. Conchubar, knowing that he would get no Ulsterman to attack the heroic sons of Usnach, had brought in outsiders to do the work.

With many a kiss and sob Levercham hugged Deirdre and told her of the treachery Conchubar was planning. Now Naoise and the others wished they had listened to Deirdre's dreams, but it was too late. All that was left for them to do was to arm themselves, to lock and bar the house, and to prepare to defend themselves.

Levercham returned to Conchubar and told him that the years and the rough life had taken their toll on Deirdre. "She is thin. Her bones stick out of her flesh. Her cheeks are pale and wan. Even her bright hair is dimmed."

Conchubar shrugged.

"Well, let Naoise have her then," he said. "She is of no use to me."

But later Conchubar wondered if Levercham had brought him a true report. He could not get the memory of Deirdre as she used to be out of his mind. He sent one of his men to report on her.

His messenger found the house locked and shuttered but managed to climb up a ladder and look through a crack in an upper window. There he saw Naoise and Deirdre playing chess, she so beautiful that he gasped out loud. She looked up and saw him and cried out. Naoise, swinging round, flung a chess piece at him and hit him in the eye.

The messenger rushed back to the king, eloquent in praise of Deirdre's beauty.

Conchubar sat staring into the flames of his hearth fire for a long time, his chin sunk on his chest. Then he rose and called the warriors that were strangers to Ulster to him. That night they encircled the House of the Red Branch and set it on fire. Iollan, son of Fergus, fought courageously but was beheaded. Buinne, son of Fergus, betrayed them and left to join Conchubar as Deirdre had foreseen. The three sons of Usnach fought magnificently, and in the end it was only because Conchubar employed Cathbad's Druid tricks that he defeated them. Cathbad made the brothers believe that they were surrounded by a dark and violent sea that they had to cross in order to escape the burning house. Naoise took Deirdre on his shoulders and tried to wade through it. When the waters reached his shoulders he tried to swim.

To swim, the three sons of Usnach had to release their swords—and when their swords were gone they were easily slain.

Deirdre was taken, weeping and keening for the two young men she had loved as sister and the one she had loved as wife.

Conchubar took her, but had no joy of her. Like a dead woman she lay in his bed, and nothing he could do would rouse her. In the day she sat weeping and keening for the three young men—and to everyone she sang their praises. Her cheeks grew pale and her body thin.

At last, exasperated, the king asked her what two things she most hated in all the world. Without hesitation she said it was he himself and the man who had killed the three sons of Usnach—Èogan, son of Durthacht.

"That is good," Conchubar said sourly, "for you will spend one year with me and one with Èogan, son of Durthacht."

Èogan stepped forward, smiling.

Deirdre stood between the two and looked from one to the other, her eyes pools of shadow.

"Ay," said Conchubar with a sneer. "Well may you look—a ewe at her two rams."

And all around her Deirdre saw the faces of men leering and laughing, and the two of them she hated the most were swaggering with the great joke of it.

Quickly she slipped from between them and started to run. Shouting with mirth, they followed her. They knew and she knew there was nowhere for her to go.

But when she reached the end of the field, she paused. Beyond the grinning circle of men was a huge rock. She lifted up her eyes and in her heart said a quick prayer of thanks to Scathach, the woman warrior who had taught her the warrior's salmon leap.

She leapt—and in her falling Deirdre dashed herself on the rock and scattered out her brains.

The men fell silent—awed and shamed.

Cathbad turned away. All had come about as he had prophesied—kings had been dishonored and heroes slain. Only this last act he had not foreseen.

——— Commentary ———

One of the main themes of the story of Deirdre is the problem of predestination, and in weeping for Deirdre we weep for our own powerlessness in the face of an implacable destiny. The Celts had a very strong belief in Fate, which, as far as I know, they did not personify but rather recognized as a pattern or scheme which underlay and shaped all their lives.

Cathbad, the Druid, foretold the treachery of kings and the death of heroes—but it is interesting to note that he did not foretell Deirdre's own suicide.

As we read the story and are carried along by the inexorable logic of it, we are waiting for Deirdre to make one decision, any decision, that would free her from the fearful web in which she is entangled. The poignancy of the story is largely due to our hope that, while we watch with horror how the story unfolds, the terrible finale can be averted. We may grasp with relief her suicide at the end, because it is the only indication we have that our ends are not completely shaped. *This* had not been foretold.

There are, as always in myth, several interlacing themes of equal importance. There is the story of the love between Deirdre and Naoise, for instance—the love that risks and sacrifices so much. He leaves his beloved Eriu for her, and she leaves the country she loves, Alban. This love is contrasted with the possessive and destructive lust of Conchubar.

Then there is the theme of honor and dishonor—and finally there is beauty. Much is made of the extraordinary beauty of Deirdre, and it is male reaction to her beauty that brings about "the sorrows." Time and again the heroes of Celtic myth demand that their women be more beautiful than any other, and time and again blood is spilled because of it. Deirdre's foster mother tried to protect her by telling Conchubar she had become old and unattractive.

But Deirdre's beauty may not be representative only of physical beauty. If she represents, as in some of the other Celtic myths, the high aspirations of the soul, Conchubar would represent the man or woman who goes after such things greedily, clumsily, and selfishly—wanting the rewards of such a quest but not being prepared to give up anything to achieve the goal. Naoise represents the man or woman who works and suffers and sacrifices to cultivate and protect that to which he or she aspires. Note that while Conchubar apparently wins, in reality he does not. He "has no joy" of Deirdre, and Deirdre will not stay with him. She goes to join Naoise on the next plane of existence.

Deirdre is kept isolated from the world, for the pursuit of her (i.e., the pursuit of higher consciousness) is dangerous and can destroy. Conchubar brings her out of her isolation but does not know how to win her. She *chooses* Naoise, who is humble and nervous at first, uneasy about what he is undertaking. But with the help of his two brothers, Naoise tackles the journey of the soul in search of its self and all its attendant deprivations and dangers. The sons of Usnach are three, as the Celts so often use this number for completion, for wholeness. Naoise and his two brothers are three aspects of the same searching, journeying soul, and only by working together can they handle the dangerous beauty represented by Deirdre.

It is interesting that the brothers are led into Conchubar's trap because they ignore the promptings of intuition and even the very strong visionary warnings they are given. They are longing for the old life of the flesh they used to have, and in the end they are destroyed because they are taken in by illusion. Hundreds of handpicked warriors cannot kill them until they fall prey to Cathbad's illusion. And *then* they are killed. It is significant that it is a sea Cathbad conjures up—a dark sea. In Celtic myths the sea is often the symbol for the greater consciousness. At this stage of their development the brothers should be able to recognize the difference between the real sea and the fake. But they do not. We are reminded that there is a fine, but important, line between an honorable and trusting nature and a naïve and gullible one. We are also reminded to be particularly careful of symbols normally used in one way to express good—and in another way, its opposite. We should never, ever, take anything for granted.

The story of Deirdre is very old. It must predate the story of the cattle raid to steal the Brown Bull of Cuailnge, because Fergus deserts Conchubar in protest against his treachery in killing the sons of Usnach—and in the story of the cattle raid, he fights on the side of Maeve against Conchubar.

The version of this story translated by Jeffrey Gantz in *Early Irish Myths and Sagas* comes from the *Book of Leinster* and differs in some ways from Lady Gregory's version.

Sources used:
    Gregory, Lady Augusta. *Cuchulain of Muirthemne.* Gerrards Cross, U.K.: Colin Smythe, 1970.

Findabair and Maeve

She stepped quietly between the tables, scarcely noticing the noise of the men shouting and arguing and bursting into ribald song as she poured their wine from a tall and heavy flagon. Many stopped their shouting when she passed and bowed their heads, following her with their eyes—but no one touched her for she was Maeve's daughter, the greatest prize in Eriu. She was small and slender, her face pale and her eyes often shadowy. Only her long hair, gleaming like white gold in the lamplight, seemed the dowry of a princess.

Times without number she glanced up at the young man playing chess with her mother and then lowered her eyes again before anyone marked her interest. She knew she would never be allowed to choose her own husband.

The shadows in her eyes became deeper as she watched her mother at play. The couple were seated on the raised platform at the center of the great hall at Cruachan. The huge columns of red yew and oak that held the vast roof high were carved with hundreds of intertwining figures, but those that surrounded the royal platform were of bronze chased in silver. Findabair watched as her mother threw back her mane of red hair and laughed as loud as any man. The couple were surrounded by tall candles in elaborate candlesticks brought by Froech himself from the land of the Sidh. Some were of silver and some were of gold— but all were richly studded with precious jewels that caught the light of the candle flames and reflected it, greatly magnified, onto the gaming board. Maeve and Froech at their game of chess were raised above the rest of the hall and seemed to be contained in brilliant light as flies are contained in amber. The chessboard Froech had brought with him was of white gold with squares of red gold. The pieces, in silver and gold, gleamed and shimmered.

They had been playing for almost three days—and for three days the spits had been turning as the game roasted, the heroes of Connacht had been feasting and carousing, and the three sons of Boand and of Uaithne, the Dagda's harper, had been playing their harps of silver and gold and white gold. Their music was strange and beautiful, and it wove such magic in the hall that some died with sorrow while they played and others wept for joy. No one noticed the passing of time.

Findabair saw the gleaming of the light on her mother's bronzed and freckled shoulders and the way she leaned across the board to touch the hand of Froech as they played, and she thought her heart would break. Since she had first heard tell of this prince—son of Idath of the Connachta and of Bé Find of the Sidh—she, Findabair of the Fair Eyebrows, daughter of Maeve, had sought him with her bird-sight across the valleys and the hills, even into his own hidden country. She had seen him in her dreams—in the flickering of sunlight through the leaves of the forest, reflected beside her in the smooth surface of a pool. She had trembled when the great gates of Cruachan were flung open and through them rode the prince's brave and colorful company, shining like the sun with gold and precious fabrics and jewels—fifty dapple-gray horses bridled with gold, their silver breastplates ringing and tinkling with golden bells. Following them were seven greyhounds on silver chains, seven horn blowers clad in shining mantles, three motley fools and three harpers . . . .

Ailell and Maeve had made them welcome, but Findabair had not been able to get near the handsome prince. Maeve herself poured his wine. Maeve herself sat talking with him at the high table.

After the first feasting the company retired to the chambers that had been prepared for them, and in the morning they were out hunting. The people of Cruachan gathered in groups to watch them. Never had they seen such sleek and well-groomed horses, so gallant and magnificent a company. Findabair stood at her window and watched them ride out, and in the evening she watched them return. Sometimes Queen Maeve was with Froech, sometimes not.

Early one morning, when the first birds were making their music, Findabair left the castle and went down to the river to bathe. There Froech came upon her, her skin as white as swan's down, her hair as bright as the sun.

"Where have you been hiding, princess?," he asked gravely, looking down at her in the water. "It is to meet you I came to Cruachan."

She flushed, but whether it was with anger or with modesty he could not tell.

"I have not been hiding, prince," she said in a low voice, "but you have had eyes for no one but my mother."

Her hair floated out around her on the clear water. "She is very different from her mother," he thought. "If Maeve were in the river there would be no stillness here." He tried not to think of Maeve—that powerful and dominating woman, that beautiful and lusty queen. "Maeve is a woman to make the earth shake," he thought. "But Findabair would make it flower."

He stepped into the water and took her in his arms. There was no one to see them—no one to carry tales. Findabair shut her eyes and lifted her face to his.

She too forgot her mother.

Later when they were resting on the bank, Froech asked the young princess to come away with him secretly.

"Secretly?" she said, lifting her chin defiantly. "Am I not the daughter of a king and queen—and you a prince with riches far beyond any I have seen? Why should we sneak away in secret when you can well afford a handsome bride-price?"

Froech was silent. He did not like to say to the girl that he feared Maeve might take it as an insult that he wanted her daughter and not herself.

"My parents will not object," Findabair said confidently, though in her heart she was not so confident. It was true that Froech was rich and noble and greatly honored both in the land of her people and in the land of the Sidh, but Maeve had always had her own plans for Findabair.

Long and lingeringly they loved and kissed, and Findabair gave him her ring to keep as pledge that she would marry no one but him. He promised to ask her parents for her, and they parted full of hope for the future.

Maeve and Ailell listened quietly to his request and then asked him to leave their presence while they discussed the matter. Ailell was in favor of the marriage, thinking how much they would benefit from the alliance, but Maeve was insulted that he sought her daughter's bed and not her own. She suggested a bride-price to Ailell that was far beyond any reasonable amount. She also demanded that he should bring all his forces and his cattle to help her in the war for the Brown Bull of Cuailnge on which they were about to embark.

Froech was called back to the council chamber, and Ailell stated the details of the bride-price. As the list rolled on—three score of dark gray horses with gold bridles; twelve cows, each with a white calf with red ears; uncountable treasure; musicians of the Sidh; warriors—Froech listened with growing anger. Maeve watched him like a hawk its prey.

At last Froech called a halt. "I would not give such a bride-price for Maeve herself!" he declared angrily, and he turned on his heel and strode out of the chamber.

Ailell looked at Maeve and Maeve at Ailell.

"If we let him go in that mood, he might well run off with the girl in secret," Maeve said. "And we will be mocked for this everywhere in Eriu."

"Findabair must not be stolen from us, whatever happens," Ailell agreed.

Ailell and Maeve had seven sons, but none were as useful to them as their daughter. Without a daughter to bargain with, how would they make alliances to confound their enemies?

That day, after the hunting when all were hot and tired, Maeve suggested they plunge into a nearby pool.

Froech was stripped off ready to dive in when Maeve said to him, "Ah, Froech, you see that rowan tree that grows on the other side of the pool?"

"I see it," he replied.

"I have never seen branches so richly laden with berries. See how they hang low over the water? Froech," she said, and her voice was like honey and her gaze seemed to touch the whole length of his body. "Froech, will you fetch me a branch from that rowan?"

Froech hesitated. There was something in her voice—some shadow of menace—and yet no more had been said about his refusal to pay the bride-price for her daughter. It seemed as though both Ailell and Maeve had forgotten all about it. He looked at Findabair. Her eyes were full of warning, but she was too afraid of her mother to step forward and speak to him openly.

"This pool is deep," he said cautiously.

"Deep it is," Maeve said smoothly, "but of no danger to a strong swimmer." She moved forward and stood close to him. He could feel the power of her, smell the strong woman-scent of her. "Fetch me the branch," she whispered, and in her eyes were promises he could not resist.

He plunged in and Findabair stepped forward with a gasp . . . like a golden salmon his leap, like pearls the drops of water that showered from his limbs.

Maeve and Ailell watched intently and with gloating anticipation. He reached the far side without incident and plucked a branch of bloodred berries.

Ailell nudged Maeve's arm and pointed to the young prince's clothes lying on the bank beside them. A ring had fallen from his belt pouch— a ring Ailell himself had given Findabair. Swiftly Maeve stooped down and flung it into the deepest part of the pool.

Froech swam back across the pool and placed the branch he had picked into the hand of Maeve.

"More beautiful than rubies," Maeve purred. "But there is another I can see even more beautiful," and she looked longingly back across the water.

Confident now that this was not a plot to kill him, Froech plunged in again and swam back toward the center. But this time he did not reach the far side. The water began to boil and churn, and a hideous monster rose from the depths and reached for him. Froech shouted at once for his sword, which was lying on the bank at Maeve's feet— but neither she nor anyone else moved to pick it up.

Three times he called as he struggled with the beast—but twice he was ignored. On the third cry Findabair rushed forward and seized the sword. Her mother reached out her hand to stop her, but she was too late. The young girl was already halfway to Froech. Her father threw a five-pointed spear at her to prevent her reaching him. It went through her two long plaits and held her back, but Froech managed to catch the sword from her outstretched hand and slay the monster.

When Ailell and Maeve saw that he was severely wounded, they feared retribution and had him carried to the castle where they ordered a healing bath to be prepared for him. Women gathered around and bathed him, and afterward he was laid on a clean and comfortable bed.

Findabair was prevented from seeing him; her parents were angry that not only had she gone against them to save his life, but she had gone behind their backs to have secret assignations with him—as the ring proved.

That night there was a clamor at the gates, and when the gatekeeper looked out he saw three fifties of women in scarlet and green, with silver bracelets on their arms. When asked whence they came, they replied that they had come for Froech, son of Idath, who was the favorite of the High King of the Sidh. Froech heard of this and requested that he be taken to them. The women bore him away and the following evening returned him whole and healthy.

When the feasting was at its height that night, Ailell demanded that all his treasures be brought to him so that he might admire them. Servants brought chest after chest of fabulous gold and gems, but at the end all Ailell could say was that something was missing—the ring he had given Findabair. He asked that it too should be brought before him.

"I have mislaid it, Father," said Findabair nervously.

"So careless with my gifts, girl!" he said coldly. "I think you have used it as a trysting present. With what youth have you shamed your parents? Tell me, girl."

"No youth, my lord, I swear. It is mislaid."

Findabair's eyes were lowered and her hands were clasping and unclasping. She did not dare look at Froech. Would he speak up for her? And if he did, what would her parents say? He seemed to be out of favor.

"If you cannot produce it, Daughter, you will forfeit your life."

A gasp went around the court like wind through fallen leaves.

"No treasure is worth such a price," Froech said. "I will give you all I have, for the girl saved my life."

"Nothing you can give will take the place of my daughter's respect for her parents," Ailell said. "Let her produce the ring and put my mind at ease."

"Let her produce the ring—if she can," said Maeve, looking hard at Froech. That he should have chosen such a green girl over her fire and passion still irked her.

"Let me leave the hall, my lord," said Findabair in a small, tense voice, "and I will look for the ring."

"No," said Maeve. "Send your maid to look for it."

So the maid went, and Findabair remained.

"Princess," said Froech quietly to Findabair. "I gave your servant a salmon I caught in the pool in which you saved my life. Will you accept it as my thanks? And while we wait for your maid to return, perhaps it could be served."

"Yes, let's eat and drink," Maeve said. "The maid might be a long time."

Findabair looked at Froech reproachfully—but she sent for the salmon nevertheless. When it came it was laid before Ailell and Maeve.

"Carve it yourself, Queen Maeve," said Froech, looking at her pointedly.

Smiling, she cut into the flesh.

"A portion for the king," Froech said, as Maeve served the visitor first. Maeve shrugged and gave the second portion to the king.

Findabair, pale and in despair, poured the wine.

The flesh of the salmon on King Ailell's platter parted, and within it lay the ring he had given Findabair. He looked at it, astonished.

Froech smiled at Findabair.

"Is this not the ring your daughter lost?" he asked quietly.

Findabair, flushed with relief, trembled and clasped her hands. She could not imagine how Froech had performed the trick.

Maeve looked hard at the young man.

"I saw the ring fall into the pool when the princess leapt in to save me," he said smoothly. "I noticed that a salmon swallowed it—and later I caught the salmon."

Ailell and Maeve were silent.

What now? They knew that Froech was aware of all they had done.

"Forgive us, Daughter, for doubting you," they said.

Findabair looked at them—and her eyes were unforgiving.

"I can no longer live at Cruachan," she said. "I will go with the first man who offers me protection."

Froech stepped forward.

"Once I asked your parents for you, Findabair, but the bride-price was too high. Now I will take you under my protection, for I see that here you are not honored as you should be."

"You have my love, prince," she said, for once her head held high and her eyes shining and proud.

"That is good news indeed," said Maeve slyly, "for there is no greater honor to our daughter than she should be under the protection of such a house as yours. But we are about to embark on a great war and need the help of all our friends. Leave the girl with us, Froech, and call for her when the war is over. Meanwhile, as surety for your good intentions regarding our daughter, bring your warriors and your cattle to help against the men of Ulster."

Froech looked at Findabair and then at Maeve—and hesitated.

"The girl will be safe with us," Ailell said. "We regret that we mis-judged her."

Findabair took the arm of Froech and clung to it.

"Take me with you, prince," she pleaded.

"You will be safer here," he said. "The hosts are on the move and the country between here and my country is full of men with battle fever. The daughter of Maeve would be a fair prize for any man to take and boast about, and I, without my army, would not be able to offer you enough protection."

Before Findabair could plead more, Maeve clapped her silver rod against the great bronze gong that stood beside her chair and called her warriors to her. Findabair was swept backward in the crush, and Froech was forced to leave without holding her in his arms again.

The war that now had the whole country on the move was one of Maeve's own making. She had set her heart on possessing the Brown Bull of Cuailnge, the most famous bull in Eriu next to Ailell's own. In every respect Maeve's personal possessions and fortune matched her husband's, for she had come to him as the daughter of the High King. But the one thing he had that excelled her own was his white-horned bull. At first she had asked only to borrow the Brown Bull for a year, but the boasting of her men and his suspicions of her had made mischief between Daire, son of Fachtna, who owned the bull, and herself—and now it was a matter of honor for her to take it by force and for him to prevent her. The whole country was taking sides, some with Maeve and some with Daire.

The hosts of Maeve and Ailell drew near to Ulster at a time when the warriors of that kingdom were suffering from a spell that made them weak. Only the young warrior Cuchulain, the Hound of Culain, escaped the enervating effect of the spell, because his true father was Lugh, the Longhand, and not a mortal man. He alone was there to defend the borders of Conchubar's kingdom against the ravages of Maeve's army. But one man or not, he was such a mighty warrior that day by day he destroyed so many men and, Maeve was in despair of making any progress against him.

One day Ailell and Maeve devised a scheme. A messenger was sent to Cuchulain to ask if he would meet peacefully with the king and his daughter to discuss terms. Cuchulain suspected a trick—but agreed. At the last moment Ailell was afraid to go and substituted his fool dressed in his royal clothes, crown and all. The idea was that the fool was to wait just far enough away from Cuchulain that he would not be recognized, and Findabair was to go to the warrior alone and plead with him to stop harassing them, offering herself to seal the bargain.

The girl was not at all pleased with this idea but was persuaded to do it to save the lives of her people.

The meeting was arranged for the evening because Ailell thought the light would be so bad that the substitution of the fool would not be noticed, and if Findabair succeeded, she would have the long hours of the night for lovemaking and persuasion.

But Cuchulain noticed that a man was wearing the clothes of a king without the bearing of a king. He noticed the nervousness of the girl. So this was Maeve's daughter. He studied her with interest as she stood before him. Her golden hair was in two long, thick plaits, bound with silver. She was pale and slender compared to her mother, with none of Maeve's vigorous beauty, none of her wildcat energy and menace. Like a young doe she stood before him, poised to flee. This was the girl kings fought for? Cuchulain smiled. It was not the girl they wanted—but access to the mother.

Quietly he listened to the words she spoke. When the battle fever was not on him Cuchulain was courteous and gentle. Her speech was beautifully cadenced, like a well-rehearsed song.

"So you would sacrifice yourself for your people?" he asked at last, leaning on his spear.

"No sacrifice, sir, to lie with the greatest champion Eriu has ever known."

"And I—what would be my reward for betraying my uncle's people?"

She flushed slightly and lowered her eyes.

"I am told," she said in a voice almost inaudible, "any king would be glad to bed Maeve's daughter."

He smiled grimly.

"I hear Maeve is as mighty in bed as she is on the battlefield. Can this be said of her daughter?"

Findabair was silent.

He reached out and took her roughly by the shoulders. He could feel how she shrank back, but he did not release her.

"If I am to be offered goods as barter," he said cruelly, "I expect them to be worth what the merchant claims for them."

He could feel her trembling in his grasp. Surely this must be the only woman in the world who would hesitate to lie with him?

He released one arm and with his free hand he flung his spear so that it whined through the air and pierced the chest of the poor fool who had been sent to take Ailell's place. Findabair was shivering now with apprehension. This man was mighty strong and beautiful to look upon, but his touch was hateful to her after the touch of Froech.

His left hand sank into her flesh until he could feel the bone.

"And as for you, daughter of Maeve, I will not kill you for I can see you are nothing more than a gaming piece in your parents' elaborate game. What were your instructions? To kill me when I was helpless and asleep in your arms?"

He lifted his dagger to her face and for a moment looked deeply into her dark and terrified eyes. She bit her lip and lowered her lids—waiting for what he would do. That her life should end at that moment was not such a bad thought to her, but that he should destroy her face so that when Froech returned . . . .

But Cuchulain cut through the two plaits of her hair and flung her from him.

"Let that be the message you bear back to your people, Findabair of Connacht. Cuchulain is no traitor to his kin."

And he turned and was gone into the shadows before she fully realized what had happened.

In the morning Ailell and Maeve found her there, crouching by the body of the fool, shivering and sobbing, her hair cropped close about her head.

After this, Cuchulain's devastations grew worse and worse, and Maeve did everything in her power to force heroes to take him on in single combat. One by one they were secretly promised Findabair if they would defeat Cuchulain. Larine, brother of Laeg, Cuchulain's chariot driver, was given wine and the promise of Findabair. Long, son of Mofebis, was offered twelve suits of armor, a chariot, *and* Findabair. To Ferdiad, son of Daire, who had trained with Cuchulain in the schools of Scathach and Aoife and was his greatest friend, Maeve offered lands and riches and honors and, finally, the greatest prize of all—Findabair—if he would go against Cuchulain for her. Even then he still refused, but he gave in when he was told that Cuchulain had been boasting that Ferdiad was the lesser champion. He bound Maeve to keep to her word that she would give him the rewards she had promised, then he set off to fight his friend. They fought day after day, and after each day's fighting they shared food and healing herbs—for it was not for enmity of each other that they fought.

On the last day Cuchulain told Ferdiad sadly that he had been betrayed, for the woman he had been promised—Findabair, daughter of Maeve—had been promised to many warriors, and many had died or been savagely wounded for her sake. It was not for love that she was offered to him but to buy his great strength. "No man will have her, for she is too useful to Maeve unwed," Cuchulain said. "If one would come who could put a harness on the sun, perhaps he . . . ."

But Ferdiad had given his word to fight Cuchulain to the death and could not go back on it.

The fighting of the two great heroes continued, and at last Ferdiad met his death by Cuchulain at the ford—as it had once been foretold by Scathach all those years before.

Then Cuchulain mourned his friend and cursed the day he had been tricked into fighting. "Yesterday he was mightier than a mountain—and today there is nothing of him but a shadow."

❖

Gradually the men of Ulster began to recover from the spell of weakness Macha had laid upon them, and, one by one, they began to come to Cuchulain's assistance.

Maeve herself rode out to challenge the warriors—a tall woman with a beautiful long face, hair of red-gold streaming out behind her, a cloak of crimson fastened with a brooch of gold, and a shining red spear. Many were the heroes Maeve personally dispatched

At this time Findabair despaired that Froech would return for her. There was no sign of him, and he had promised to return with his men and his cattle to help her parents in their war. Rumors reached her that he had a wife and children who had been stolen away and he was out searching for them. Findabair sat in the camp day after day and would talk to no one. Kings and princes brought her gifts and spoke fine words to her—but she would not reply.

One day a man came to her notice who, for the first time, stirred her heart and eased her pain. Rochad, son of Fatheman, from Rachlainn in the north. He was an Ulsterman come to help Cuchulain, tall and well-formed, with red-gold hair and gray eyes full of kindliness and mirth. Findabair had ventured out for once with the women who went every day to peer at the heroes gathering for the battle. Maeve noticed her interest and called her to her side.

"What is this, girl—eyes for one of our enemies?"

"Ay," said Findabair, "but *such* a man, Mother."

"There is no reason why you should not have him, Daughter," Maeve then said. "I will give permission for your marriage."

"How can that be? He fights with Cuchulain."

"These are but trials of strength, Daughter. The real battle is yet to come. Go to him in the night, lie with him, make him love you, and then promise him marriage if he will return to the north and leave us alone. These skirmishes are weakening our forces. If he must fight us, let him come back for the great battle at the end. And then— whatever happens—when all is finished, you shall have him. That I promise you."

That night Findabair secretly visited the camp of Rochad. He was already asleep, so it was at first as though she was part of his dream that he encountered her. She roused him with such passion that all night long he could not leave her alone. At first birdcall she told him who she was and how her mother was queen of Connacht.

"Bad news that," said Rochad, "for Maeve has raided our lands and carried off our cattle and our women and children."

"She knows I love you and has promised me to you after the great battle if you will return north now."

Rochad looked at the woman in his arms. He had held other women but never one that made love so hungrily. It would be no bad thing to be in the favor of Queen Maeve, and it would be no hard thing to lie every night with such a woman as Findabair. He promised her he would withdraw his men now, but he would not promise that he would not join in the great battle if he were needed. When the fighting was done and peace had come again—he would come for her.

Findabair returned to her own camp, her cheeks flushed and her eyes starry. The dew was fresh against her bare feet, the grass springy. The world looked very beautiful indeed for the first time since Froech had held her in the river beside Cruachan. She longed for the killing to be over—and to be back in the arms of a man such as Rochad.

Her women found her singing that morning and, surprised at her change of mood, asked her what had happened. She told them about the night she had spent and how Maeve had promised that she should marry Rochad when the fighting was done.

One of her women carried the tale to her lover, who was one of the attendants to one of the kings of Munster. He in turn carried it to his master.

"Queen Maeve has promised *me* her daughter!" he shouted angrily.

Then it came out that twelve kings had been bound to fight for Maeve on the surety that they would have Findabair to wife when the fighting was over.

The camp of Connacht was in uproar—each king, as they discovered the deception, attempted to destroy the others who also claimed Findabair. The girl herself slept through it all, dreaming of Rochad, smiling as she relived his touch, thinking that at last she would be free of Maeve.

She woke to the shaking of her shoulder.

"What is the matter?" she asked sleepily, noticing her woman's distraught face.

"Lady, lady!" the woman cried. "There has been such a slaughter done in the camp. Seven hundred at least have died, and my love amongst them!"

"In the camp?" said Findabair in amazement, rising hastily from her bed and pulling on her robes.

"Come and look," the woman wept, tugging at her arm.

They went outside the royal tent and looked around. No battlefield could have been bloodier. Headless bodies lay strewn about, severed arms and legs, women weeping and keening.

"Why?" cried Findabair, who, though well used to the sight of war, was not prepared for such a carnage among her friends.

"It was for you, mistress," her woman said bitterly. "All these men are dead because of you."

Then she was told how she had been secretly promised to so many and how, when they found out, they began to slaughter one another.

Findabair put her hands to her ears, her face white with horror. She ran from the dreadful scene, ran from the sound of the weeping and keening. She ran to the river in the valley and stood on its bank in despair. She was shamed, deeply shamed. How she hated her mother for what she had done! How she pitied the men who had died for her! Now she remembered little things she had taken no notice of before—gifts given, flattering words said, knowing nods and smiles. She remembered enough to know that her women had not lied to her, that there really were several men who believed she would be their wife.

Then she began to scream. She screamed and screamed—trying to shut out the groaning and the weeping, the blood and the gore, the pity and the shame. Quiet and modest she was no longer. She shook her fists at the sky. She would never be free! Maeve's promise to Rochad was as false as the others—as false as the promise to Froech!

When they found Findabair's body, it was caught in a tangle of branches in the still part of the swiftly flowing river, her face covered in long scratches as though she had tried to tear it away.

Commentary

I chose to write primarily about Findabair instead of Maeve because I began to wonder how it must have been to be the daughter of Maeve. I built her story from bits and pieces embedded in the story of Maeve— sometimes no more than a throwaway line, sometimes a whole vignette. Maeve is practically the most written about of any of the Irish heroines; she is forceful, strong, proud, devious, bloodthirsty. Daughter of Eochàid, the High King, she married a relatively minor king, Ailell, son of Ross Ruadh, King of Leinster. Their castle, or dun, was on the plain of Magh Ai in the province of Connacht. They had seven sons and only one daughter. Although Ailell was no weakling, he was without a doubt secondary to Maeve in many ways. She had property of her own, cattle and treasure and land that matched anything he had. In fact the whole bloodbath of war to steal the Brown Bull of Cuailnge was brought about because there was one possession Ailell had that outshone her own: Ailell had a better bull. The story of this immense cattle raid in all its elaborate and bloodthirsty detail comes from the *Táin Bó Cúailnge,* a twelfth-century manuscript that preserves much that predates the Christian era. In fact, in *Irish Sagas* (M. Dillon, ed.), David Greene suggests that the two bulls are more than animals and hark back to the age of the great bull cults.

The indication that Maeve was clever and devious appears in other tales besides this. In the story of the argument as to who is the champion of Ulster—Conall, Laeghaire, or Cuchulain—Maeve devises a clever ruse to save Ailell from the dangerous consequences of naming any one of them champion when he is asked to arbitrate. On her suggestion, Ailell tells each one in turn that he is the champion and gives him a token to take back to Emain Macha to prove it. He charges each with secrecy. Each man returns to Conchubar's court convinced he has the one and only champion's token. Laeghaire reveals that he has a drinking cup of bronze with a silver bird at the bottom. Conall produces his token—a drinking cup of silver, with a bird of gold at the bottom. Cuchulain caps them both by bringing out his token—a golden cup with a bird made of precious stones. Ailell is well out of the way when his judgment is delivered.

Maeve plays a very similar game with the kings whose support she wants in the war of the Brown Bull of Cuailnge. She offers them each the prize of Findabair, and each believes he has won her. Maeve no doubt believes that if any survive the war she'll have time enough then to think up something to sort out the problem.

Maeve is the queen most quoted to show the privileged position of Celtic women in the Iron Age. They were equal in every respect to men, and in some cases they were superior. They could own property; they could, as kings did, "divide gifts" and "give counsel"; they could ride chariots, fight battles, dispose of lives. As one of the six daughters of the High King, Maeve brought her own army with her to her marriage. And with all this power and freedom went the recognition that women's sexual needs were as legitimate as men's. Maeve chose Ailell for her husband from her many suitors because, like her, he was generous and brave. But even more important, he was not prone to jealousy. "For," she said, "I am never without one man being with me in the shadow of another."

It is strange, therefore, that Maeve does not see that her daughter should have the same rights and privileges as herself. She treats her most insensitively. But if we are to look for underlying meanings in this story, as we have been doing in the others, we might well say that Maeve, Ailell, and Findabair are aspects of the same being: Maeve—the driving force, the will, the animal self; Ailell—the balancing mind, also part of the "little self"; Findabair—the higher, spiritual self seeking a real and lasting love and continually being frustrated by the machinations of the lower self.

Findabair's first and primary love is Froech, who is half Other Worldly. Their meeting is in a river—often a symbol of the flow of spiritual exploration and power. Froech suggests they go away together secretly, for the spiritual quest is almost always pursued in secret away from the jeering interference of others. Findabair is not ready to do that. She still trusts her mother—her ordinary, animal nature— and she still wishes the world to know what she is doing.

Froech is set some dangerous initiative trials including the fetching of the rowan berries from across the water inhabited by a dangerous monster. The rowan is one of the most magical trees in Celtic myth. To reach the magic berries Froech must brave the monster. Maeve, the lower self, refuses him help because she wants him destroyed. His presence brings uncertainty and disturbance into her life. Findabair, the higher self, leaps in and risks her own life to save him—by doing this she passes an initiative test of her own. Maeve's interest in the rowan berries is not at all because of their spiritual/magical associations but because of a purely worldly desire to keep her daughter firmly on the lower plane where she can be used for material purposes. Maeve is attracted to Froech but only for superficial reasons.

Froech has taken Findabair as far as he can while she is still under the domination of her mother—she still obeys her mother, though it goes against her conscience to do so, as in the case of the incident with Cuchulain.

At last Findabair realizes Froech is not coming back. On the quest nothing is repeated in exactly the same way. The path is spiral; we go round and round but are always either higher or lower than we were before. She believes rumors about him and stops looking for him.

Rochad is a strong and honorable man. Findabair loves him and reaches after him, but he has not the Other World connections of Froech. She is on a slightly lower level than she was before, but at least she is starting to reach up again.

Unfortunately Findabair is still following the instructions and advice of her mother instead of taking her life into her own hands. Finally realization comes, and she is shocked to see how much damage has been done because she allowed herself to stay under the domination of her lower self. The horror of facing up to it destroys her.

It is interesting that Findabair is found in a river—for it was in a river that her first great encounter with the higher-self initiation took place. It is also poignant that she is caught up in a tangle of logs, representing the obstacles to the quest she was not strong enough to overcome.

There are many other meanings hidden in the story. For instance, Findabair's ring is found in the body of a salmon—the symbol for wisdom in Celtic myth. Her pledge that she would follow the spiritual quest is thrown away by her lower self but is found again in the body of wisdom.

In Lady Gregory's rendering of the championship of Ulster, Findabair is shown to have "bird sight." Hearing the thunder of approaching men and horses, Findabair goes up to her sunny parlor above the great door of the fort at Cruachan and looks out. She gives her parents a graphic and detailed description of the distantly approaching men and chariots. That she should see so far and so clearly is yet another hint that she represents the far-seeing aspect of the soul.

Twice Findabair's hair is the occasion for some special attention—once when she is trying to rescue Froech in the pool and her father throws his spear and pins her back by her long plaits, and second, when Cuchulain cuts her plaits off and sends her back to her parents, shorn. In throwing the spear and pinning his daughter's hair,

Ailell is performing a symbolic act—the act of restraining his daughter's capacity for individual choice and freedom. Cuchulain shears her hair—as the French did to Nazi collaborators after the Second World War—to mark her as "unclean," to shame her and her parents. Findabair had shamed herself by doing what her parents demanded, even though she knew it was wrong—and so she no longer had the right to wear the symbol of freedom: her hair.

Incidentally, it is said that Maeve is buried under a huge cairn at the summit of Knocknarra, "visible to all Sligo, and to this day unexcavated." It is also said that her warrior ghost has been seen on many occasions. I am not surprised, for she was a woman of most forceful personality and one to whom the things of this earth were particularly important. I can believe she did not want to leave them.

Sources used:
Gantz, Jeffrey. *Early Irish Myths and Sagas*. New York: Penguin Books, 1981.

Gregory, Lady Augusta. *Cuchulain of Muirthemne*. Gerrards Cross, U.K.: Colin Smythe, 1970.

Grania

Grania was the daughter of Cormac, grandson of Conn of the Hundred Battles, High King of Eriu. She was brought up in the great royal enclosure on the Hill of Temuir, a lively and wayward girl. Her father despaired of finding a suitable husband for her, for she refused all suitors. And they blamed the king himself for the refusals.

When Oisin (son of Finn of the Fianna) and Diorraing the Druid came to Temuir to ask Grania in marriage for Finn, King Cormac said they must ask her themselves, for he had no control over her and he did not want to be blamed yet again for a refusal.

King Cormac brought the two messengers to her sunny bower and explained what they were asking. For some reason, that day Grania was in the mood to be dutiful and cooperative, and she said that if Finn, son of Cumhal, was acceptable to her father as a son-in-law, he would be acceptable to her as a husband.

Pleased, but somewhat astonished, the High King set about arranging the wedding feast, and Oisin and Diorraing returned to Finn with the news that the old enmity between his family and the family of Cormac was now at rest, and Finn was accepted as Grania's betrothed.

Grania knew of the power of the Fianna—a band of the greatest heroes and champions both Alban and Eriu had ever known—and was looking forward with some excitement to meeting the famous Finn, son of Cumhal, the mighty leader of them all. Finn's grandfather was Baiscne, a former leader of the Fianna, and his mother was Muirne, granddaughter of Nuada of the Tuatha de Danann and his wife Ethlinn. Thus in Finn's veins flowed both Milesian and Tuathan blood.

Since she was a child Grania had heard tales of Finn's courage and daring. It was also said that he had fed on the salmon of knowledge and the nuts of the nine hazels of wisdom and that his two favorite hunting hounds, Bran and Sceolan, were actually the pups of his mother's sister Tuirenn, who had once been changed into a hound by the jealousy of a former mistress of her husband. Grania was fascinated by the stories and felt that at last she had found a husband worthy of her.

Finn's arrival was greeted with a fanfare of trumpets from the ramparts. People had gathered at Temuir from far and wide to celebrate one of the most important weddings in a long time.

It was known that Finn had been married before—a marriage which had ended tragically and from which he had taken a long time to recover. Once when he was out hunting and in pursuit of a fawn, his two magical hounds, Bran and Sceolan, had refused to harm the fawn, realizing that, like themselves, it was no ordinary animal. The fawn followed them back to the dun at Almhuin and, once inside, it changed into a beautiful young woman named Sadbh. A dark enchanter of the Tuatha, Fear Doirche by name, incensed by Sadbh's refusal of him, had changed her into a fawn. She had been hunted like a wild animal for three long years, and the enchantment could only be broken if she was brought alive into the dun of the Fianna.

Finn and Sadbh loved each other deeply. He gave up hunting and all his usual pursuits just to stay with her. But one day the men of Lochlann came against Eriu and Finn had to lead the Fianna out to battle. When he returned, his beautiful, and by now pregnant, wife was gone.

He was told that Sadbh, looking out for the return of Finn, saw him and his two hounds approaching. Before anyone could stop her she ran out of the dun to greet him. Those who were watching saw her start and give a terrible cry when she came up close to the man, and she turned to run back to the gate. She stumbled, and in that moment the man brought out a hazel rod from beneath his cloak and touched her with it. At once she was changed into a fawn. Still she tried to regain the safety of the dun, but the two dogs ran after her and pulled at her neck savagely, herding her back into the forest. That was the last anyone saw of her—though they went out at once to look for her.

Finn was heartbroken and searched everywhere, never showing interest in any other woman.

At the end of seven years, a young naked boy was found living wild in the forest. By the reaction of Finn's two hounds, and because the boy resembled Sadbh, Finn took him in and questioned him. The boy knew nothing of his parentage, saying that the only mother he had ever known was a gentle fawn who had taken care of him.

"What became of her? Where is she?" asked Finn at once.

The boy shook his head sadly.

"There was a dark and cruel-looking man who used to come to us," he said. "Sometimes he spoke in a gentle voice to the fawn and sometimes he spoke angrily. He seemed to be trying to entice her to follow him, but she always backed away from him in dread. One day he struck her with a hazel rod, and she followed him—but all the time looking piteously back over her shoulder at me as though she were going against her will."

Tears came to the great Finn's eyes then and he took the boy, his son, into his arms. He called his name Oisin.

Everyone was pleased that at last Finn had decided to put an end to many years of sorrow and loneliness in choosing a new wife. Grania was not known to him, but she was the daughter of an important house, and the marriage was to be celebrated with the greatest gathering and festival at Temuir for a long time. As head of the Fianna, Finn was a worthy husband for the High King's daughter.

Grania first walked and talked with her prospective husband on the green beside her father's house. She was shocked to see how old he was—tough, grizzled, and shaggy, he was not at all as she had imagined him to be and not at all as the heroic tales about him had led her to believe. He, in his turn, looked at the green girl before him and, beautiful as she was, wondered if she could take the place of Sadbh. She had a reputation for a sharp wit and quick answers, and he decided to test this out.

"What are the best of jewels?" he asked.

"Those on a dagger's hilt," she replied at once.

"What is sharper than a sword?"

"A woman's wits between two men," she said, glancing at him sideways.

"And faster than the wind?" he asked.

"A woman's mind!" she replied.

That night at the feasting, she watched him as he and her father, of an age, sat side by side, leaning together, boasting, and laughing—gray-haired and heavily scarred by old and savage battles.

On either side of the two old men sat young men, straight and firm of limb, their arms gleaming with gold and their hair with living light.

Beside Grania sat Diorraing, one of Finn's Druids.

"Tell me," she said to him. "Who is it that is sitting on the right hand of Oisin?"

"That is Goll, son of Morna," the Druid answered.

"And beside him?"

"Osgar, son of Oisin."

"My husband's grandson!" muttered Grania under her breath—but aloud she continued to ask for the names of the young men who had come with Finn.

"Caoilte, son of Ronan . . . Lugaidh's son of the Strong Hand . . ." the Druid continued in response to her prompting.

"And who," Grania asked as innocently as she could, "is that?" She indicated the handsomest of all of them, a dark-haired and gentle-speaking man sitting on the left side of Oisin.

"That is Diarmuid, son of Donn, grandson of Duibhne. His mother was closely related to Finn."

Grania questioned the Druid further about him.

"It is said he was fostered by Angus Og himself, son of the Dagda, and brought up in Brugh na Boyne among the 'lasting rocks' and the Tuatha de Danann. But there is some kind of curse on him for something his father did. There is a wild boar without bristle, ear, or tail that will be the death of him one day."

"Sad to think of it," said Grania.

"He has taken a vow that he will never refuse a woman who asks for help," Diorraing added.

"What does his wife think of that?" Grania laughed.

The Druid smiled. "Diarmuid is not wed," he said. "Too many women love him. But there is a tale that once he took an old hag to bed who was refused shelter by all other men, and she proved to be a young and beautiful princess, daughter of the King of the Sea, and they lived and loved many years before he lost her."

Grania asked no more questions but looked thoughtfully along the line of young men the Druid had just named for her.

She called her most trusted serving maid to her and asked her to bring from her private chambers the great golden cup that held so much wine it was said a host could drink from it. Into it she slipped a sleeping draught. Then she instructed her maid to offer the wine to Finn and all the others—all, that is, except Oisin, Osgar, Caoilte, Diarmuid, and Diorraing the Druid.

All who drank from Grania's golden cup were soon asleep.

Then, one by one, she spoke in soft and seductive tones to the young men who were left awake—asking them for their love, promising to marry them instead of Finn. One by one they refused out of loyalty to Finn their leader. But to Diarmuid she said: "I beg of you to take me out of my father's house and away from Finn this very night."

He protested, but she reminded him that he was bound by a Druid oath to help any woman who asked for help.

"And I," she said quietly, "have asked for your help."

Diarmuid was greatly troubled by this and took his friends aside and asked them what he should do. He could not break a Druid oath; on the other hand, he had great love and respect for Finn and could not, for his honor, do what Grania asked.

His friends agreed that he could not break his oath and there was nothing for it but that he should take Grania away. "Though you will meet your death for it," Diorraing said.

"I shall take her from her father's house and from Finn as I am bound," Diarmuid said, "but I will do no more. I shall not break my loyalty to Finn of the Fianna. I shall not take her as my woman or my wife."

He tried once more to escape from the trap she had set for him by telling her that they could not leave Temuir that night because the place was guarded by Finn's men, his own companions, and he could not, for his honor, trick them into letting him through. Their punishment for failing in their duty would be upon his head.

"No matter," she said quickly. "There is a secret door from my summer house that is not guarded. We can escape through that."

"I will not sneak out of a side door like a thief in the night," Diarmuid said.

"Well, then," said Grania relentlessly, "leap over the walls on your spear shafts as behooves a warrior of the Fianna. There would be no dishonor in that."

Diarmuid gave in.

Once outside, he tried again to persuade her to return to Finn. "For I shall not take you as my wife," he warned, "but will keep faith with him whatever happens. If we go now, there will be no place on earth we will be able to hide from his just wrath. But if we go back now— he will know nothing."

But she would not be persuaded and swore that she loved Diarmuid so much she wanted to be with him no matter what happened. She could not live without him.

"It is said there is an enchantment about you, a spot on your forehead, given you by a sorceress, to make women love you."

Diarmuid sighed. "It is said," he admitted heavily, "but . . . ."

"Take me away from Finn's wrath," she said hastily, lest he tell her that he had seen the way she was looking at him before she noticed the spot on his forehead. "Let us not waste a moment longer. I fear even now I hear the first bird singing!" She tugged at his arm and hurried him away across the fields.

Later, when she was tired and had to rest, Diarmuid tried once more to persuade her to return. "There will be no rest for either of us for as long as we live," he said. "It is not too late to return."

But again she would not listen and held him to the oath he had sworn.

That night Diarmuid laid out a piece of unbroken bread as a sign to Finn that he had not broken Grania's virginity.

When they were a good way from Temuir, Diarmuid made a house of woven twigs for Grania, with seven doors and a little fence around it. He laid a bed for her of soft rushes and the finest twigs of the birch tree. But he did not lie with her.

Grania lay a long time staring in to the dark, certain that he would weaken in his resolve and come to her. But he did not.

Never mind, she thought. There will be other nights.

Meanwhile Finn found out that his bride had run away with Diarmuid and was furious. There was hardly a person in the land who did not know how he had been shamed and insulted—and he determined to seek vengeance for his shame. He sent trackers off at once to find where the runaways had gone, and within a short while they were sure they had gone to ground in Doire da Bhoth, the Wood of the Two Huts.

Oisin, Osgar, Caoilte, and Diorraing, hearing of Finn's preparations to capture them, sent Bran, Finn's hound, to warn them—for besides Finn himself, Bran loved Diarmuid.

Diarmuid woke to find Bran licking his face, and he knew at once that Finn must be near. For the first time Grania seemed to realize just what danger she had put them in and urged Diarmuid to take her away at once.

"No," said the young man. "I have kept my bond. I have taken you away from your father's house and from Finn—and now I will not hide from him."

"Are you mad!" she cried, shaking and pulling at his arm. "It will be the worse for us if Finn finds us here."

"You may go," said Diarmuid. "But I shall not."

Then Oisin, Osgar, Caoilte, and Diorraing, still worrying about Diarmuid being found by Finn, told Caoilte's serving man to shout a warning to him because he had a voice that carried very clear and far. Again Grania pleaded with him to flee, and again Diarmuid refused. Now she was terrified and bitterly chided him for putting her at risk.

Finn sent the sons of Neamhuin into the wood to see what they could see. They brought back a report of the house woven of twigs and the seven doors. They had seen Diarmuid there with a woman.

Finn armed himself and declared that Diarmuid would not leave that forest without giving him satisfaction for all that he had done to him. Oisin tried to soothe him, saying that if Diarmuid had done anything to dishonor Finn, he would surely not be waiting for Finn to catch up with him, as he was clearly doing.

Finn would not listen and ordered his men to surround the house.

At this moment Angus Og of the Tuatha de Danann, foster father to Diarmuid, saw that Diarmuid was in danger and, as swift as a winter wind, flew to Doire da Bhoth—entering the house without Finn or any of his men spotting him.

"What have you done, grandson of Duibhne?" he asked his foster son, and Diarmuid told him the whole story.

"I will take you both away from here," said Angus. "Come under my cloak."

"No," said Diarmuid. "I shall not flee. I am a warrior of the Fianna. But take Grania to safety. If I live, I will follow her. If I do not—return her to her father."

"Do not leave me, Diarmuid," cried Grania. "For if I go without you I cannot be sure you will follow. I need you! I need your help!"

She clung to his hand and tried to pull him under the cloak—but he withdrew from her.

"Take her, foster father. Take care of her."

"Only until you come for me. Only until you come!" she cried.

Angus put his arm around Grania's waist and swirled the cloak around her so that she could no longer see Diarmuid.

Then, at each of the seven doors, there was knocking—and at six of them were friends of Diarmuid trying to persuade him to escape and run. But he would not leave through any of those doors, for he said it would bring down the wrath of Finn on their own heads if he did so.

At the seventh door was Finn and his armed men, and it was only at this door that Diarmuid would make his bid to escape. He put his two hands on the two staves of power Manannan had given him when he was a youth and leapt light and high over the heads of Finn's warriors. Then he put his shield to his back and ran before they had realized enough of what had happened to pursue him.

That night Diarmuid came upon Angus and Grania in a cabin with a fire at the hearth and meat on the spit. Seeing him, Grania leapt up and took a step toward him, her cheeks flushed with pleasure that he had indeed followed her. He did not take her in his arms, however, but greeted Angus quietly and sat down to eat. He was weary and disheveled, and when he had satisfied his hunger he sat slumped at the table with his head in his hands.

Softly Grania came up to him, stroked his hair, and washed the sweat off his brow with a cool cloth.

Angus rose and stood before him. "I am leaving you now," he said, "for I cannot live your life for you, and you have chosen a hard way. You will have no peace, my son, for what this woman has asked you to do. Never relax your vigilance. Never stay in one place long."

He put his hands on his foster son's shoulders and looked deeply into his eyes. And then he left.

Grania looked at Diarmuid. The young fresh face she had loved at the feast in her father's hall was pale and tired, the sparkle in his eyes gone. What had she done?

"It will be all right," she whispered. "As soon as we are far enough away from Temuir, Finn will forget. He will tire of chasing us. He will forgive."

Diarmuid looked at Grania. She was more beautiful than she had been as a thoughtless young girl flirting with him and his friends in her father's castle. Her lips no longer pouted but trembled.

"Ah, Grania," he said sadly. "We have indeed chosen a hard way."

Seeing how his expression had changed toward her, she tried to take him in her arms, but he pushed her gently aside. That night—as before—he slept away from her.

Angus was right. There was no peace in the world for them. They moved from place to place; Finn did not forget, and he did not forgive.

Finn had a way of scrying where they were by peering closely into clear water in a bowl of pale gold—and wherever they went, he was not far behind. Every time he was about to come upon them, he found a piece of unbroken bread laid out by Diarmuid as a sign to him that he had kept faith with him. But it did not soften his heart toward them.

Champions of many different countries took it as great sport to hunt them down for Finn of the Fianna, and Diarmuid's ingenuity and courage were stretched to the utmost to avoid them. He tried to use tricks as much as possible—not wanting their blood on his hands. But there came a time when tricks would no longer serve, and Grania woke one morning to find Diarmuid fully armed.

That night and the next and the next, Diarmuid returned to Grania, wounded and weary, falling down at her feet too exhausted to remove his weapons and his arms. She struggled to get the hard metal away from him while he slept, and she slept close beside him.

Each morning when she woke, he was standing again, fully clothed, and ready to fight. It worried her that he did not cut the heads off his enemies when he defeated them, as was the custom, but bound them and left them alive. It did not take Finn's woman-Druid of the Black Mountains long to release them and for them to come after him again.

One day, as they watched their enemies approach, Grania noticed a handsome young man in a green cloak ahead of the troop, and Diarmuid noticed the way Grania looked at him.

"Will you fight beside me, Grania?" he asked, seeing that she had a knife in her hand.

"No," she said. "I will not." And she handed it back to him.

"I think you have love for that young man in the green cloak," he said then.

"I have not," she said sharply. "But I wish I had given my love to no man before this day."

This time Diarmuid attacked in anger and put down so many champions and warriors and their hounds that Finn grew discouraged and returned to Almhuin, his home in Leinster.

For a while the fugitives were left in peace, moving through the country unhindered.

One day they came to the Wood of Dubhros, and there they saw, for the first time, the extraordinary quicken-tree of the Tuatha de Danann, which This had grown from a rowan berry dropped accidentally by a musician of the Tuatha. Around it in spring a cloud of bees continually hummed, and in summer, when the berries glowed red, clouds of birds fluttered. The more berries that were eaten, the more berries there were. Any mortal who chanced to eat a berry enjoyed good health, youth and beauty. They were as sweet as honey to taste and more intoxicating than the strongest mead. If anyone ate more than one he would be likely to lose his wits.

The Tuatha decided the tree should be guarded night and day, and for this purpose they searched out Searbhan Lochlannach, the Surly One of Lochlann. They placed a ring of iron around his huge neck and told him that he would never die until there had been three strokes on that iron ring made by his own iron club. He took his duties so seriously that no one dared enter the wood where the tree was, and the place became a wilderness.

Diarmuid managed to befriend the Surly One and made a pact with him that he would never touch the berries if he was allowed to live and hunt in the wood. Then he built a cabin for Grania and himself, and the two of them lived there in the wood quite safely for some time.

One day two warriors came to Finn and asked to join the Fianna. Finn agreed that they could, on condition that they brought him either the head of Diarmuid or a handful of the berries from the quicken-tree of the Tuatha in Dubhros Wood. Oisin took them aside and warned them that both conditions would be equally impossible to fulfill, but they would not listen and set off for Dubhros.

After a time the warriors came to the cabin Diarmuid had built and hammered on the door. Grania listened as Diarmuid exchanged words with them. She learned that they were to take either Diarmuid's head or a handful of quicken-berries back to Finn.

"What are these berries?" she asked—and Diarmuid told her about the quicken-tree and the arrangement he had with the Surly One not to touch them in exchange for being allowed to live in the wood. The two sons of Morna, who had been consulting with each other while Diarmuid was telling Grania the story, now shouted out that they intended to fight Diarmuid for his head rather than go after the berries.

They chose to fight with their bare hands, and a good fight they put up. But in the end they were defeated and bound by Diarmuid.

Meanwhile, Grania had been thinking about the magic berries, and the more she thought about them the more she wanted them. When Diarmuid returned she asked his help in getting a handful of them. Again Diarmuid was trapped by his vow that he would assist any woman who asked for his help. He tried to dissuade her—but she would not be dissuaded.

Hearing that Diarmuid was to go to the quicken-tree for the berries, the two sons of Morna pleaded to go along to help him get them. He refused their help, for he said it would be their certain death, but agreed to unbind them so they could be on their way.

Diarmuid found the Surly One asleep and, instead of taking the berries there and then, touched him with his foot so that he awoke. The huge man looked at Diarmuid suspiciously.

"I do not want to break our agreement, Searbhan Lochlannach," said Diarmuid, "but I must ask you for a handful of the quicken-berries for the princess Grania."

"I swear I will die rather than give her any of the berries," said the guardian of the tree.

Diarmuid sighed. "If you will not give them to me willingly," he said sadly, "I must take them from you unwillingly. I do not intend treachery, so I give you fair warning of my intentions."

The Surly One stood up at once and gave Diarmuid three mighty blows with his iron club, which made the young man reel back. The Surly One was so pleased with his work that he relaxed his vigilance. In that moment Diarmuid threw down his own weapons and leapt at the big man, seizing his club in his own hands and striking him on the iron ring around his neck three times.

At this the two sons of Morna, who had been watching the fight, came out of hiding, full of admiration for the young warrior. Diarmuid set them to burying the Surly One and then asked them to fetch Grania, while he sat a while and tried to recover from the blows he had been dealt.

When Grania came, Diarmuid told her she could eat as many of the berries as she wanted. She stared at the tree—the beautiful, magical, shining tree—and she was afraid to touch it.

"Pick me some of the berries, Diarmuid," she said. "I will not eat them unless they come from your hand."

So Diarmuid reached up and picked the berries for her. And he ate some too.

He then told the two sons of Morna to return to Finn with some of the berries and say that they themselves had killed the Surly One and taken the berries—that way he would be obliged to take them into the Fianna.

But Finn was suspicious when he received the berries, knowing that the two sons of Morna could not have slain such a fearsome guardian by themselves. He claimed that he could smell Diarmuid's hand in it all and raised a huge troop of warriors to advance on the Wood of Dubhros.

Diarmuid, satiated with the berries, had climbed up into the tree and gone to sleep in the bed of the Surly One—dreaming dreams.

Finn and his men came to the tree and found it unguarded, and they ate their fill of the berries. Then, in the heat of the day, they lay down to dream their dreams also.

It seemed to Finn he was playing a game of chess under the tree—and against him were Oisin, his son; Osgar, his grandson; Lugaidh's son, and Diorraing the Druid. Time and again he was about to win the game when Diarmuid threw a berry from the tree and knocked his opponent's piece so that it fell into a square and brought about Finn's defeat. He could do nothing to win a game—and every time he lost, the Fianna gave a great shout of mocking laughter.

When he woke Finn stood up angrily and looked up into the tree.

"Diarmuid is here in the tree," he said to his men.

"Why would he stay there, knowing that you have been sleeping at the foot of it?" asked Osgar.

"Am I right, Diarmuid?" shouted Finn into the tree. "Or is my grandson?"

"You always had good judgment, Finn," Diarmuid replied—and showed himself. His arm was around Grania and he gave her three kisses—the first he had given her since they ran away from her father's house.

Seeing this, Finn went wild with rage.

"It was bad enough," he roared, "that the seven battalions of the Fianna saw how you took away my bride at Temuir when you yourself were supposed to be guarding my safety—but for those three kisses alone you will lose your head!"

He commanded his men to surround the tree.

At this moment Angus Og, in Brugh na Boyne, became aware of the danger Diarmuid was in and came to his help.

One by one, nine men climbed the tree, intent on killing Diarmuid. One by one, nine men fell out of the tree and were killed by Finn, who thought he was killing Diarmuid—for Angus Og had put the likeness of Diarmuid upon them.

At last, discouraged, Finn called back his men while he thought what his next move would be. In the hiatus Angus Og took Grania under his cloak of invisibility and flew off with her to Brugh na Boyne—Diarmuid promised to follow if he was still alive.

When she was safely away, Diarmuid called out to Finn.

"I am coming down now to fight," he said, "for I see there is no place on earth where I may have peace until we settle this score. I have fought for you all my life, and if that cannot turn your heart toward me—nothing can."

"Come down, son of Donn," Finn shouted. "My heart will not turn toward you before the end of time itself!"

"Forgive him," said Osgar, Finn's grandson, "for he is a great and honorable man and has done you no wrong but to keep a vow he had to keep."

"I will not!" said Finn.

"I will fight beside him then," said Osgar, "and anyone who raises a weapon against Diarmuid, raises a weapon against me."

Then Diarmuid leapt from the branches of the tree and landed beyond the fighting men, beside Osgar. Those who attacked, Diarmuid and Osgar attacked—but soon they were clear away.

Bitterly and broodingly Finn returned to Almhuin to bury his dead and heal his wounded, vowing never to forgive Diarmuid.

Diarmuid fetched Grania from Angus and they continued on their travels. They found a good cave by the sea and lived there for a while.

One night a storm blew up, and they sheltered deep in the cave, the waves of the sea breaking in where they had once had their hearth.

Late at night a curragh came washing into the cave, and out of it climbed a big fellow, a Formorian—his name Ciach, the Fierce One. He shared their shelter with them, and, as none of them could sleep for the raging of the storm, Diarmuid and he sat down to a game of chess by the flickering light of the lamp.

Ciach won the game and asked for Grania as his prize. He put his arm around her and drew her to him as though he were going to carry her away there and then. Instead of pulling away from him, Grania seemed to nestle in closer and, looking straight at Diarmuid, said that she had been all this time with one of the best men of the Fianna, and he had never given her as much satisfaction as she was now getting from the arms of this Formorian.

"Perhaps it would be better for me if I went with him," she said provocatively.

Ciach grinned and held her closer.

Diarmuid leapt up and seized his sword.

Grania, in bitter anger, threw her dagger at him and pierced his thigh.

White with rage, Diarmuid, in spite of the wound, attacked the Formorian and made an end of him. And then, without a backward glance at Grania, strode out of the cave into the storm.

Horrified at what her frustration had made her do, Grania rushed after him, calling his name. The storm crashed around her and the rain drenched her to the skin—but she could find him nowhere.

The next day, when the rain had stopped and light had come back to the earth, she found him, seated on a rock by the sea, brooding.

She stood a little way from him, afraid to step nearer.

He did not look at her.

A heron cried out—a wild and lonely cry.

"What is that?" she asked.

And for the first time he turned his head and looked at her, his eyes dark with his suffering.

"It is a heron that cannot fly. It is a heron that has lost its way."

"Diarmuid, grandson of Duibhne, I ask your forgiveness for what I said and did last night. I sought to make you jealous because you will not lie with me."

"Oh, Grania, daughter of the High King, how many steps have you taken that should not have been taken?"

She hung her head.

"Grania of the beautiful hair," he said sadly, "princess lovelier than a green tree in blossom, your love is as passing as a cloud, as deadly as a storm. What are you asking of me now? You have taken me from everything and everyone I have known. I have nowhere to lay my head in peace. I long for the bright days among the Fianna, for the loving companionship of my friends. It were better you had given me your hatred than your love."

"Oh, Diarmuid," she said. "My love for you is beyond my control. I saw you and I could not live without you. Each day it grows like a tree in the warmth of the sun."

"You are a woman full of sweet words that mean nothing. You gave your promise to the leader of the Fianna and it meant nothing. You tell me with words that you love me—but with deeds you mock me! I am the heron who has lost its way. I am the heron who cannot fly."

"Come back with me, grandson of Duibhne. You are my love— my only love. Your way is with me."

He looked at her for a long time—and he knew that he could not leave her. He rose and followed her and they returned to the cave. She lit the hearth fire and asked if he would eat.

"The meat is not cut," he said quietly.

"Give me the knife and I will cut it," she said.

"Take it then from where you have sheathed it," he said—and he showed her that it was still in his thigh where she had plunged it.

She shrank back, but he made no move to take it out himself. She knew then that this was something she had to do. This was something she could not avoid.

She pulled it out. She staunched the bleeding. She washed and bound it.

When she had finished she offered her shoulder for him to lean on and he stood up and leaned on her. He was close to her and she could not look at him for shame of all that she had done to him.

He looked down at her and saw her lip tremble and her eyes lowered. He stooped his head and kissed her—and this time when they went into the cave and lay on the bed of soft young rushes, he made love to her as man to wife.

That day when he put the sign of the bread out for Finn as he always did, it was a piece of broken bread.

And so time went by, and this time when Diarmuid and Grania fled from place to place, they were lovers and together, and it was no longer so hard to bear. When he slept, Grania would keep watch, singing to him that to be parted from him would be like life parted from a body. When she woke him she sang another song. She sang of the wakefulness of all the creatures of the wild—for Grania and Diarmuid shared the dangers of being hunted with all birds and beasts.

Wherever they hid they could not stay for long, for Finn, with his scrying, found them out. But now Grania was more alert than she had been, and there were times when she saved Diarmuid's life by noticing things he had not noticed.

At last Finn's obsession with making Diarmuid pay for what he had done—and his belief that the young couple were being helped by his friends in the Fianna—drove him to seek help from the King of Alban, a man who carried a grudge against Diarmuid for the killing of his father and his two brothers in a battle.

Finn sailed with the men of Alban up the Boyne River until they came to the dun of Angus Og, where Diarmuid and Grania and Osgar were at that time taking shelter.

The Brugh stood on the top of a green hill—a mound of silver-white crystal with a stone wall around its base carved with power symbols and, surrounding it again, a circle of standing stones. It was a place no mortal man dared approach too closely without the invitation of the occupants. The very air around it seemed to hum with magic.

Finn stood at the foot of the hill and shook his spear and shouted his challenge to Diarmuid to come out and fight. He knew he could not touch him if he chose to remain with Angus.

Within the Brugh, Diarmuid and Osgar consulted together, and when the dawn came and the first red light touched the waters of the Boyne, the two warriors stepped forth, their weapons gleaming fiercely, their shields together like one shield.

By the day's end Finn had to climb back into his ship and sail away. Diarmuid and Osgar were still alive.

Now he was in despair of ever defeating Diarmuid by force of arms and went to the Land of Promise and called on the help of his old nurse to work enchantment on Diarmuid. This she did—first by covering the hills with a Druid mist so that when Diarmuid went out hunting no one could find him to come to his aid. Then she made a hole in a leaf and aimed deadly spears at him through it. Though he fought them off as best he could, Diarmuid found he could not touch her with his own spears. At last, badly wounded and almost destroyed, he had the presence of mind to aim his last spear through the hole in the leaf she was holding—and this found its mark. With a shriek she and her mist disappeared.

Finn stepped forward but his way was barred by Angus Og, who persuaded Finn that his enmity toward Diarmuid must end, and Finn, seeing that he had failed by force of arms and by enchantment, reluctantly agreed. Angus then went to the High King, Grania's father, and extracted a promise of peace from him. Back at the Brugh he healed Diarmuid's wounds and lulled him with the enchanted music of his silver harp, two birds plucking the strings of red gold as they hovered over it. He told Diarmuid that Finn and Cormac had agreed to peace, and Diarmuid said that he would only accept it if he were given his grandfather's lands back and certain other lands he named as Grania's marriage portion.

This was finally accepted, with Angus as go-between, and Diarmuid and Grania came out of hiding. The home they built for themselves was far from Temuir and Almhuin, and for sixteen years they lived in peace. During this time Grania bore four sons and one daughter.

One day, her sons out to fosterage and time hanging heavy on her hands, Grania told Diarmuid that she was going to prepare a feast and invite Finn and her father to attend. Diarmuid protested, for in those sixteen years no word had been exchanged between them. But Grania pleaded, saying that she had never fully relaxed all that time because, although they were no longer enemies, they were not friends. She sent messengers to invite the two men and prepared the feast.

Diarmuid and Grania's hospitality to Finn and Cormac and their households lasted the whole length of a year, and Grania was convinced that at last the ghost of the old enmity between Finn and Diarmuid had been laid.

On the last night of the year Diarmuid woke from his sleep hearing the sounds of hounds on the hunt.

"What is it?" Grania asked.

"I hear the hounds on the hills—hunting," he said.

"I hear nothing," she said. "It was a dream. Go back to sleep, my love."

He went back to sleep but started up once more saying that he had heard the sounds of the hunt again.

"Nonsense," she said. "Hounds do not hunt in the middle of the night. It is enchantment."

Once more he lay back. The third time the sounds of the hunt woke him it was dawn, and because it was now light, Grania could not stop him from going out to see for himself what was going on.

"Take your best weapons," she said. "There is something strange about this."

But he did not listen to her and took only his light weapons for hunting small game.

He followed the sounds of the hunt and came to the top of Beinn Gulbain, where he found Finn sitting on a rock alone.

"What is this hunt?" he asked coldly, without greeting.

Finn shrugged. "One of my hounds scented a boar in the night and insisted on hunting it. Several of my men have been killed and several of my hounds. It were better you went back to the dun and kept yourself safe."

"I do not hide from danger," said Diarmuid. "You should know that."

"It is better you did this time," Finn said slyly. "For it is the earless

Green Boar of Beinn Gulbain we are hunting, and it is said that it is he who will bring about your death."

"If he is here, I will face him," Diarmuid said. "But lend me your two best hounds."

"I will not," said Finn, rising from the rock. "I go back to the feast your wife has prepared for me." And he started back down the mountain, leaving Diarmuid alone.

"I see it is you who have arranged this for my death," Diarmuid called after him. "But I defeated your schemes before—and I will again."

Finn's laughter echoed among the rocky crags mockingly, and he and his hounds were soon out of sight.

Then Diarmuid met head-on the boar that had been destined for his death. He drew his sword, but with one blow of the boar's fearsome tusks the metal of the blade was snapped away. Diarmuid wished he had taken Grania's advice. The weapons he had with him were useless against this huge and fearsome beast.

The boar charged again and Diarmuid leapt onto his back, clinging while he tried to stab the boar with his dagger. The boar tossed and bounded and ran all over the mountain, trying to shake the man off his back, crashing him against rocks and into streams. At last he flung Diarmuid off and drove his deadly tusks deep into him. With the last strength that was in his arms Diarmuid beat at his head with the hilt of the sword that was in his hand—and killed him.

Finn stood looking down at the dying man with a smile of pleasure.

"If only the women could see you now, son of Donn," he said with satisfaction. "All your handsome looks turned to filth and ugliness!"

"Save me, Finn," Diarmuid pleaded. "Now is the time to remember all the times I saved your life in the days when I fought with the Fianna."

"No one can save you," said Finn coldly.

"You have the gift of healing. I have heard that a drink of water from your hands can heal whatever wound a man has."

Then the men who were with Finn pleaded for Diarmuid's life, reminding Finn of the great deeds Diarmuid had done in the old days and how it was Grania who had held him under bond to help her and not Diarmuid himself who had chosen to go away with her.

"I would give you water," said Finn then, "but there is no water here."

"Nine paces from you there is a spring," whispered Diarmuid.

"Is there indeed?" said Finn, and walked slowly, slowly, toward it.

He raised water in his hands and began to walk back toward Diarmuid. But just before he reached him Finn let the water slip through his fingers.

"Go back," shouted his men—and back he went, slowly as before.

The second time he let the water slip through his fingers—and again went back to the spring.

The third time he carried the water safely—but when he reached Diarmuid he was dead.

When Grania saw the men returning to the rath, she knew at once that Diarmuid was dead and that Finn had brought it about, even before Oisin told her the full story.

She sent out her men to bring back Diarmuid's body from the mountain, and while they were gone she wept and keened for her lost love and vowed vengeance on the man who had tricked him into his death—forgetting that she herself had brought him to this end.

When the men who had gone to fetch Diarmuid's body reached it, they found his foster father, Angus Og, already there.

"I cannot bring him back to life in your mortal world," he said. "But he can live with me in my world."

And Grania's men stood back in awe as the shining and shimmering Tuatha de Danann gathered up the corpse of their master, laid it on a golden bier, with the tall staves of Manannan at each corner. They watched as he was carried down the mountain, fading into golden mist before he reached the bottom.

Grania never saw him as Finn would have liked her to have seen him, gored and broken by the boar. Her memory of him was as he was when he left her—tall and beautiful, his black hair in thick curls, his eyes the blue of a summer sky.

In the beginning it had seemed to Grania that Diarmuid was too gentle, too honorable. She had longed for his touch—longed for him to show to her some of the passion she felt sure must be smouldering in his heart as it was in hers. It had taken a bitter crisis in which he had nearly lost his manhood before he would take her in his arms. She thought back to that night and felt that whatever had happened before or since, all the suffering, the hiding, the danger, the fear, and the discomfort—all, all was worth it for that first lovemaking on the floor of the cave the night when they had heard the lost heron cry.

Angus Og had taken Diarmuid to Brugh na Boyne, and he could live on there among the spirit people, but she would never again feel the hardness of his body against hers nor see him smile as he looked into her eyes in the morning when he woke. Life and Death are interchangeable and there is no sense of mourning either . . . but oh, she would not feel his kiss again.

For *this* she would have vengeance!

Grania called her four sons back from fosterage and shared out their father's weapons between them. She told them about the boar of Beinn Gulbain and how it was their father's destiny, for something *his* father had done, to be killed by it. "But," she said bitterly "it was Finn, under bonds as our guest and under bonds of peace, who made the hunt to flush the beast out of cover and set him at your father. It is Finn who must pay for his death—and it is you who must extract the payment. Go now," she said. "Learn everything there is to learn about fighting so that when the time comes you can take on Finn of the Fianna as your father did. But do not be soft as your father was, binding enemies so that they live to fight again. When you have Finn at your mercy—kill him!" Her voice rose and her eyes gleamed. She felt that if she had Finn before her at that moment, she would kill him herself.

Months passed and Grania lived on at the rath, bored and lonely. Diarmuid had chosen a place to build his home as far as he could from the court of the High King at Temuir and from Finn's fort at Almhuin. Even when he was alive and she was busy with her children, she had resented being so cut off from the social life she had been used to as a young girl. The strain of being a fugitive over, she had enjoyed the first years of peace and quiet with Diarmuid—but as the years went by she grew more and more restless. It was this very restlessness that had inspired her to invite her father and Finn to visit. She had hoped to be properly reconciled with them and invited back to the festivals and gatherings at Temuir that she missed so much.

Now she was worse off than before. She did not have either Diarmuid or her children to break the monotony of the days.

One day her servants reported seeing a single chariot coming toward their remote valley. Her first reaction was fear. Was Finn determined to kill her too? She wished her sons were near and looked impatiently at the men in her employ. None of them were capable of standing up to Finn.

She took the knife she had flung at Diarmuid so many years before and concealed it in her sleeve. She sent her daughter into the woods with her nurse and took her stand at the great front door, ready to meet whatever her fate decreed.

As the sound of the horses came nearer, Grania's heart was beating very fast, the color high in her cheeks.

At last the waiting was over. Finn himself thundered forward and stopped the chariot in front of her, its iron wheels grating on the pebbles of the courtyard.

"Greetings, Grania," he said calmly. He was smiling, and she could not tell if it was the smile of a cat to a mouse or of a lover to a lady. His hair that had been gray when she first saw him was now silver-white, thickly framing a suntanned face with many lines. His eyes were the eyes of a young man—shrewd and bright. There was a gold torc at his hard neck and golden bracelets on his muscular arms.

"You are not welcome here, Finn of the Fianna," she said icily.

"Ah, lady, there are many things that have happened since I first met you—but all because I loved you."

Grania bit her lip and clutched the cold blade in her sleeve.

"A strange way to show love to a woman," she said.

"A strange way to show love to a man," he parried.

"Diarmuid was my love!"

"And you destroyed him."

"*You* destroyed him!"

"No, lady, it was you. But what is past is past. My horses are tired and hot. Send me a groom to care for them."

"I have not invited you to stay."

He smiled and stepped down from the chariot. He stood close before her. She could have stabbed him then. But she did not.

He looked at her closely, up and down, the woman who had caused him so much humiliation and trouble. In maturity she was even more desirable than she had been as a girl. He noticed that she did not object to having a man look at her that way again.

Flushing slightly, Grania turned and called out to the grooms to come and attend to his horses. Then she ordered the cooks to prepare a meal.

That night the two sat on either side of the great long table in the great long hall, empty now apart from the few serving maids.

Finn tore at the venison and lifted the wine to his lips—and never once took his eyes off Grania.

She wanted to speak haughtily to him. She wanted to tell him that her sons were at this very moment training so that one day they would kill him. She wanted to throw the dagger across the table at him—but each opportunity she got, she lost by hesitation.

As the evening wore on she found she could no longer speak, no longer look away from him; his eyes were holding her and she was longing for his touch as once she had longed for Diarmuid's.

In the small hours of the morning Finn was with her in her bed, and the roughness of his lovemaking pleased her more than all the gentleness of Diarmuid.

Finn stayed with her many months and the Fianna did not know where he was. They searched across the country, but not one of them thought to look at Rath Grania—nor did they expect to see him coming, as eventually he did, with Grania clinging to his arm as loving as any new bride to a new husband.

The Fianna laughed and joked as she passed among them so that her cheeks burned red with shame.

"Keep tight hold of her this time, son of Cumhal," Oisin said. "We do not want to lose any more of our honorable men."

Finn grinned at his son. "Don't worry," he said. "I know now how she is to be held."

Seven years later Grania's sons returned from the far countries where they had been training in feats of arms and were astonished to find their mother at Almhuin, mistress of their enemy's household.

Diarmuid had always said she was good with words—and it was with words she now diverted their enmity from Finn and persuaded him to take them into the Fianna.

—— Commentary ——

The story of Diarmuid and Grania is one that is as familiar to the Scots as to the Irish. Many Scotsmen claim that the famous band of warriors, the Fianna, were based in Scotland and only went to Ireland because the hunting was better there. The Irish tradition, however, claims that the Fianna were based in Ireland and only went to Scotland for the hunt. Whatever the truth of it is, it is almost certain that the story is very old and belongs to the Celts before they split into Scots and Irish. The main waves of Irish settlers went over to Scotland between the second and fifth centuries A.D.—and as near as we can get it the Fianna were defeated and disbanded in the third century at the Battle of Gabhra in Ireland in A.D. 277 or 294 (according to J. F. Campbell's sources). Probably the oldest written copy of the story we have is in a manuscript of 1651 by Daíbhí Ó Duibhgeannáin, now in the Royal Irish Academy. J. F. Campbell includes the story from various oral Scottish sources in his *Popular Tales of the West Highlands,* and Lady Gregory has a version in her *Gods and Fighting Men.* It is from the latter that I have drawn most for my version of the story.

Grania is sometimes called the Celtic Eve, for in this story there is forbidden fruit on a tree that the woman persuades the man to pluck— this time with the added twist that she persuades him to pick the fruit himself and give it to her, presumably in the hope that if there is any retribution to fall, it will fall on him and not on her. But, though the Adam and Eve parallel must inevitably run through the reader's mind and the theme is certainly, on one level, one of the destruction of a noble, honorable man by a scheming temptress, there are more complex ways we can read the story.

Grania strikes us as a healthy young woman with a strong sexual drive. She is continually presented with unsuitable suitors by her father and finally gives in. Her mind tells her that Finn is suitable for her—and it is interesting that it is *her* mind he tests out when he first meets her. This is an arranged marriage—arranged by the mind and, finally, rejected by the body.

Grania seeks a younger man. She considers the available young men one by one, settling at last for the one who was her choice in the first place—Diarmuid, who has been foolish (or noble) enough to make a Druid vow that he will always assist a woman if she asks for help. A Druid vow is no ordinary and idle promise but a binding and solemn oath rather like one for the ministry or the presidency—and probably accompanied by fearful spells against its breaking.

It is clear that Diarmuid represents the noble depths of the human being, that mysterious part where the conscience resides and where the urge is for the growth and upward evolution of the spirit. Grania is that restless, cunning, devious side of us, always seeking ways for self-gratification no matter what the consequences—the side that holds us back from our spiritual growth, that thwarts our attempts to be noble and honorable. For all that, Diarmuid's plunge into the whole dangerous and difficult experience with Grania is what makes it possible for him to translate his theoretical nobility into the real thing. The conflict and tension between these two sides of ourselves is perhaps vital to our spiritual growth.

At the beginning of the story these two protagonists (contained in each and every one of us) seem clear-cut. Grania is bad. Diarmuid is good. But as the story progresses good versus bad ceases to be the only issue—and it ceases to continue to be so clear-cut.

Grania and Diarmuid are driven from place to place. They are faced by danger after danger. Diarmuid comes nobly through test after test— while Grania becomes fearful and petulant. Her bold thoughtlessness is gone—and she becomes the fearful, whimpering, less-than-noble part of ourselves. But all the time, while we admire Diarmuid for his steadfast loyalties, his compassion to his enemies, and the nobility with which he comes out of every trial, we sometimes feel that he is a little too good to be true. We even begin to have a sneaking sympathy for the selfish and scheming Grania. We empathize with her needs and wish he would take her to bed. We cannot condone that she throws a knife at his genitals in a fit of passionate frustration, but . . . .

At the beginning we get the feeling that Diarmuid is doing what is good and right because it conforms to a code of honor imposed from the outside. He does not even make up his own mind about Grania's request to leave Finn but consults his friends and goes by their advice. The turning point comes, I think, with the eating of the forbidden fruit. For the first time Diarmuid kisses Grania. This, like everything else in myth, as in life, has complex motives and causes which can never be properly unraveled. It is Diarmuid's first act outside the code of honor. He may have been moved by desire to kiss her (at last!) or it may be that for the first time he is taking a step to recognize the other, the earthy, the physical side of himself—without which he is not, after all, fully human. It may be that, as in the Biblical story of Eve, sin has entered his pure soul for the first time by eating the forbidden fruit—and he taunts Finn openly. It may be that, on the ordinary level of the adventure story, the man Diarmuid realizes for the first time that he does love Grania after all and does not want to return her to Finn. He kisses her so ostentatiously in front of Finn to make sure that now there can be no going back.

It is after eating the fruit of the quicken-tree that the situation begins to dramatically change between the two. A violent quarrel, sparked off by Grania's frustration and Diarmuid's jealousy, brings about the third great turning point in the story—the first turning point is their flight from the familiar, safe, and comfortable world they had known; the second, the eating of the forbidden fruit. Because of Grania's irritation with Diarmuid for doggedly sticking to the letter of the code of honor, she almost deprives him of his potency as a man. Because there is not a close and dynamic relationship between the physical and the spiritual sides of him, Diarmuid risks impotency as a spiritual being as well as a physical being.

After the storm in which Diarmuid realizes he can no longer deny the existence of that very powerful side to his nature represented by Grania, he sits by the ocean in despair and confusion. Note—the ocean of consciousness. He is beginning to be conscious of his own nature, the complexity of the decisions he has to face. Before, everything seemed simple because he had a code by which to live. Now he has broken the code—he has killed a man in a jealous rage. He thought he had done everything right for Grania and here she is, not grateful at all, but trying to maim and/or kill him!

The heron is a bird much used in Celtic myth to evoke the numinous—the Other World—the supernatural. Druids were known to keep their shamanistic artifacts in a bag made of crane or heron skin. The heron can be seen at dawn sitting on rocks or low-hung branches for long periods of time—just watching and waiting (meditating?) until at last it skims the waters of consciousness, gracefully and expertly, making a sudden and apparently effortless dive for a fish (truth/wisdom). At this crisis point in their lives, both Grania and Diarmuid hear the heron cry. Grania doesn't understand what it is and asks Diarmuid. Diarmuid understands that he has lost his way on the journey to the upper realms he thought was so clear-cut for him before.

Grania is becoming conscious of her higher self by hearing the heron beside the ocean. Diarmuid is becoming conscious of his lower self by experiencing passion and jealousy. The heron reminds him of something greater than any code—but which as yet he can't see how to obtain. Neither of them will ever be quite the same again.

When they return to the cave (the subconscious), Diarmuid says that Grania must remove the knife from his thigh. For the first time he is not protecting her from the consequences of her actions. Remember, he asks the two sons of Morna to bury the Surly One *before* Grania arrives, and he has always let Angus take her away so she will be protected no matter what he has to endure.

For the first time Grania realizes she must face up to what she has done. When she gives him her shoulder to lean on, we feel that at last they are sharing their lives, each helping the other. Now their love can be consummated because it is a real love, rooted in the full complexity of their nature as human beings.

It is interesting that before this Angus (the god) never tries to bring about peace between them and Finn. He only helps them out in a very temporary way because of his love for his son. It is when he sees they are truly united in a very real love that he deems the time right to speak about reconciliation with Finn and her father.

Now—how does Finn fit into all this?

Finn may represent the dark side of the god as Angus Og represents the light side; the two sides of the god complement the two sides of the human being. The Celtic gods are part of a loosely defined hierarchy reflected from the society they serve. There are kings—but there are also High Kings. There are gods (which Finn and Angus represent) and there are High Gods.

Finn is vengeful, pursuing, judging, and punishing. Angus is understanding, forgiving, helpful, rescuing, and peacemaking. Both are undeniably supernatural. Both can "see" where the couple are, no matter where they hide. Finn is vengeful because his pride has been hurt. Angus is helpful because he *loves*.

It is interesting that Finn cannot destroy Diarmuid no matter how hard he tries, as long as Angus is watching over him.

The forbidden fruit is not the only resonance of the Bible we find in this story. Diarmuid is destroyed by "the sin of his father." Donn, Diarmuid's father, jealous of another young boy who was receiving more attention than his own son at the court of Angus Og, took him between his knees and squeezed the life out of him. The little corpse was then turned by enchantment into a earless boar that was one day destined to kill Diarmuid.

Diarmuid is always referred to as the grandson of Duibhne. His father, for that terrible deed, was not someone to be proud of—and was best forgotten. Finn is the only one who calls Diarmuid "son of Donn"—to indicate that, like his father, he is treacherous and sinful.

What of the end of the story: Grania and Finn together at last?

On one level it is the story of a fickle woman who lets her libido rule her life. On another it might indicate that Finn and Grania, who represent the earthy side of the human and the god, join together after the harrowing trials they have both been through—and in the end make up a being greater than the sum of its parts. They live in peace together—their love fully realized in an earthly sense. As always in Celtic myth the Other World is not some faraway heaven but is instead a realm or state occupying the same space as our own—outside time and resonating to a different frequency.

This story, like so many of the stories in mythology, is about the inner journey of the human soul/psyche/spirit—the facing of tests and trials for the initiation into a better, or higher, state of being. Angus and Diarmuid live on in the Other World in a fully realized spiritual sense.

At the same time this myth is also a good adventure story of passion, rivalry, and murder.

Sources used:

Gregory, Lady Augusta. *Gods and Fighting Men.* Gerrards Cross, U.K.: Colin Smythe, 1970.

Rolleston, T. W. *Myths and Legends of the Celtic Race.* London: Harrap & Co., 1917.

The Farmer's Youngest Daughter

There was once a farmer who lost his cattle and searched all day for them through the mists of the hills. At the turn of day into night, as he wearily made his way home, he saw a dog watching him from the top of a cliff.

He took no notice and walked on.

Then the dog came down to where he was and stood before him on the path. "What will you give me," asked the dog, "if I get back your cattle for you?"

"I do not know," said the farmer. "What do you want? I will give you anything you ask if it is within my power to do so."

"Will you give me your daughter to wed?" the dog asked.

The farmer laughed. "I will give her to you," he said, "if she herself will have you!"

The two went back to the farmer's house—the man and the great black dog together.

The farmer explained to his three daughters what had

happened and asked the eldest of them if, to save his cattle and there-fore his livelihood, she would marry the dog. She tossed back her head and laughed loudly and said she would not. The second likewise re-fused, saying that she would not, though his cattle would never be found. The third and youngest looked at her father and looked at the dog—and said that she would.

As the dog and the young girl walked away to the jeering of her two elder sisters, the cattle began to return from the hills.

The young girl drew her woollen cloak about her shoulders in the chill night air and walked beside the dog, wondering what was to become of her.

"Do not be afraid," the dog said in the darkness. "We will soon be under shelter."

She walked on, looking neither to the left nor the right.

At last they came to a big house looming out of the darkness, with light in every window, the door open, and light streaming out from inside. As she stepped over the threshold she looked back at her com-panion for the first time and started. The dog had been transformed into a tall and handsome man, dark-haired and dark-eyed, with a smile that warmed her heart.

The young woman lived with him a long while very happily, but one day she told him that she missed her father and would like to visit him. Her husband agreed that she should go—but warned her not to stay long. She was pregnant and he told her she must, what-ever happened, be home before the child was born. She agreed that she would.

He gave her a silver-white mare to ride and told her that as soon as she arrived at her father's house, she was to take the bridle off and set the mare free to wander in the hills. When she was ready to re-turn, all she had to do was to shake the bridle outside the house and her steed would come back to her at once.

Her father was delighted to have her home, having spent many a sleepless night worrying about her since she left. He was now a fat and prosperous man.

Her sisters questioned her day and night, eager to hear what it was like to be married to a dog, but, though she was there many days and nights, she managed to avoid telling them anything about her life with her husband.

One day she became ill, and before she knew it she was in labor and her child was born. As she lay with it in her arms—her family and friends sitting round the hearth fire—strange and haunting music was heard. One by one all who watched fell asleep.

Into the chamber came her husband. He stooped and kissed her but said no word. He took the infant from her arms and left the room.

In the morning everyone was anxious to know what had happened to the child—but she would say nothing. As soon as she was able she slipped out of the house and shook the bridle in the air. Within moments her lovely mare presented itself and bowed its head for the bridle to be fastened. Then—as swift as the March wind—they flew away to her own home.

"You have come," her husband said.

"I have come," she replied. But nothing more about the incident did either of them say to each other. He took her in his arms and she was glad to be back with him.

Some months later the young woman grew restless again to see her father, and, as before, her husband gave her the silver-white steed and warned her that she must return before their child was born.

As before, she slipped the bridle off the mare—and the beast galloped off into the hills. But this time, the very first night, the young woman stumbled and fell and went into labor. As before, a beautiful child was born, but by the morning it had disappeared. The faint and eerie music had done its work, and all had slept while her husband took the child.

Her father was angry and demanded to know where his grandson had gone—but again she would not say. As soon as she could, she slipped out and shook the bridle and returned to her husband.

"You have come," he said.

"I have come," she replied. And again no word was said about how she had broken the condition of her going. He took her in his arms and she was happy.

A third time the young woman went to see her father, with the same conditions upon her, and again she had a child. All happened as before—but this time her father was so angry he threatened to kill her if she would not tell him what was going on. Frightened, she told him everything.

This time when she went to shake the bridle the mare did not appear. She shook and shook, day after day—but there was no sign of the beautiful and magical steed.

Her father tried to persuade her to stay, but her love for her husband would not let her be at peace in her father's house.

When she finally accepted that the steed was not ever going to come for her, she set out on foot and, wearily, at last came to the home she had shared with her husband. She found it empty, apart from his old mother, who told her that he had left. She suggested that she might catch up with him if she went quickly.

She walked all day in the direction the old woman had indicated, but found no trace of him. Night came on and she was exhausted.

In the distance she saw a light and hurried toward it. She found a house, spotlessly clean and well kept—a woman sat spinning beside the hearth.

The young woman was greeted at once and invited in. "Sit down and eat, and warm yourself by the fire. I know about your journey. You are looking for your man, who has gone off to marry the daughter of the King of the Skies."

The young woman was shocked. "He has?" she gasped. How could this be? Tears filled her eyes.

Then the spinning woman gave her food and washed her feet and showed her where she might sleep comfortably for the night. In the early morning she woke her and gave her food and drink for her journey.

"You will find yourself spending tonight with my middle sister," the spinning woman said. She gave her a gift of a pair of scissors that could cut by themselves.

All day the young woman walked, her heart anxious and sorrowful. At nightfall she saw a light in the distance and hurried toward it. Again she found a clean and well-kept house, with a woman spinning at the central hearth. As before, she was given food and water and rest; the woman knew without being told about her search for her husband. In the morning, when the spinning woman set her on her way, she gave her a gift of a needle that sewed by itself and told her she would find shelter that night in the house of her younger sister.

For the third day running the young woman walked and walked until she could walk no further, and at the coming of darkness she saw a light and found a house and a spinning woman who gave her food and shelter, knowing everything about her search for her husband. In the morning, the third sister gave her a gift, and this time it was a thread that could thread itself through the eye of a needle. The spinning woman told her that that night she would be in the town where the King of the Skies lived.

When the young woman reached the town she asked for shelter for the night from an old crone who kept the geese of the king. She asked if the old woman could find her work in the palace, but she was told there was no work to be found at the moment because everyone was preparing for the princess's wedding. Then the young woman asked if the old woman could find something for her to do, because she was so unhappy that she could not sleep. The old woman gave her a shirt to mend and the young woman set about it with her magic needle, thread, and scissors. At that moment one of the princess's maids came visiting and noticed how the needle, thread, and scissors were working by themselves, and she carried the tale back to her mistress.

The next day the maid was sent back to find out what the young woman would take in exchange for the magical scissors.

The young woman replied that the only thing she would consider in exchange for the scissors would be one night in which she would take the place of the princess in her bed.

The princess agreed, but when the night came she gave her lover a sleeping potion so that when the young woman took the place of the princess, the man beside her was deeply asleep and did not wake at all the whole night. She lay beside him and stroked him tenderly and pleaded with him to wake—telling him that she was the mother of his three children and asking his forgiveness for breaking the geiss that he had put upon her.

First thing in the morning, the princess came in and chased the young woman out before the man woke.

The next day the princess sent her maid to ask for the needle that sewed by itself and was given the same condition for the exchange as for the scissors.

Again the princess gave her lover a sleeping potion so that no matter how hard the young wife tried to wake him she could not.

But the three children were sleeping nearby and the eldest son heard the woman talking to his father all night. In the morning when he was out walking with him, the eldest son told him all that he had heard.

That night the princess allowed the young woman to take her place in bed in exchange for the thread that threaded itself. She poured the sleeping potion for her lover, but he only pretended to drink it.

When the young woman kissed him and stroked him and whispered that she was the mother of his three children, he turned over and took her in his arms and made love to her.

When the dawn came and the princess returned, the young man told her that it was the young woman who was the mother of his children that he truly loved. . . .

The family returned to their own home and planted the seed in the fields for the new summer crop.

Commentary

This story, in the version told to J. F. Campbell and reported in his *Popular Tales of the West Highlands,* borders on the folk tale—unlike pure myth and legend because the original essence has become so watered down, so trivialized, that it has become almost whimsical and has lost its original powerful, disturbing, and transforming character. The working man of Islay who told J. F. Campbell this story, learned from his grandmother, speaks of "a little doggie" who asked the farmer for his daughter in marriage in exchange for the return of his cattle. Of course, this could not have been an ordinary "little doggie" but the great black supernatural beast that guards the way to the Other World.

The youngest daughter of the farmer, who agrees to marry the dog in order to save her father's livelihood, is in the same tradition as Cordelia in Shakespeare's *King Lear* (which, incidentally, is based on a Celtic story), but the thread of memory that draws this tale from remotest antiquity has not borne with it the names of the protagonists. That does not matter; the woman is there—strong, tender, loving—never giving up until she has achieved reunion with her beloved. The man is at once her husband on a physical level, the guardian of the way in an Other Worldly sense, and the object of her spiritual quest.

The young woman flags from time to time and needs a rest from her quest, back in the old familiar world of her childhood. Her spiritual mentor allows her to return on certain conditions (the geiss, the taboo, the conditions inevitable in a mythic tale). She is not to bear their child there, and when she does, it is taken away from her at once. This taboo may be connected with the old teaching that esoteric matters have to be kept secret—that to tell them to the uninitiated risks having them misunderstood and contaminated.

The first two times the young woman breaks the condition, she is forgiven because it seems she cannot help herself—but the third time she tells the secrets of her own free will, and the magical steed no longer comes to take her back. She has gone too far back into the material world and cannot, except by great personal effort, return to the spiritual level she was at before.

She chooses to make the effort and struggles back painfully on foot to her home. If she were a lesser person, she would have given up when she found that her man had left. But the old crone, his mother, encourages her to go on—the mother goddess, the force of feminine intuition that drives as hard as any force of rational and masculine will. . . .

The young woman goes in the direction the goddess has indicated, but during each of three days she has to make her own decisions about which paths to take, what hills to climb. Mercifully, each of the three nights she is allowed to rest. Again there are three women—the three aspects of the Celtic mother goddess. They help her to wash off the dust of the journey; they give her nourishment and rest; they set her on her way again at dawn—but not without a mysterious and magical gift. At the time they are given to her, the young woman has no idea how valuable these gifts will prove to be.

She cannot now directly achieve her goal. When she first went to live with her man, she did so by grace—simply as a reward for the loving and trusting kindness of her heart. But now she has to pass through three periods of trial and training followed by rest. Even when she finally reaches the town, the princess does not ask for the three gifts at once but one by one. Two nights have to pass in struggle and frustration before the young woman achieves reunion and redemption. It is interesting that it is their son who brings them together at last—someone who is a combination of the two of them. We get the feeling that her man had left her for the princess not because he was fickle but because his role is as circumscribed as hers—only in a different way. She frees him by freeing herself, and together they return with their three truly magical gifts—their children—united and happy and ready to make the earth spiritually fertile by planting the new season's crops.

From:

Campbell, J. F. *Popular Tales of the West Highlands*. Aldershot, U.K.: Wildwood House, 1983.

The Sea-Maiden

One day a poor old fisherman was bringing in his nets, and they were as empty as they had been for many a day past. He felt the boat rocking, and beside it he saw a sea-maiden.

"What will you give me if I fill your nets with fish?" she asked.

The old man shook his head. "I have nothing to give," he said.

"Will you give me your firstborn son?"

"I have no son—nor am I ever likely to have one."

"Who is there in your family?" the sea-maiden persisted.

"No one but my wife, who is past childbearing, my mare, and my dog, who are as old as the both of us."

"Then take these grains," the sea-maiden said. "Give three to your wife, three to your mare, three to your dog, and plant three in the ground behind your house. Your wife will bear three sons, your mare three foals, your dog three puppies, and behind your house three trees will grow. The trees will be a sign. When one of the sons dies, one of the trees will wither. Go off home now and do as I say. Your nets will be full of fish and you will prosper. But remember me—in three years' time bring me your firstborn son."

Everything happened as the sea-maiden said it would, and the fisherman prospered.

In three years to the day he looked at his firstborn son, and he could not bring himself to take him to the sea-maiden.

She arose beside the boat as before and asked for his son. He pretended that he had forgotten that this was the day he should have brought him.

"Never mind," said the sea-maiden. "You may keep him four more years. Perhaps it will be easier for you to part with him then."

She had in her arms an infant of the same age as the fisherman's son and she dived into the sea and was gone.

The fisherman continued to prosper, and in four years' time, the sea-maiden again appeared and found that he, once more, had "forgotten" to bring his son. She gave him another seven years—but stressed that the next time he must bring him for sure.

The man went home happy, for he was confident he himself would be dead before the seven years were up, and he would not have to face the sea-maiden again. But the seven years passed and the old man was so restless and miserable that his son questioned him as to what the trouble was. At first the old man refused to tell him, but at last the young lad got the story from him. He offered at once to go to the sea-maiden and spare his father whatever consequences there might be if he did not—but the fisherman pleaded with him not to go.

"Well, then," said the son, "there is nothing for it but that I must go far away. Go to the smith and let him make me a sword."

The fisherman went to the smith. The first sword he made was too light and splintered when the young lad shook it; the second was still not right and broke into two halves; but the third stood the testing and the fisherman's son accepted it. The next day the son took the black horse, the firstborn of his father's old mare, and the black dog, the firstborn of his father's old dog, and he set off on his travels.

He had not gone far when he came upon the carcass of an animal freshly slain. He divided the meat between a great dog, a falcon, and an otter that were there, and each, as he received his portion, promised help to the boy if he ever needed it.

He rode on and came upon a king's house, where he took service as the herder. The grass was so poor in the region, however, that the milk yield was very low. He went farther and farther in search of better grazing and eventually came upon a fertile green glen. Unfortunately, it was in the domain of a very mean-spirited giant, and the boy had to fight for his life. The giant was killed. The boy looked into his deserted house and saw great riches—but he took none. The cows, however, yielded such good milk that evening that the king was very pleased with him. When the cows had consumed all the green grass of the glen, the boy pressed on further and there met a second giant he had to fight and kill before his cows could safely graze.

One night the boy returned with his cows to find the king's household in an uproar. It seemed there was a three-headed female monster in the lake demanding sacrifices—and the sacrifice it demanded this time was the king's daughter. "But," said the dairymaid, "all is not lost because the princess has a brave suitor who is going with her and will fight the beast."

The next day the princess and her suitor set off bravely enough, but when the monster rose from the loch the suitor fled, and it was the fisherman's son who came to the rescue of the princess. The boy had worked hard all day, and with the long wait he grew sleepy. He lay down beside the princess and told her to wake him when the beast approached by putting her gold ring on his finger. This she did. The fight was long and hard but the fisherman's son managed to cut off one of the beast's heads with his sword, string it on a withy, and send it screeching down the loch, whipping the water up into bloodred spindrift as she went.

The boy then returned to tend his cows, and the princess returned to her father's house. On the way she met the suitor, who bullied her into letting him claim that it was he who had severed the monster's head.

The second day all happened as before. The suitor fled. The fisherman's son slept, and this time the princess woke him by putting her earring into his ear. He fought bravely and well and managed to sever the second head and put it on the withy—and, when he departed to tend his herd, the suitor again claimed the deed.

On the third day all happened as before. This time the princess roused the fisherman's son with her second earring.

When all the heads were off the monster and the cowardly suitor

209

claimed the princess, the young girl said she would only marry the man who could take the heads off the withy. The suitor tried and failed, and many other men besides—no one could get them off but the one who had put them there: the herder. The princess set one more test by saying that she would marry the man who had her ring and her earrings.

The princess and the herder were happily married for some time, until one day they were walking by the loch when the same monster with three new heads, more fearful than the last, leapt out of the loch and seized the young man and dragged him under the water. Sorrowfully, the young woman mourned her husband until an old smith gave her some advice. She was to spread all her jewels and all her fine things beside the loch at the place where the young man had been taken from her.

This she did, and the beast surfaced and looked at the fine things laid out on the shore.

"I will give you any one thing you choose if you will give me a sight of my man," the young woman said.

The monster dived and returned with the fisherman's son, whole and handsome.

"I will give you all that you see here, if you will give me back my man," the princess said.

The monster looked at the treasures—and made the exchange.

All went well with the young couple for a while, until one day they were walking by the loch again, and this time the young wife herself was seized by the monster and dragged under the water.

Sorrowfully, the fisherman's son consulted the old smith who had been so helpful before. He told the young man there was only one way to kill the monster. "At the center of the loch is an island, and on the island is a white-footed hind, slender and swift. If she were caught, a black crow would spring out of her mouth; if the black crow were caught, a trout would fall out of her; in the mouth of the trout there would be an egg. The soul of the monster is in the egg. If you crush that egg, the monster will die."

The young man set off, but he could see it was no easy matter to reach the island with the monster waiting in the gray water to seize any boat that passed over it. So he sat on his fine black horse, and with his dog beside him, made a prodigious leap and landed on the island. He hunted the white-footed hind and had her cornered but still could not reach her. He thought back to the great dog with whom he had shared the meat at the beginning of his journey and wished that he was there to help. No sooner did he wish than the dog was there. Between them they captured the hind—but as soon as they did so, a crow sprang from her mouth and flew off.

If only I had the help of the falcon that shared the meat with me, the young man thought. No sooner thought than the falcon appeared and chased the crow. As the falcon caught her, a trout fell from her mouth into the loch and swam away. Then the young man called for the otter, and it was the otter that brought the trout to him from the midst of the loch.

The young man took the egg from its mouth and put it on the ground, with his foot on it.

The beast rose from the water, pleading with him to spare the egg.

"Give me back my wife," he demanded.

At once the princess was returned, and when he had her safely in his arms he crushed the egg and the beast died.

He was now a great man in the land and he and his wife lived happily together.

But one day when they were out walking they saw a dark castle in a wood beside the loch, and the young man was curious about it. "No one has ever come back who has entered it," said the young woman. "Leave well alone."

But he would not and that very night went up to the door.

There he was met by a little old crone who greeted him with flattering words and invited him inside. As soon as he entered, she struck him on the head with a club and he fell to the ground.

Back at the fisherman's house, one of the three trees of the sea-maiden withered. The fisherman mourned his eldest son, and his middle son persuaded him to tell him why he thought he was dead. As soon as he heard the tale he set off to find his brother, taking the second horse and the second dog. He came upon the king's house and heard the tale of his brother and the castle in the wood. Nothing would stop him—he had to go and see for himself if his brother was indeed dead.

He met the crone, accepted her flattering invitation, and was felled in the same way as his brother.

Back at the fisherman's house, the second tree withered—and the third son insisted on setting off in search of his two brothers.

The king and his eldest brother's wife told him about the castle, and he at once set off for it.

"All hail and good luck to thee, fisher's son," said the old crone to him, as she had to his brothers, and started to say all kinds of hospitable and flattering things.

"Go in," said the young man sharply, "I will hear your flattery when we are inside." And he saw to it that she went in ahead of him. When her back was turned the young man drew out his sword and cut off her head—but quickly she seized it and crammed it back on. The dog sprang at her—but she clubbed it as she had the two brothers with her magic club, and he fell down. The youth then wrestled with her for the club and managed to get it away from her. He struck her with it and she dropped to the ground.

The young man searched the castle and found his two brothers lying side by side. He touched them with the magic club and they stood up.

Then there was rejoicing among the three brothers, and they returned to the king's house with all the gold and silver they could carry from the castle.

At the death of the king, the eldest son became king in his place.

Commentary

This tale was told by a fisherman of Kenmore, near Inverary, to J. F. Campbell in 1850, and I give it here because, like "The Farmer's Youngest Daughter," it is such a beautiful microcosm of a myth. J. F. Campbell had heard the same story with minor differences from many different people, and it rings true to the most ancient of tales.

It is a sort of Faustian story where an impoverished old man sells his soul for worldly riches. It is his eldest son he proposes to sell, but I think his soul resided in his son as the sea-maiden's did in the egg. The idea of the soul, or life force, being kept separate from the body is not uncommon in myth.

The hind, the crow, the trout, and the egg are all creatures highly charged with magical significance for the Celts. The hind with white feet suggests a phase of purity and innocence. From this, the soul passes through the experience of darkness, violence, evil—symbolized by the carrion crow. Coming out of this, the soul is more aware—wiser. The fish (trout and salmon in particular) usually denote wisdom because they swim in the rivers and the seas of consciousness. With the egg the life cycle is completed. The soul is back at the beginning—about to be reborn. The crushing of the egg that ends the life of the monster releases the life of the young woman.

It is interesting that in each case the creature has to be caught by someone working in its own medium. We see much the same idea in the fact that the heads cannot be taken off the withy except by the one who put them there, and the brothers cannot be revived but by the club that felled them in the first place. Also in each case the fisherman's son has earned the right to use that particular animal to help him.

The monster is no simple antediluvian creature but a highly evolved and complex being serving a very important and complex purpose.

In Celtic myth there is no sense of death ending life—but rather of changing it or translating it from one form into another. The egg is crushed and the monster is dead. And yet—is she? I am sure the old crone at the gate of the dark castle is another form of the beautiful sea-maiden who offered the old fisherman prosperity in exchange for his son. She appeared as the betrayed, avenging, destroying beast with three heads. She was defeated and her heads were cut off. But her heads grew again and she reappeared. Crushing the egg that contained her life force destroyed her in one form—but she sprang back into life and continued her efforts to claim the young man she had been promised as a holy sacrifice.

The third son understands more than his brothers. He knows he cannot trust flattery. He knows he has to use the crone's own magic weapons against her. Spiritual beginnings can only be made in spiritual ways. The club is no ordinary club as shown by the fact that it is wielded by a very old crone who could not possibly have had the physical strength to fell the two healthy young men—even from the back. In Irish myth it was said of the famous club of the Dagda that he could kill men with one end of it and restore them to life with the other. We are reminded of the balance of creation and destruction that keeps the universe stable.

The two young men are dead and become alive again—another instance of the Celtic refusal to accept death as an end. It is also another instance of three apparently separate people actually being one person. While one part of this composite person is still alive—that is, the youngest son—the others cannot be destroyed.

The three-in-one return to the king's house, free at last. The sea-maiden has been defeated. Maybe she was not a ravening beast after their blood at all but a goddess who was putting them through trials to make them strong and whole.

It was perhaps not quite fair that the fisherman did not keep his side of the bargain, but the sea-maiden gave him extensions and seemed to understand his reluctance to part with his son. She no doubt watched the progress of the boy with interest and noted his kindness to the three creatures who eventually helped him. She is a mixture of generosity and dangerous, punishing violence.

There is a refrain of three sons, three horses, three dogs, three trees, three heads, three attacks by monsters (if you count the old lady at the door of the castle as the third). We are in magic time and everything is charged with meaning and profundity.

Note that the trees wither when the sons "die." Green nature and human nature are of one piece, and their lives are interdependent.

It is a smith who forges the sword for the son when he sets off to find his own life (and it is only the third forging that is good enough), and it is a smith who gives wise advice both to the princess and to the young man. In very ancient times smiths were thought of as sages, wisemen, magicians—because through fire they forged the vital implements needed for survival. To the ancient people it was almost a kind of magic that metal appeared out of stone. It is possible that the famous story of Arthur drawing the sword out of the stone in order to prove that he was the rightful king had something to do with this ancient awe and reverence for the iron smelter and smith's work. The fact that the smith plays such a role in this story is one of the clues that the story has its roots way, way back in ancient times.

In the "happy ever after" ending, the sea-maiden has returned to her benign aspect, and her sea-riches are the young man's reward for being kind to creatures, for being steadfast and hardworking, for being courageous in facing danger, and, finally, for using his wits and understanding.

Maybe the princess who finally and safely gathers her man into her arms and makes him king of her father's kingdom is actually the daughter of the sea-maiden—the babe "of like age" the fisherman saw in her arms the first time he refused to deliver his son. The fact that she was released in connection with an egg that contained the life force of the sea-maiden/monster also suggests that she may well have been her daughter.

Sources used:

Campbell, J. F. *Popular Tales of the West Highlands*. Aldershot, U.K.: Wildwood House, 1983.

The Celtic Book of Days
A Guide to Celtic Spirituality and Wisdom

Caitlín Matthews • ISBN 0-89281-565-5 • $24.95 hardcover
Color illustrations throughout

With the look and feel of a rare illuminated manuscript, this beautifully illustrated book offers thoughts for each day of the year, organized around the four major Celtic festivals: Samhain (ancestral communion and introspection); Imbolc (beginnings and primal innocence); Beltane (creativity and powerful expression); and Lughnasadh (maturity and consolidation). The daily entries are drawn from Celtic myth, poetry, prayers, and customs from many eras, including both pagan and Christian streams of Celtic spirituality.

The Celts
Uncovering the Historic and Mythic Origins of Western Culture

Jean Markale• ISBN 0-89281-413-6 • $14.95 paperback

"Markale has created a vivid picture—poetic and philosophical—of this deeply spiritual people. Here are the prophecies of Merlin and the druids, Celtic mythology, the Britons and Bretons, the Celtic Christian church, the history of the Gaels. This is a well-researched, erudite study of Celticism and its core beliefs."

The Book Reader

From the author of *Women of the Celts* comes one of the most comprehensive treatments of Celtic civilization ever written. This history positions the Celts as the primary European civilization, who occupied the whole of Western Europe for more than a thousand years before the Greco-Roman hegemony. Markale restores the Celtic civilization to its true importance in the development of European social, political, and literary values.

WOMEN OF THE CELTS
Jean Markale • ISBN 0-89281-150-1 • $14.95 paperback

Journey deep into the mythic world of the Celts, where both men and women become whole by realizing the feminine principle in its entirety. The Celts, who at one time were spread throughout Europe, left permanent traces of a culture in which women were the spiritual and moral pivot. Through legends and literature, *Women of the Celts* reveals the impact of this heritage on modern attitudes toward marriage, sexual liberation, and love, and shows the Celtic woman to be an enduring symbol of human freedom.

King of the Celts
Arthurian Legend and Celtic Tradition

Jean Markale • ISBN 0-89281-452-7 • $14.95 paperback

In this absorbing book, Jean Markale places King Arthur at the center of a brilliant revisioning of Celtic culture and history. Through close examination of the legends, the mythic elements of ancient histories, and the names of people and places, Markale provides new insights into the identity of Arthur and the society in which he flourished.

Sorting through the many variants of the Arthurian romances, Markale strips away the religious and political embellishments added to the tales by medieval monks and court storytellers to reveal a different kind of king—a Celtic warrior-hero who resisted the Saxon invasions in fifth-century England. From this vestigial core of genuine Celtic myth, the author reconstructs a new version of the life of Arthur.

Finally, bringing the reader into the present, the author uses Celtic Britain as a lens to examine the pretenses and ills of our contemporary society and offers the Celtic model as a way to integrate the often competing values of unity and diversity.

Merlin
Priest of Nature

Jean Markale • ISBN 0-89281-517-5 • $16.95 paperback

Once again drawing on his extensive knowledge of Celtic and Druidic cultures, Jean Markale offers a radical new interpretation of the literary and historical texts that speak of Merlin. The result is a revealing portrait of the archetypal Wild Man and shaman known as Merlin, who lived in the lowlands of Scotland late in the sixth century. A "divine madman," Merlin found refuge in a sacred clearing in the forest, and with his companion Vivian sought enlightenment and union with nature. When the Merlin legend resurfaced in the 12th century, his message of the universal brotherhood of all beings called out to a rapidly urbanizing society that was losing touch with nature. His warning, which went unheeded in his own time, is no less relevant to us today.

These and other Inner Traditions titles are available at many fine bookstores or, to order from the publisher, send a check or money order for the total amount, payable to Inner Traditions, plus $3.00 shipping for the first book and $1.00 for each additional book to:

Inner Traditions
P.O. Box 388
Rochester, VT 05767

Be sure to request a free catalog.